AMERICAN
GOVERNMENT

AMERICAN GOVERNMENT

READINGS FROM ACROSS SOCIETY

QUENTIN KIDD
Christopher Newport University

New York   San Francisco   Boston
London   Toronto   Sydney   Tokyo   Singapore   Madrid
Mexico City   Munich   Paris   Cape Town   Hong Kong   Montreal

Publisher: Priscilla McGeehon
Senior Acquisitions Editor: Eric Stano
Marketing Manager: Megan Galvin-Fak
Senior Production Manager: Eric Jorgensen
Project Coordination, Text Design, and Electronic Page Makeup: UG / GGS Information
  Services, Inc.
Cover Designer/Manager: Nancy Danahy
Cover Photos: © PhotoDisc, Inc.
Manufacturing Buyer: Al Dorsey
Printer and Binder: Courier-Stoughton
Cover Printer: The Lehigh Press, Inc.

For permission to use copyrighted material, grateful acknowledgment is made to the
copyright holders on pp. 241–242, which are hereby made part of this copyright page.

Library of Congress Cataloging-in-Publication Data
American government: readings from across society/[compiled] by Quentin Kidd.
        p. cm.
    Includes bibliographical references.
    ISBN 0-321-06677-4 (pbk.)
    1. United States—Politics and government.   I. Kidd, Quentin.
JK21.A4464 2000
320.973—dc21   00-056689

Please visit our website at http://www.ablongman.com

ISBN 0-321-06677-4

1 2 3 4 5 6 7 8 9 10—CRS— 03 02 01 00

CONTENTS

Part III   Political Behavior   133

PREFACE

THEME AND PURPOSE

At the end of class one day, a student approached me and asked about the supplemental readings I had assigned. They were classical political science readings from a very traditional political science reader. "I know that these are important," he began with an apologetic tone in his voice. "But I'm going to be a physical therapist and I just can't seem to get interested in these readings." As much as I was dismayed with this student's comment, I understood exactly what he was saying. Tocqueville and Madison were not easy reading, especially for the 95 percent of the large lecture class who were not political science majors but were taking the class in order to fulfill a general education requirement. I had noticed for several weeks that only a few students were actively engaging in class discussion about the reading. Most of the students seemed to be disengaged rather than engaged in the readings and discussions about them.

Because of this experience and the realization I was not going to make political scientists out of a class of non–political science majors, I set about compiling a group of readings that would speak to the nonmajors. This reader is the result of that work. My goal in *American Government: Readings from Across Society* is to gather a collection of readings that are current and easy to read, and that make the point that government and politics are both present and relevant throughout society. In other words, government and politics are important to all students, not just political science majors. To many of us who teach American government and politics, this is not a new revelation. For many of our students, however, who came of age during a time when even the president of the United States condemned government as a bad thing, this may indeed be a new revelation.

The target audience for this reader is thus the increasingly large and diverse group of non–political science majors taking introductory courses in government and politics. The reader is intended to be used as a tool to communicate better to this audience that government and politics are relevant and important to them. Many of these nonmajors do not necessarily understand or appreciate the extent to which government and politics are both present and relevant throughout society, including in their own chosen disciplines of accounting, engineering, or sports medicine.

Because of the increasing use of Introduction to American government as a service course, and the resultant change in the student body of the course, readers with the traditional political science–oriented selections are becoming less and less relevant to students. The selections in this reader are purposefully not traditional. They are taken from diverse sources in an effort to attract the interests of students who are not political science majors and still need some understanding of government and politics and how they work. This reader is not an effort to throw in the towel. It is an effort to open a new front and connect with students in another way and to help them understand the role of government and politics across a diverse society.

By focusing on government and politics across society, this reader does not promote government or defend it; nor does it necessarily praise or disparage government and politics. Some selections defend government and politics, and other selections criticize government and politics. Some selections are very provocative and others are not. The theme of the reader and the articles selected for inclusion follow one simple premise: Whether one likes or dislikes it, government and politics are present and play an important role across society. Engineers, nurses, and accountants interact with government at the local, state, and/or national level extensively, and it is important that they have some understanding of how government works in order to interact effectively with it.

By providing students with the opportunity to read about government and politics from many different perspectives, it is hoped that students will gain a more thorough understanding of the role that government plays throughout society. In the end, it is hoped that these readings will play a part in helping students become better citizens.

STRUCTURE AND CONTENT

This reader is divided into four parts:

- Foundations
- Institutions/Structure of Government
- Political Behavior
- Public Policy

The structure of the reader is consistent with the structure of many introductory American government textbooks. Each part, with the exception of the fourth, contains ten selections, carefully screened for readability and timeliness. Since the selections in this reader are drawn from a variety of sources, many of which are not traditional sources for political science readings, each part contains an introduction that places the group of readings into a larger historical or contemporary political context. In addition, individual readings are introduced and placed into a larger historical or contemporary political context as well. These introductions provide the thread that holds the diverse set of readings together.

PEDAGOGICAL FEATURES

- *Head Notes with Section Questions*. Each part is introduced with Head Notes and Section Questions that place the part into a larger historical or contemporary political context and stimulate critical thinking.
- *Article Summaries*. Each article is introduced with a short summary that places the article into a larger historical or contemporary political context.
- *Critical Thinking Questions for Each Article*. Two or three critical thinking questions are included after each article summary which can be used for class discussion or homework purposes.
- *Learn More on the Web*. World Wide Web addresses relevant to the topics covered in the part are included so that students may easily go to the Web and continue their exploration.

COMMENTS

I have put this anthology together as a partial response to a growing problem in large introductory courses with significant numbers of nonmajors in them. Some will find the approach and selections a perfect response, while others may find it lacking. Whatever your thoughts on this reader, I would appreciate any suggestions or comments you have concerning it. My e-mail address is qkidd@cnu.edu.

ACKNOWLEDGMENTS

As with any work, this anthology would not have become a reality without the help of many people. Tops on the list are my students, first at Texas Tech University and currently at Christopher Newport University. They are the reason for this project, and continue to serve as "reviewers" to this day. Two colleagues, John Camobreco and Michelle Barnello, provided invaluable feedback at a critical juncture in the life of the project. Corey Mickleberry, a student at Christopher Newport University, helped by obtaining permissions. Eric Stano, my editor at Longman, guided the project with a very patient hand and Terri O'Prey made sure the production of the manuscript went off without a hitch. A number of colleagues reviewed the manuscript: Edmund P. Carlson at Virginia Wesleyan College; Chris Grant at Presbyterian College; Jan Hardt at University of Central Oklahoma; Steven Holmes at Bakersfield College; Johanna Hume at Alvin Community College; Edward G. Moore at University of Texas-Brownsville; Elizabeth M. H. Paddock at Drury College; Scott Peters at Illinois Institute of Technology; Steve Sandweiss at Tacoma Community College; Paul Savoie at Long Beach City College; and Amy R. Sims at Goldengate University.

Finally, I would like to thank my wife Holly and son Brandon, both of whom watched this project go from idea to reality, and never once complained along the way.

Quentin Kidd

PART I

FOUNDATIONS

CONSTITUTIONAL GOVERNMENT

HEAD NOTES/SECTION QUESTIONS

The U.S. Constitution, ratified in 1788, is the blueprint of our political system. Two of the most fundamental characteristics of our constitutional government are democracy and federalism.

As a democracy, America has been a unique experiment in majority rule without mob rule. When the Founders were debating the kind of government the new country should have, James Madison made the argument in *Federalist No. 10* for a democracy. But, Madison was keenly aware that if he and his fellow nation-builders were not careful, they could create a political system where the majority could abuse the rights of the minority. And they did not want that.

To prevent this from happening, Madison advocated a republican form of democracy, where representatives could filter the will of the people. The development of a constitutional democracy was brilliant and seems to have worked rather well so far. As the selection by James R. Barber suggests, one reason it has worked well is because democracy itself is very flexible and able to adjust to the demands that citizens place on it. The reading by Michael Lind argues that one particular area where more democracy is needed is in the U.S. Senate, which he claims is not democratic at all.

As a federal system, America has been a unique experiment in evolution. Initially, the Founders created a federal system because the Articles of Confederation had failed. Under the Articles of Confederation, each state was equal in power to the others, and the national government was weaker than any individual state. The result was disunity and social instability. So, when the Constitution was written, the Founders created a federal system, whereby the national government would be strong enough to foster unity and create stability, yet still left the states significant power.

One reason that the individual states were willing to join a federal system was because they felt certain that in the constitution, the limits of the national government's powers were clearly spelled out. However, as Martha Derthick points out, there is a great deal of ambiguity in federalism about how powerful the federal government is in relation to the states. Carl Tubbesing discusses the centralizing tendencies of federalism as they exist today, and Noam Chomsky defends the federal government's powers, arguing that a strong federal government is needed today to protect individuals from big business.

Both democracy and federalism, two core elements of constitutional government, are continuously debated. As you read the selections in this section, consider these questions:

1. Do you think that the Founders would be pleased or displeased with the extent to which America is democratic today?
2. Do you think that the Founders would be pleased or displeased with federalism as it exists today?
3. Oddly enough, while democracy has expanded to include nearly all Americans, power has become more centralized in the federal government. In your view, could the expansion of democracy have happened without the centralization of power at the federal level?

LEARN MORE ON THE WEB

U.S. Constitution
http://www.law.cornell.edu/constitution/constitution.overview.html

Documents from the Continental Congress
http://lcweb2.loc.gov/const/ccongquay.html

U.S. Historical Documents
http://kuhttp.cc.ukans.edu/carrie/docs/amdocs_index.html

National Archives
http://www.nara.gov/exhall/exhibits.html

National Constitution Center
http://www.constitutioncenter.org/

The Federalist Society
http://www.fed-soc.org/

National Governor's Association
http://www.nga.org/

National Conference of State Legislature
http://www.ncsl.org/

The Council of State Governments
http://www.csg.org/

MORE DEMOCRACY!
MORE REVOLUTION!

BENJAMIN R. BARBER

CONTEXT

In establishing a democratic nation, the Founders were committed to the notion that people should participate in their own ruling. This commitment to rule by the people is what caused them to create a government that was at least conceptually democratic. Yet, as we know, the Founders had a different view of "the people" than the view we hold today. The people who really participated in their own ruling back then were a select few that included white landowning men. All others, including women, slaves, natives, and non-landowning men, were not a part of this early concept of democracy.

Yet, as Benjamin R. Barber argues in this selection, the wonder of democracy is that it can withstand revolutions that actually make it more democratic. Democracy is very capable of expanding. Today, as when the colonists first broke with England, the cry from people to be let in—to be able to share in the ruling of themselves—continues to be heard. Indeed, throughout our nation's history the concept of democracy has been expanding because with every move toward greater emancipation, inclusion, and equality, comes an expanded definition of democracy. We would never think of defining democracy today as rule by white landowning men, as was the case in the early years of our nation's existence, because the concept of democracy is much broader than that today.

Barber argues that as much as the concept of democracy has been expanded over the last 200 years, it can and should be expanded even more. In particular, he claims that our politics can be more democratic by cultivating a greater sense of citizenship among those who currently do not participate in governing themselves. He also claims that we can expand the meaning of democracy by encouraging a sense of civic responsibility within our economy. Finally, he claims that we can be more democratic in our civil society by expanding our commitment (via resources) to civil society in general.

● *THINK CRITICALLY* ●

1. When Barber says "more democracy," is he saying America is not democratic? What does he mean by this?

2. What are some of the specific ways that Barber thinks we could use more democracy in politics, economics, and civil society? Do you agree? Why or why not?

3. Can you think of any specific examples today where efforts are being made to increase democracy in politics, economics, or civil society?

For all its undeniable prosperity, in part precisely because of its undeniable prosperity, there are many things amiss in America today. For each thing that is right, something has gone wrong. For all the prosperity, there is far too much inequality; for all the practiced tolerance, there is too much incivility; for all the push to the center, there is too much recrimination, too much polarization; for all the productivity, there is too much disemployment, too much meanness, too much commercialism; for all the rollback of bureaucracy and welfare statism, there is too much antigovernment paranoia, too much distrust of democracy. In a word, for all the democracy, there is not enough democracy.

Yet the left appears to have neither an obvious constituency nor a persuasive political program to contend with these ills, and the disarray caused by the Clinton crisis can only exacerbate the difficulties it faces. The old coalition that created the New Deal and the Great Society represents an ever-tinier minority of voters. The old programs embody living ideas but dead policy options too wedded to vanished notions of nineteenth-century capitalism. Are there new "first principles" that can make a difference? Or will old first principles do? Although we progressives often make sport of our historical legacy, America's most promising progressive principles have in fact always been its first principles; for America's first principles (if not its practices) have always been fundamentally progressive. Foremost among those principles is Jefferson's bold claim that the remedy for all the defects of democracy is simply more democracy.

MORE DEMOCRACY

"More democracy!" has from the outset been the American battle cry—the cry of colonialists against the British, of tenants against landowners, of farmers against bankers, of disfranchised women against men, of slaves against slaveowners and of workers against those who would expropriate their labor. Radical proponents of democracy have historically made war not on American ideals but on hypocrisy—the distance power elites have put between those ideals and the nation's actual practices. Where Europeans have seen in politics the rationalization of class hegemony and called for a revolution against the political, Americans have seen in politics the means of their emancipation and have used political means to forge revolutions of inclusion. Revolution has taken the form: "Let me in!" "More democracy" has been the American ticket to emancipation, inclusion, equality and social justice. For more democracy means institutions and attitudes that are more democratic, and so means a more democratic democracy and thus a better democracy.

In the years before the Civil War when the women at Seneca Falls sought a place in the American sun, they refused to assail the rights language that had empowered men. Instead they held that language up to the test of its own entailments, asserting that the "self-evident truths" of the Declaration made all men *and women* equal. William Lloyd Garrison proclaimed he would "strenuously contend for the immediate enfranchisement of our slave population" precisely on the basis of those "inalienable rights" vouchsafed by America's founding documents. To abolish slavery required—more democracy. Martin Luther King, Jr. assailed the American nightmare of racism by embracing the American dream. More democracy.

What does such a broad formula mean today? More democracy, yes, but how? Where? Well, as Walt Whitman would say, everywhere! "Did you suppose," he queried in his *Democratic Vistas*, "democracy was only for elections, for politics and for a party name? I say democracy is only of use there that it may pass on and come to its flower and fruit in manners, in the highest form of interaction between men, and their beliefs—in religion, literature, colleges, and schools—democracy in all public and private life."

If democracy is, as John Dewey insisted, less a form of government than a way of life, then more democracy means specifically more democracy not only in the domain of government but in the domain of business and the domain of civil society. More democracy in each of these domains could engender three small revolutions and compel significant progress toward more equality, more justice and more security for all.

MORE DEMOCRACY IN POLITICS

To make our politics more democratic is the easiest (and, because we refuse or are unable to do it, apparently the hardest) of the tasks we face. For all the influence of money, special interests and transnational markets, our politics remains formally and legally democratic—which is to say, generically democratic. One person, one vote. That half of the eligible electorate does not vote and that those who do not vote are those who would benefit most by more political democracy (the young, people of color, the poor) is ironic and fateful. Ironic because nonvoters compose a significant proportion of the missing left constituency, and if they voted, their numbers would crucially alter the composition of our representative bodies. Fateful because by not voting they surrender the very power that could break the cycle of despair that paralyzes them politically.

The conservative cynic says to the homeless person soliciting a handout, "Get a job!" The progressive says, "Vote!" We know from Richard Cloward and Frances Fox Piven that nonvoting is about far more than apathy or complacency, that—disempowered economically and socially by a system that seems closed—the marginalized find it hard to feel that an occasional vote for mostly indistinguishable candidates will be very empowering. But they are in error: What they feel is truly false consciousness. For politics remains the sovereign domain, which means its rules are universally regulative. The law creates corporations and the marketplace and can contain and moderate them as legislators and their constituents please. Bill Gates, it appears, can be tamed if the political will is there. Legislators are first chosen in primaries, and if they lack excellence or ideological variety, participation in the political process can change that.

However useful as an explanation for the failures of the left, there is something disingenuous about a sociology that claims the referendum and the ballot box are somehow irrelevant to the challenges of social and economic injustice; that those very injustices destroy the viability of the processes by which they might be remedied. A vote *is* a vote, and the majority still carries the day. Our problem is winning the majority.

If we did no more than use the democratic means (federal, state, local) in front of our very noses, we could bring a great deal "more democracy" to the political domain. The Christian right figured this out a long time ago and made inroads first into local and then into national politics. The Rainbow Coalition registered a lot of people but too few of them ever actually voted. Getting out *its* vote apparently remains the left's greatest challenge.

Changing demographics compound the difficulties. As the natural constituents of the New Deal and the Great Society grow old and disappear from the voting rolls, as organized labor becomes a fraction of what it once was, as suburbanites become more numerous than city dwellers and successful minority groups become more politically variegated, and as people without kids at home are increasingly asked to support children's programs, progressives need to rethink how to advance an agenda of inclusion, social equality and justice in terms that do not make enemies of those in the Democratic Party's evolving base.

The key to meeting each of these challenges is cultivating citizens—through programs of civic education, voluntarism, community service and social responsibility that teach the young and old alike the arts of liberty and the competencies and responsibilities of self-government. The Corporation for National Service has been a vital tool of civic education, as have the dozens of campus-based programs of community service. The fight for public schools and against vouchers is in part a struggle for civic education, a battle to preserve the civic role of schools as creators of citizenship and social responsibility.

MORE DEMOCRACY IN THE ECONOMY

Among the reasons for the failures of political democracy is the changing nature of the deeply undemocratic commercial sector, which today controls not only the production and distribution of durable goods but the production and distribution of ideas, information, knowledge, pictures, news and entertainment as well as the means by which they are transmitted. It is time to recognize that the true tutors of our children are not schoolteachers or university professors but filmmakers, advertising executives and pop culture purveyors. Disney does more than Duke, Spielberg outweighs Stanford, MTV trumps MIT. It is not from their schools that children learn to obsess over the President's private sexual conduct.

As tutor to our commercialized civilization, consumerist culture has been teaching antipathy to government and a misplaced faith in privatization and markets. Rather than serving personal needs in the name of social goods, the market has turned to the manufacture of human needs at the expense of social goods in an economy of endless consumption. It replaces citizens with consumers, urging us to regard ourselves, even in civic clothes, as "customers" of state bureaucracies and clients of government. But as consumers we get choice without power: individual selections from an agenda we do not control and with social consequences we cannot deal with.

Corporations have nurtured an ideology of privatization that has diminished the power of the democratic institutions by which public agendas are forged and common decisions taken. The marketplace must then be democratized: not deregulated but decentralized; not rendered safe and secure by corporate welfare but rendered competitive and self-sufficient; not made merely profitable but made more fair.

This means corporations must now themselves become more democratic. Ideally, this entails workplace democratization—minimally via employee stock ownership plans, cooperatives and stronger (and more internationalized) unions. Democracy is about obligations as well as rights, however. And as the government sector is diminished, corporations will be obliged to assume some of the responsibilities of citizens. Corporate responsibility can no longer be a discretionary policy of those occasional companies headed by civic-minded CEOs. It becomes the price of privatization, an obligation incurred by the private sector's complicity in curtailing democracy in the political domain. As governing institutions (prisons, schools, telecommunications) are privatized, private corporate institutions willy-nilly will become more public.

Rapacious capitalism that brutalizes workers and rides roughshod over the common goods of civil society in the long run befouls its own nest. Capitalism needs competition, democracy and civility, which means it needs to democratize its practices and civilize its executives—especially if it pursues a politics of privatization and government delegitimation.

But I am not so naïve as to think that corporations will take to civic responsibility merely because it is a good thing, or because they have a long-term interest in doing so even where it unbalances quarterly profit sheets. Government can act here as a jawboning partner—as it did in the Apparel Industry Partnership against child labor in foreign plants; as a provider of inducements, through tax breaks for corporations that agree to responsible work practices (now they get tax breaks in return for nothing at all); and as an enforcer, by negotiating effective workplace standards, meaningful protection for labor organization and citizen-friendly policies for international institutions like the WTO and the IMF that depend on US cooperation.

MORE DEMOCRACY IN CIVIL SOCIETY

The disillusionment with politics makes political democratization difficult. The private character of the commercial sector makes economic democratization voluntary and thus improbable. The civic domain is, however, democratic by its very nature. It is local, composed of voluntary members committed to association and common goods, and it is by definition not for profit. It contains those "free spaces" where we learn to be citizens. It is in the arena of civic education. In these spaces, democracy does not depend on the reputation of leaders, only on the competence and civic responsibility of citizens.

Strong democratic civil society shares with government a sense of publicity and a regard for the general good and the common weal, yet it also partakes in that liberty that is the special virtue of the private sector. It is a voluntary and thus private realm devoted to public goods—the realm of church, family, education, culture, recreation, art and voluntary association.

Without civil society, citizens are suspended between big bureaucratic governments they no longer trust and private markets they cannot depend on for moral and civic values. Where the public square once stood there are only shopping malls and theme parks. In the absence of a vibrant and pluralistic civil society, formal democratic institutions atrophy. What is central democratic government but civil society organized for common action? Government is civil society's common arm, just as civil society is government's restraining hand. Civil society calls for decentralization rather than privatization, sharing rather than abdicating common power. At the same time, it can dissipate the atmosphere of solitariness and greed that surrounds markets. Both government and the private sector can be humbled by the expansion of civil society, for it absorbs some of the public aspirations of government (its commitment to public work) without being coercive, and it maintains liberty without yielding to the anarchy of commercial markets. A reinvigorated civil society can rehabilitate democratic government, now in such low repute. Indeed, to a considerable degree, democratization of civil society is the so-called third way being touted by Tony Blair and Bill Clinton—a condition for democratization of both politics and commerce.

For this to happen, however, requires programmatic action by citizens and by government. Civic space is at a premium in a commercial culture that privileges theme parks, malls and suburban developments. At the Walt Whitman Center we are working with architects, developers and urban planners to create a model of multi-use public space in consumption-dominated commercial malls. We have also designed a civic Web site that features a moderated civic chatroom for political deliberation that is both serious and entertaining. Why should the new technologies profit only the private sector and become the medium exclusively of commerce and entertainment? Why should civil society not have its own educational, cultural and political sites, if necessary, supported by an independent government-sponsored organization like PBS or NPR. Arts education is also an important way to nurture civil society, for the arts are its very soul and the source of that creative imagination indispensable to both culture and democracy. This may be reason enough to fund the NEA.

MORE DEMOCRACY, MORE REVOLUTION!

In old, well-entrenched democratic states, it is easy to forget that democracy is a radical principle, perhaps the most radical of all principles. It derives from the root claims that people have a right to govern themselves and that no one has the right to govern another. Together, these claims legitimize revolution: a people's right to seize the power necessary to govern themselves. Liberty is rarely a gift of the powerful. It must be wrested from them in democratic revolutions that are just because they are democratic and effective because they are revolutionary.

Jefferson summed up the inherently revolutionary spirit of democracy when he insisted that each generation repossess its first principles anew, observing that the tree of liberty had to be nurtured from time to time with the blood of patriots. You cannot inherit freedom. You may be "born free" in the abstract, but to possess your birthright, you must fight for and earn it. Yet as prudent democrats from Hannah Arendt to Bruce Ackerman have noticed, the revolutionary democratic moment in America has had to contend with an equally potent establishmentarian moment averse to change and popular empowerment. Our real problem may be that we are immersed on the left in one of America's cyclic establishmentarian moments. Feeling swamped by a placid popular culture and its obsession with sex and money, dazzled by a wildly productive if ethically indifferent economy and frightened by a globalization process that seems to remove choice not only from individuals but from democratic nations, we have lost touch with democracy's revolutionary American core. This moment of stasis and uncertainty is the moment to reclaim our radicalism—our *radice*, or root, principles—and bring the fervor of democratic rebels back to our cause: Jefferson writing the Declaration, John Brown at Harpers Ferry, America's disfranchised women at Seneca Falls, Martin Luther King at the Lincoln Memorial. These Americans did not wait for America to give them the liberty they claimed as a birthright. In the name of America, and with the collaboration of coalitions of citizens they mobilized and took it.

At the end of the last century, a fearful Frenchman cried, *Trop de zèle!* Too much zeal! Our plea at the [beginning] of this century must be *Plus de zèle! More zeal!* More democracy! More ardor, more rebelliousness, more gumption in the struggle for more votes, more corporate responsibility, and more civil society. Never mind what the President did or didn't do—what are *we* going to do?

Just a few yesterdays ago, Marxist revolution failed because it refused to take democracy seriously, thinking it had first to establish revolutionary economic and social justice by hook and by crook. It would be a perverse irony if democracy were to fail a few tomorrows from now because it refused to take revolution seriously—refused to enlist America's great revolutionary ideals in the ongoing and never-ending struggle for more democracy.

2

75 Stars: How to Restore Democracy to the U.S. Senate

Michael Lind

CONTEXT

In the previous reading, Benjamin R. Barber suggests that democracy is a concept that over time has expanded in meaning and now applies to many more people than it did 220 or so years ago. Early on, democracy applied to white landowning men, and today it applies to nearly everyone over eighteen-years of age not convicted of a felony. He further suggests that its meaning can be expanded even more.

In this selection, Michael Lind contends that the U.S. Senate is one institution in particular that is increasingly undemocratic and in need of an expansion to allow for more democracy. Lind argues that if democracy means anything, it means one person, one vote. People who live in states with smaller populations have much more influence per vote in the Senate than people who live in states with larger populations. The disproportionate amount of influence is the result of the fact that each state gets two seats in the Senate regardless of the state's population. This is undemocratic, Lind claims, because two votes in the Senate from Wyoming are equal to two votes in the Senate from California regardless of the fact that California's population is much larger than Wyoming's population.

How do we solve this problem? Lind suggests that one way to make the Senate more democratic, in other words to equalize the weight of each vote in the Senate as it relates to the population of people the vote represents, is to create new states. In particular, Lind says that the most populous states, such as Texas, California, and Florida, ought to be divided into several states. This would increase the number of senators, but would make the Senate more democratic in the process.

● *THINK CRITICALLY* ●────────────────────

1. Why is the Senate structured the way it is, and was the Senate supposed to be democratic in the way Lind argues that it is not democratic?
2. How would expanding the number of states affect the House of Representatives? Would this be good or bad for democracy in America?

75: STARS:

How to restore democracy in the U.S. Senate (and end the tyranny of Wyoming)

Here's a quiz question for you: What American institution has used its power to thwart desegregation, campaign finance reform, health care reform, New Deal programs, gun control, and midnight basketball—and gave Adolf Hitler time to conquer most of Europe without American opposition? The answer: the United States Senate. Because of our Senate—the least representative legislative body in the democratic world except for the British House of Lords—an ever shrinking minority of voters has the power to obstruct policies favored by an overwhelming majority of the American people. The Senate is the worst branch of government, and it's going to get even nastier in the century ahead.

If democracy means anything, it means one person, one vote—a principle flouted by the Senate's very design, which is based on an antiquated constitutional provision that provides equal suffrage in the Senate for government units (states) rather than suffrage based on the size of a constituency. As a result, a dwindling minority of Americans elects a majority of senators.

California has 66 times as many people as Wyoming—and yet on any given vote Wyoming's two senators can neutralize California's two senators. Texas, with more than 19 million people, has only two senators—as many as Montana, which has less than 1 million citizens. New York, the third most populous state in the union, can be outvoted by tiny Rhode Island (the true Empire State).

This malapportionment favors inhabitants of Rocky Mountain and New England states at the expense of Americans who live in densely populated megastates—not only Sun Belt states such as California, Texas, and Florida, but also states in the Northeast and Midwest such as New York, Illinois, and Pennsylvania. True, the big states have more members in the House. But this misses the point: Why should Idahoans be represented in the House and the Senate, while Californians, Texans, and New Yorkers are effectively represented in the House alone? It's not an even trade. The majority of Americans get nothing in return for forgoing their right to democratic representation in one-half of their national legislature.

From the 18th century to the present, the ratio of large- to small-state populations has grown from 19-to-1 to 66-to-1. Today, half of the Senate can be elected by 15 percent of the American people—and the problem is only getting worse. Almost all of the population growth in the United States in the foreseeable future will be concentrated in a few populous states (chiefly California). By the middle of the next century, as few as 5 percent of the population, or even 1 percent, may have majority power in the Senate.

Even now, only 10 percent of the U.S. population elects 40 percent of the Senate. By filibustering, senators representing little more than one-tenth of the nation can block reforms supported by the House, the president—and their fellow senators, who represent the other 90 percent of the population. This is not democracy. It is minority rule. For example:

The Republican Party held the Senate from 1980–86 only because of Senate malapportionment. During that period, Republican senators as a group received fewer votes nationwide than Democratic senatorial candidates. If the Senate had been elected on the basis of population, President Ronald Reagan would have faced a Democratic Senate throughout his eight years in office.

In 1991, the Senate voted 52–48 to appoint Clarence Thomas to the Supreme Court. The senators opposing Thomas (including those from California, New York, New Jersey, Ohio, and Texas) represented a majority of the American people—but found themselves in the minority in the Senate.

In order to pass his budget package in 1993, President Clinton had to cave in to demands by senators from Montana, Arkansas, and Louisiana to lower the gasoline tax.

Likewise, Clinton's 1993 domestic stimulus program, which was targeted at metropolitan areas in megastates like California, was killed by conservative Republican and Democratic senators from underpopulated states such as Oklahoma.

While the Senate exaggerates the power of anti-urban, anti-government conservatives in domestic policy, when it comes to foreign affairs, the Senate has always been the command post of isolationism. As late as 1940, a bipartisan team of isolationists in the Senate blocked the efforts of President Franklin Delano Roosevelt and the House to revise the country's misguided neutrality laws and rescue Britain from defeat at the hands of the Nazis. Thanks to the unrepresentative Senate, Hitler came close to winning World War II.

The only Americans whose views are consistently magnified by Senate malapportionment are white, rural, right-wing isolationists. If you are non-white or of mixed race, if you live in a major metropolitan area, if you are liberal or centrist, if you support an internationalist foreign policy, or even if you are a conservative who lives in a populous state, you should look on the Senate with loathing and apprehension.

Because of its role in screening executive and judicial appointees, the Senate also has a disproportionate influence on all three branches. To make matters worse, the senators' staggered six-year terms—intended to insulate the enlightened statesmen of the upper house—have merely ensured that the Senate would be out of touch with the times, as well as out of touch with the American majority.

ORIGINAL CONTEMPT

Most of the Founding Fathers hated the Senate, which they created to satisfy small states, like Rhode Island, that demanded equal representation in the new federal government. In "The Federalist No. 22," Alexander Hamilton, criticizing the Senate by implication, identified equal representation of the states in the national government as one of the worst defects of the Articles of Confederation. Allotting representatives on the basis of statehood rather than population, he wrote, "contradicts the fundamental maxim of republican government, which requires that the sense of the majority should prevail." Hamilton predicted that "two-thirds of the people of America could not long be persuaded, upon the credit of artificial distinction and syllogistic subtleties," to be governed by a third of the population. "The larger States," he concluded, "would after a while revolt from the idea of receiving the law from the smaller." If Hamilton returned today, he'd be amazed to learn that the citizens of large states have not yet revolted against the excessive power of the statelets in America's upper house.

In the early 1960s, the Supreme Court struck down malapportioned state legislatures as unconstitutional, arguing that they violated the principle of one person, one vote. In 1963, the Supreme Court declared in *Gray v. Sanders* that "the conception of political equality from the Declaration of Independence to Lincoln's Gettysburg Address to the 15th, 17th, and 19th Amendments can mean only one thing—one person, one vote." There you have it: The federal judiciary determined that the structural principle underlying state senates at that time—and the U.S. Senate today—was unjust and unconstitutional.

For much of American history, white Protestant rural constituencies were deliberately overrepresented in state legislatures in order to dilute the political influence of urban dwellers, who were more likely to be European immigrants. In the 21st century, the built-in corruption of our Senate may cause a constitutional and racial crisis. Just as European immigrants in the cities were stymied by rural Anglo-Protestant "rotten boroughs" in state legislatures in the 19th century, so the coming Hispanic, black, and Asian majorities in the megastates will have their votes diluted by the overrepresentation of the white microstates in the Senate. As the Chicago lawyer and writer Tom Geoghegan has pointed out, the House will soon look like multiracial metropolitan America; the Senate will continue to look like white rural America.

The Senate has always functioned as the last bastion of white supremacy. The balance of slave states and free states in the Senate permitted the South to preserve slavery and weaken the federal government for a generation after its population had been surpassed by that of the North. In this century, Southern senators filibustered anti-lynching legislation, and later blocked civil rights reform. The gridlock they caused was one reason the federal courts eventually seized the initiative on desegregation. If the emergent multiracial majority in the United States perceives the Senate as the tool of selfish white obstructionists, pressure will grow on the judiciary or the president to take control and push through reforms that the majority needs and approves—at the cost of further weakening our constitutional order.

DIVIDE AND RULE

Can anything be done about the Senate and its weighted vote for white reactionaries? A distinguished New York senator once grumbled to me over dinner, "You should write an article saying we should combine all those Western states into one." Alas, we can forget about creating a single populous "state of Deseret" by forcibly consolidating all those states with right-angle corners. The microstate delegations to the Constitutional Convention of 1787 managed to booby-trap the Constitution to protect themselves. Article V states that the American people cannot amend the Constitution to get rid of equal suffrage for the states: "No State, without its Consent, shall be deprived of its equal suffrage in the Senate." And Article IV, Section 3, provides that no state can "be formed by the Junction of two or more States, or parts of States, without the consent of the Legislatures of the States concerned as well as of the Congress." Not one, but two poison pill provisions.

Yet there is a way to address the problem of Senate malapportionment, one that doesn't require us to abandon the Constitution or to alter the two-senators-per-state rule. Let's go back and read Article IV, Section 3, in its entirety:

> New States may be admitted by the Congress into this Union; but no new State shall be formed or erected within the Jurisdiction of any other State; nor any State be formed by the Junction of two or more States, or Parts of States, without the Consent of the Legislatures of the States concerned as well as of the Congress.

Why not form new states within the jurisdictions of the existing megastates? Why not divide in order to rule? This is not as crazy as it sounds. Commentator Walter Russell Mead has suggested that no American should have to live in a state with more than 4 or 5 million citizens. If the 4-million-population rule were applied to the large states, California might be subdivided into eight new states; Texas, five; New York and Florida, four; Pennsylvania, Illinois, and Ohio, three; and Michigan and New Jersey, two.

Eight Californias? Five Texases? Four New Yorks? Why not?

With 25 new states in the union, the Senate would be far more representative of the American people. The citizens of the nine largest states, who today send a mere 18 senators to Washington, would soon have a total of 68 senators to defend their interests against senators from microstates like Vermont and Wyoming. The overall Senate representation of the voters in present-day California, Texas, and New York alone would jump from 6 to 34. The House functions with 435 representatives; a Senate with 150 members would be quite manageable.

This scheme would be perfectly constitutional under Article IV—as long as the small states as well as the populous states consented. Obviously the megastates would have to strike a deal with the microstates, so that they did not then subdivide into still tinier units (nanostates?). Under this proposal, states like Wyoming would still have roughly four times greater representation in the Senate than California's eight new states of 4 or 5 million citizens apiece—and would have reason to be grateful that California didn't divide into 32 new states. How could the microstate politicians be persuaded to go along with the dilution of their unjust authority in the Senate? Perhaps the megastate majority in both parties would give the microstate senators no choice. The moment the Senate's malapportionment becomes a popular political issue, both parties are likely to sacrifice the wishes of their Rocky Mountain and New England minorities in order not to offend the megastate voters who will decide which party controls the House and the presidency. Lose a State, Gain a Caucus.

In 1997, British conservatives paid the price for ignoring an equally vexing problem of constitutional reform. The Conservative Party was decimated when voters in Scotland and Wales flocked to the Labor-Liberal Democrat alliance that promised local legislatures for the two regions. In this country, the direct election of U.S. senators was proposed in minor-party platforms as early as 1876; it became part of the Democratic Party platform in 1900; and it was not achieved until the 17th Amendment passed in 1913. This proves that, even in the United States, once a national majority is aroused, the Senate can be reformed—eventually (for 20 years, the Senate did not even let the amendment come to a vote, even though the House had approved it five times).

Selling subdivision to residents of Florida, New York, California, and other populous states should be much easier. (I am referring to legal and consensual division, of course, not to militiamen declaring that a ranch is a republic.) The states of the American union do not correspond to real geographic, social, or economic groups—and never have. Most of the state boundaries were drawn by surveyors, with little or no regard to the actual contours of the landscape. The map of the American states is like a section of wire mesh pressed down atop an abstract expressionist painting. The high mobility among Americans, coupled with the present high level of foreign immigration, renders state patriotism tenuous. Indeed, the voluntary division of some states would delight many of their inhabitants. In the 1960s there was a proposal to make New York City a state. In 1992, voters in a majority of California counties voted in favor of splitting California in two. Citizens of adjacent counties in Kansas, Colorado, Oklahoma, Nebraska, and Texas recently sought to form a new state, West Kansas. In Texas, it would be sad to see the Lone Star flag lowered for the final time. But though the state song calls Texas an "empire wide and glorious," Texas is not an arbitrary political unit, but a distinctive cultural region, like New England or the Pacific Northwest. Lose a state, gain a caucus.

Conservatives and populists who today denounce the centralized rule of the statehouses in Sacramento or Albany or Austin should be delighted with the idea of two dozen smaller states, whose legislatures would be more responsive to their smaller, more manageable constituencies. Liberals, too, should be pleased—voting power would shift away from almost exclusively white hinterland electorates toward urban, Hispanic, black, and immigrant voters. Libertarians could celebrate the choice of lifestyles offered by the states of Orange and Marin. And neo-Progressives who want to eliminate redundant levels of government might at last get their wish—at least in unitary city-states like those based on New York City, Los Angeles, and Philadelphia. Provision might be made for any state, once its population reaches 8 or 10 million, to split into two new states of 4 or 5 million citizens. Depending on the growth of the U.S. population and its density, the number of stars on the American flag might rise from 50 to 75 to 100. Short of scrapping the Constitution altogether, the voluntary division of the big states into new, smaller states is the only way that the citizens of megastates can end their semicolonial subjugation to an electoral minority in the microstates. It may also be the only way to avoid a race war between the two houses of the U.S. Congress in the 21st century, when the real "white house" will be the Senate. If the majority cannot rule by constitutional means because of the Senate, then it will rule by extraconstitutional measures, through an imperial presidency or an imperial judiciary. We can use the Constitution to reform the Senate—or trash the Constitution to get around the Senate. The choice is ours.

③

AMERICAN FEDERALISM, HALF-FULL OR HALF-EMPTY?

MARTHA DERTHICK

CONTEXT

America has a federal system of governance, one where a national, overarching government shares power with the state governments. Federalism is one of the great innovations to come out of the failure of the confederation established by the Articles of Confederation. Prior to the approval of the U.S. Constitution in 1787, many thought that a federal system was unworkable because it was thought that political power could not be effectively divided between the states and the national government. In fact, in the debates leading up to the ratification of the Constitution, one side, the anti-federalists, feared that rather than divide power, the Constitution would create a strong central government at the expense of the states. The other side, the federalists, argued that this would not happen.

Over time, the anti-federalists have been proven right more than have the federalists, as power has shifted to the federal government, often at the expense of the states. In this reading, Martha Derthick discusses the ambiguity of federalism. Derthick notes that American federalism is long on change and confusion, but short on fixed and immovable solutions to problems. She explores this ambiguity in American federalism by looking at three spheres of activity: constitutional interpretation by the Supreme Court, electoral politics, and the everyday work of the government.

Derthick argues that in terms of constitutional interpretation by the Supreme Court, there appears to be less than meets the eye. Granted, the Supreme Court has made some important decisions to preserve federalism, but the court's pro-federalism majority is slim, and the court has made many other decisions supporting federal supremacy. With regard to electoral politics, the 20th century has seen a nationalization of electoral politics and while the recent ascendancy of governors to the While House might signal a slowing down of this nationalization, it doesn't appear to be on a reversed course. Finally, with regard to the everyday work of government, centralization of power appears to be proceeding at a steady clip.

● *THINK CRITICALLY* ●——————————————————————————

1. What does Derthick mean when she says "American federalism is a highly protean form, long on change and confusion, short on fixed, generally accepted principles"?
2. Of the three areas Derthick discusses (constitutional interpretation by the Supreme Court, electoral politics, and the everyday work of the government), which do you see as being most dominated by federal power, and which least dominated by federal power? Why?

Last August the *Wall Street Journal* noted that some taxpayers were claiming that they did not have to pay federal income tax because they were residents of a state, not the United States. A few weeks earlier the *New York Times* carried a story describing Vice President Albert Gore's plan to have detailed positions on a wide range of issues in his quest for the Democratic presidential nomination in 2000. At the top of his list was education, a function not long ago considered a preserve of state and local governments.

Gore's "blizzard of positions" included preschool for all children, a ban on gang-style clothing, teacher testing, "second-chance" schools for trouble-prone students, back-to-school parent-teacher meetings where a strict discipline code would be signed, and "character education" courses in the schools. Gore proposed to amend the Family and Medical Leave Act to permit parents to attend the parent-teacher meetings during working hours.

As these contrasting conceptions suggest, American federalism is a highly protean form, long on change and confusion, short on fixed, generally accepted principles. In the event, a tax court judge fined the taxpayers who claimed not to be citizens of the United States. And the *Times* reporter hinted that many actions Gore planned to "require" would need local school board cooperation to take effect.

As the 21st century begins, public commentators often suggest that this is a time of decentralization in the federal system. The view derives mainly from a series of Supreme Court decisions that have sought to rehabilitate the states in constitutional doctrine and from passage of a welfare reform act in 1996 that office-holders and analysts alike interpreted as radically devolutionary.

But matters are more complicated than that. American federalism was born in ambiguity, it institutionalizes ambiguity in our form of government, and changes in it tend to be ambiguous too.

To sort out what is happening, I will distinguish among three spheres of activity: constitutional interpretation by the Supreme Court; electoral politics; and the everyday work of government as manifested in policies and programs.

THE SUPREME COURT

A narrow majority of the Rehnquist Court led by the chief justice attaches importance to preserving federalism. To that end, it has made a series of daring and controversial decisions that purport to limit the powers of Congress or secure constitutional prerogatives of the states.

In *Printz v. U.S.* (1997) the Court invalidated a provision of the Brady Handgun Violence Prevention Act that required local law enforcement officers to conduct background checks on all gun purchasers. The Court objected that the provision impermissibly violated the Tenth Amendment by commandeering the state government to carry out a federal law. An earlier opinion, *New York v. U.S.* (1992), had begun to lay the ground for the anticommandeering principle. In another leading case, *U.S. v. Lopez* (1995), the Court held that Congress had exceeded its commerce clause power by prohibiting guns in school zones. Still other decisions signaled a retreat from federal judicial supervision of school desegregation, prison administration, and the judgments of state courts. Another line of cases has secured the state governments' immunity from certain classes of suits under federal law.

Some analysts profess to see a revolutionary development here, but qualifications are in order. The Court decides many cases in which it does not give primacy to federalism, as for example a 7-2 ruling in 1999 that state welfare programs may not restrict new residents to the welfare benefits they would have received in the states from which they moved. This ruling struck down a California law and by implication a provision of federal law that had authorized it. Moreover, the majority that has decided the leading federalism cases is narrow (often 5-4) and tenuous, inasmuch as it includes some of the oldest members of the Court. The decisions have not exactly been hailed by legal scholars, even some who might be thought sympathetic. Charles Fried of the Harvard Law School, a former solicitor general in the Reagan administration, denounced the series of decisions last June on immunity from suits as "bizarre" and "absurd."

If this is a revolution, it is one that may not last.

ELECTORAL POLITICS

Speaker Thomas P. O'Neill's famous aphorism that "all politics is local" applied to virtually all structural aspects of U.S. electoral politics for a very long time. Determining electoral districts and voter qualifications, mobilizing voters, and financing campaigns were the province mainly of state laws and customs and were locally rooted well into this century. But that has ceased to be true under the impact of 20th-century constitutional amendments extending the electorate, as well as federal statutes and judicial decisions governing apportionment and voting rights. Federal supervision now extends even to such matters as ward-based versus at-large elections in local governments. And changes in technology and in social and economic structures mean that candidates for congressional seats or even lesser offices do not depend exclusively on funds raised from local constituencies. Candidates may get help from party committees and interest groups organized on a national scale.

Nationalization of electoral practices proceeds apace at century's end. The Motor Voter Act of 1993 requires states to allow all eligible citizens to register to vote when they apply for or renew a driver's license. It also requires states to allow mail-in registration forms at agencies that supply public assistance, such as welfare checks or help for the disabled. The costs are borne by the states.

Nevertheless, one hesitates to insist that our electoral processes are being comprehensively nationalized at a time when governors seem to have gained an advantage in access to the presidency, growing, arguably, out of the public's now chronic distrust of the national government. Of the four last presidents in the 20th century, three were governors before they were elected, and in the run-up to the 2000 election, a governor, George W. Bush of Texas, secured the Republican nomination. He owes his success partly to other Republican governors—of whom there were 32 after the election of 1998— who have backed him under the lead of Michigan's John Engler. To find a presidential nomination that originated in the action of elected state officials, one must go all the way back to 1824, when several state legislatures put forth candidates.

POLICIES AND PROGRAMS

It is necessary to be selective because there are so many policies and programs. I will concentrate on three sets—welfare, schools, and criminal justice—that have traditionally been regarded as quite decentralized. Indeed, for decades they constituted the bedrock of local government activity.

The welfare reform legislation of 1996 is everyone's leading example of decentralization in action. The law converted what had been an open-ended matching grant, with federal funds tied to the number of cases, to a fixed-sum ("block") grant and explicitly ended individuals' entitlements to welfare. States gained freedom to design their own programs, a change already largely effectuated by White House decisions during the Reagan, Bush, and Clinton administrations to grant waivers of certain federal requirements to individual states. The decentralization of program authority in this case was an important change in intergovernmental relations. Still, its significance must be put in perspective.

Whatever may have happened with welfare in 1996, income support, which is the core function of the modern welfare state, has been largely federalized in the United States in the six decades since 1935. Social Security, Supplemental Security Income (SSI), and food stamps accounted for $431 billion in federal spending in 1998, compared with $22 billion for welfare, now known as TANF (or Temporary Assistance for Needy Families). I pass over the earned income tax credit, weighing in at a volume comparable to that for welfare, a use of federal tax law for income support that would take us too far afield here.

Welfare could be decentralized in 1996 in large part because, unlike income support for the aged and the disabled, it had never been fully centralized. The main change in 1996 was a national policy change that strongly discouraged dependency and certain behavior, especially out-of-wedlock pregnancies and lack of child support from fathers, that had come to be associated with welfare. To carry out this policy change, the new law imposed some stringent federal requirements, such as time limits for receipt of welfare, on the states. Surprisingly, a liberal president and conservative members of the new Republican majority in Congress coalesced in support of legislation, but the national coalition was so frail and incomplete that it became necessary to lodge discretion in the states to achieve a result.

That is one of the traditional functions of American federalism: in the absence of agreement at the national level, discretion can be left to the states. Typically, through *inaction* by Congress, matters are left with the states, which have initial jurisdiction. What was new in 1996 was that AFDC (Aid to Families with Dependent Children) had become sufficiently centralized in the generation since the mid-1960s that giving discretion to the states required an affirmative act. It required giving back some portion of what had been taken away, as much by federal courts as by Congress. "No more individual entitlement," the most arresting phrase in the act, was directed at altering relations between Congress and the federal judiciary. I would argue that the law had at least as much significance for what it said about interbranch relations at the federal level as about relations among governments in the federal system.

Elementary and secondary education, far from being off-limits to national politicians as a local matter, has risen to the top of their rhetorical agenda. It took a year for Congress to reauthorize the Elementary and Secondary Education Act in 1993-94. The resulting law consumed 14 titles and 1,200 pages, covering subjects as wide-ranging as academic standards, racial desegregation, language assessments, migrant education, teacher training, math and science equipment, libraries, hate-crime prevention, vouchers, school prayer, sex education, gay rights, gun control, the handicapped, English as a second language, telecommunications, pornography, single-sex schools, national tests, home schooling, drugs, smoking—and more. The level of detail was minute. Any state receiving federal funds had to require that any student who brought a gun to school would be expelled for at least a year. Local officials could, however, modify the requirement on a case-by-case basis. School districts also had to refer offenders to local law enforcement officials. Developmentally disabled students were subject to the expulsion rule, but if school officials established that their behavior was related to their disability, the students could be placed in an alternative educational setting for up to 45 days instead.

In 1999, when the act was again up for reauthorization, Congress by wide margins enacted "Ed-Flex," the Educational Flexibility Partnership Demonstration Act, which authorized the Secretary of Education to implement a nationwide program under which state educational agencies could apply for waivers of certain federal rules. To be eligible for Ed-Flex, states had to develop educational content and performance standards and procedures for holding districts and schools accountable for meeting educational goals. One could point to this law, of course, as an example of decentralization; members of Congress naturally did so. But in education as in welfare, the subject of waivers would never have arisen had not a vast body of law and regulation developed from which relief had to be sought.

In criminal justice, it remains true that most police and prosecutors are state and local officials. Ninety-five percent of prosecutions are handled by state and local governments. Yet federal criminal law has grown explosively as Congress has taken stands against such offenses as carjacking and church burning, disrupting a rodeo and damaging a livestock facility. A 1999 task force report of the American Bar Association documented and decried this development but is unlikely to stop, let alone reverse it.

THE "MORES" OF INTERGOVERNMENTAL RELATIONS

In everyday affairs, how do we and our officials think and talk about governments in the federal system? Without having any evidence to support my point, I would argue that citizens and journalists routinely refer to "the government" as if there were only one—the Big One. That this is a country of many governments, though a patent fact, is nonetheless a fact that it takes a pedant or a lawyer to insist on.

Moreover, we are now accustomed to reading that Washington is giving orders to the states, or at least exhorting them to act in regard to one or another matter in which they have been found deficient. Some sample headlines from end-of-century stories in the *New York Times* would appear very odd to a student of American government who had gone to sleep in, say, 1955 and just awakened: "Clinton to Require State Efforts to Cut Drug Use in Prisons" (January 12, 1998); "White House Plans Medicaid Coverage of Viagra by States" (May 28, 1998); "Clinton to Chide States for Failing to Cover Children" (August 8, 1999). None of this is to say that the states promptly act on orders or admonitions from Washington, only that Washington is accustomed to giving them, without pausing to question the appropriateness of doing so—as is evident from an executive order on federalism that the Clinton administration issued, suspended when state officials angrily protested, and then issued in much revised form.

The offending order, issued in May 1998, contained a set of criteria for policymaking by federal agencies that was broad and inclusive enough invariably to justify federal government action: "(1) When the matter to be addressed by federal action occurs interstate as opposed to being contained within one State's boundaries. (2) When the source of the matter to be addressed occurs in a State different from the State (or States) where a significant amount of the harm occurs. (3) When there is a need for uniform national standards. (4) When decentralization increases the costs of government thus imposing additional burdens on the taxpayer. (5) When States have not adequately protected individual rights and liberties. (6) When States would be reluctant to impose necessary regulations because of fears that regulated business activity will relocate to other States. . . ." Only the most obtuse and indolent federal administrator could not have put this list to use.

The revised executive order, issued following consultation with state officials, was completely different. The section on policymaking criteria called for "strict adherence to constitutional principles," avoiding limits on policy-making discretion of the states except with constitutional and statutory authority, granting "maximum administrative discretion" to the states, encouraging states to "develop their own policies to achieve program objectives," where possible deferring to the states to "establish standards," consulting with appropriate state and local officials "as to the need for national standards," and consulting with them in developing national standards when such were found to be necessary.

It is hard to imagine a more complete about-face. It is also hard to know how to interpret the event. One can cite the original order as evidence of the imperious attitudes that high federal officials actually bring to intergovernmental relations, or one can cite the revision as evidence of the continuing power of the states. In studying American federalism, the analyst is forever asking whether the glass is half-empty or half-full. That is the appropriate question as the century turns, and the answers are to be found more in the day-to-day operations of intergovernmental relations than in either Supreme Court decisions or executive orders. It requires a blind eye to call ours an era of devolution. But even with two sharp eyes, it is hard to detect a plain answer. Everywhere one looks, the answer remains murky and many-sided.

THE DUAL PERSONALITY
OF FEDERALISM

Carl Tubbesing

CONTEXT

In the last reading, Martha Derthick discussed the ambiguity of American federalism, pointing out that in many ways it is difficult to determine whether we are in a time of centralization of decentralization of power.

Over time, however, we can see broad challenges to the centralizing tendencies of federalism. For instance, in the late 18th century, Thomas Jefferson crusaded against Treasury Secretary Alexander Hamilton's efforts to centralize the national government's role in economic development and banking. During the Civil War, the size and power of the federal government exploded as Abraham Lincoln's Republican Party became known as the party of big government. Within a decade, however, the federal government's power was under assault by both southern conservatives interested in preserving states' rights and business interests within the Republican Party itself. In the early part of the 20th century, progressives used government to redistribute income and regulate wages and working conditions, among other actions, which led to a centralization of power at the federal level. However, advocates of a weaker central government, led by Herbert Hoover, reversed much of that trend. The federal government saw its powers greatly expanded during the Great Depression and World War II, but a conservative Congress curbed some of those powers in the 1940s and 1950s. More recently, efforts to curb the federal government's size and power have been led by Republican presidents Ronald Reagan and George Bush, and a Republican-controlled Congress in the 1990s. These more recent efforts to slow or reverse the centralizing tendencies of federalism have been called "devolution."

In the following selection, Carl Tubbesing argues that after a brief respite in the early 1990s when devolution was in full swing, centralization of policymaking is again on the rise. Tubbesing says there are five reasons why the federal government is again trying to centralize policymaking, ranging from politics to the demands of new technology.

● *THINK CRITICALLY* ●

1. Tubbesing's premise is that federal preemption of state activity is nearly always a bad thing. But for whom is it bad? Can you make the argument that preemption is good for individual citizens and business, even if states do not like it?
2. In your view, will the Internet accelerate centralizing forces in the United States, or make federal preemption a thing of the past? What would Tubbesing say?

This has been a Dr. Jekyll and Mr. Hyde decade for state governments. The Dr. Jekyll side of the 1990s has gotten more publicity. This is the side of the decade's personality defined by devolution, flexibility and more responsibility for state legislature. Dr. Jekyll has presented the states with landmark devolution legislation: most prominently, welfare reform, a new safe drinking water act, the children's health program and Medicaid reforms.

The Mr. Hyde aspect has received less attention. Preemption of state authority and centralization of policymaking in the national government characterize this half of the decade's dual personality. It restricts state options and promotes uniformity. The Mr. Hyde half has preempted state authority over telecommunications policy, federalized criminal penalties and given the federal government more responsibility for regulation of banks.

Dr. Jekyll is devolution. Mr. Hyde is counter devolution. Devolution trusts state officials and relies on them to be responsive and responsible. Counter devolution says state boundaries are archaic. Devolution subscribes to Justice Brandeis' premise that states are laboratories of democracy. Counter devolution raises the question, "Are states really necessary?"

The devolution trend may have lost momentum. (Only new legislation on work force training and surface transportation pending this year would continue devolution.) On the other hand, there are at least a dozen proposals before Congress this year that have the potential for more preemption and greater centralization in Washington of policymaking.

Is there something about the last decade of the 20th century that is accelerating the trend toward preemption? Yes and no. There are five primary explanations of why federal officials propose to preempt state activity. Two of these are more or less unique to the 1990s. Three, however, are permanent components of the preemption debate.

PREEMPTION BECAUSE OF TECHNOLOGY

There is no doubt that technological advances have altered the way the country conducts its business and the way people communicate. The Internet, computer networks, cellular phones and all of their technological and telecommunications cousins have shrunk the world. They ignore state boundaries, present daunting challenges to state regulatory schemes and tax structures, and tempt federal officials to supplant state regulation and taxation with national approaches.

Turn on your computer. Get on the Internet. Access the Barnes and Noble home page. Type in your Visa number. Order a hundred dollars worth of books. Do you pay your state and local sales tax? Probably not. Get in your car and drive to the mall. Go into Barnes and Noble and buy the same books. Do you pay your state and local sales tax? Absolutely.

Sign up with America Online. Pay the monthly fee. Do you pay a local government Internet access tax? Maybe, but probably not. Decide that you want to be the first in your neighborhood to use on-line telephony. Do you pay the telecommunications tax? Now, that's a really tricky one.

"Electronic commerce poses a long-term threat to the current tax system. The threat is that consumers will increasingly use electronic media for purchasing goods and services—circumventing conventional sales taxation," writes Thomas Bonnett in *Is the New Global Economy Leaving State-Local Tax Structures Behind?* State legislators are only just beginning to grapple with the tremendously complex and politically charged questions of whether and how to tax transactions on the Internet.

Federal officials are concerned about how state and local governments will tax the Internet. Some, like California Congressman Christopher Cox, Oregon Senator Ron Wyden and the Clinton administration, worry that any rush by state and local governments to tax it will stifle a burgeoning new industry and dampen economic activity. Senator Wyden argues that taxation of Internet activities would prevent "small high-tech businesses from prospering."

Wyden and Cox are pushing federal legislation that would prevent state and local governments from enacting new Internet taxes for six years. They argue that a lengthy moratorium is necessary to give the industry a chance to grow and to provide time for government and industry officials to work out a systematic approach. North Dakota Senator Byron Dorgan, a former state tax commissioner, strongly opposes the Cox-Wyden bill. "Federal preemption is inappropriate," he says. "The federal government should keep its nose out of the states' business."

Technology, combined with a dramatically evolving economy, also explains federal attempts to preempt state regulation of the banking and insurance industries. State legislatures initiated the revolution in financial services industries in the 1980s when they began allowing interstate banking. In 1994, Congress approved the Riegle-Neal bank reform bill that largely substituted federal interstate branch banking rules for the ones states had developed. Legislation to modernize banking pending before this session of Congress would further erode state control of financial services. The bill, whose chief sponsor is House Banking Chairman Jim Leach, would limit states' regulatory authority over insurance and securities.

Iowa Congressman Leach argues that technology and the changing financial services marketplace make state regulation of the industry virtually obsolete. In a March 1997 speech before the Institute of International Bankers, the Banking Committee chair argued: "The global financial services industry is evolving at a rapid pace, and legislation is needed in part to reflect marketplace changes, in part to set the ground rules for the next generation of change."

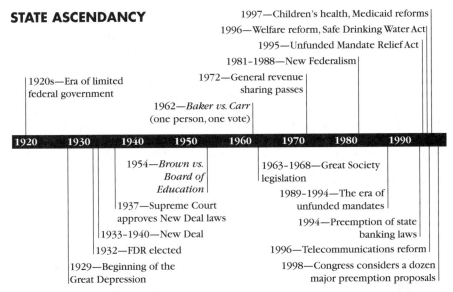

STATE ASCENDANCY

1997—Children's health, Medicaid reforms
1996—Welfare reform, Safe Drinking Water Act
1995—Unfunded Mandate Relief Act
1981-1988—New Federalism
1920s—Era of limited federal government
1972—General revenue sharing passes
1962—*Baker vs. Carr* (one person, one vote)

1920   1930   1940   1950   1960   1970   1980   1990

1954—*Brown vs. Board of Education*
1963-1968—Great Society legislation
1937—Supreme Court approves New Deal laws
1989-1994—The era of unfunded mandates
1933-1940—New Deal
1994—Preemption of state banking laws
1932—FDR elected
1996—Telecommunications reform
1929—Beginning of the Great Depression
1998—Congress considers a dozen major preemption proposals

FEDERAL ASCENDANCY

Since 1932 American federalism has largely been an era of predominance of the federal government in establishing domestic policy. The 1990s, marked by passage of legislation devolving some responsibilities to state governments, have seen some reversal of this trend. At the same time, the federal government also has taken authority away from the states in several key areas.

The Office of the Controller of the Currency, an executive branch agency, has made similar arguments in a series of recent rulings that have eroded the ability of states to regulate banking and insurance.

Despite the changing financial marketplace, defenders of state banking and insurance laws argue that state regulation is necessary to ensure a financial system that makes the most sense for each state. "Banking needs in Arkansas are just not the same as they are in New York," says Arkansas Representative Myra Jones. She fears that "continued nationalization of banking will prompt the exodus of investment capital from certain states, especially rural ones."

PREEMPTION AND POLITICS

Congressional politics have changed over the past decade. There are more competitive congressional districts. And congressional campaigns are becoming more and more expensive. It is plausible to argue that both of these developments have exacerbated the congressional tendency to propose legislation that would preempt state authority.

According to American Enterprise Institute scholar Norman Ornstein, congressional elections have become more competitive in the 1990s. More seats are changing parties from election to election. There are greater fluctuations in election margins. (An incumbent may win with 60 percent of the vote one year, then lose two years later.) And the number of safe seats has come down from the high mark of the 1988 election.

More competition presumably means that congressional candidates are actively on the lookout for issues that will appeal to voters. They need popular ideas that set them apart from their opponents. What better place to look than state legislatures?

For several years, legislatures have responded to consumer concerns about managed care. According to NCSL's Health Policy Tracking Service, 32 states have adopted legislation that gives patients in managed care direct access to OB/GYNs. Twenty-six legislatures have passed laws requiring that insurers cover emergency care. Recognizing the popularity of these and similar laws, Georgia Congressman Charles Norwood has introduced comprehensive legislation to regulate a variety of managed care practices. If approved, Norwood's bill would preempt all state legislation in this area.

The 1997 gubernatorial race in New Jersey drew national attention to consumers' concerns about the costs of automobile insurance. Since the 1970s, 15 state legislatures have attempted to control insurance costs by adopting no-fault laws. Kentucky Senator Mitch McConnell, asserting that "the nation's auto insurance system desperately needs an overhaul," introduced legislation in the 105th Congress that would preempt state laws and impose a national no-fault system.

State legislatures have responded in various ways to consumer complaints about fees that banks charge for using automatic teller machines. A few have banned the fees altogether. A few others have required banks to inform customers that they will be assessed a fee for using the machine. Bills currently pending in Congress copy these two approaches. New Jersey Congresswoman

Marge Roukema takes the warning message approach. New York Senator Alfonse D'Amato would ban the fees. Either would preclude state regulation and variations among states.

The cost of running for Congress has continued to rise in the 1990s—substantially more than the rate of inflation. A cynic might link the increase in preemption proposals to an incumbent congressman's nearly insatiable need to raise campaign funds. Some legislative and regulatory proposals, which almost coincidentally preempt state authority, are worth billions of dollars to companies. The companies naturally marshal their lobbying resources in support or opposition to the bills and favor their congressional allies with political donations.

In 1995, the New Hampshire legislature became the first in the nation to restructure electric utilities. Since then, nine other legislatures have approved similar legislation. In 1996, Colorado Congressman Dan Schaefer introduced legislation that proposes to impose national deregulation and to preempt state efforts. Such a massive change in the electric industry would be worth millions, if not billions, of dollars to companies effected by restructuring. For example, the Edison Electric Institute, a trade association for investor-owned electric utilities, opposes federal mandates that would require states to restructure. Enron, a power marketing company, supports such federal action.

It is not surprising, therefore, that campaign contributions from companies in this fight have increased dramatically since Congressman Schaefer first introduced his bill. For example, Enron and its PAC in 1993 reported soft money contributions to the various congressional campaign committees and the two national parties of $47,000. By 1995, this figure grew to $120,000. And in 1996, the year the deregulation bill was filed, Enron's soft money contributions totaled $286,500—a sixfold increase in three years.

Contributions to individual congressmen also increased in this period. Congressman Schaefer chairs the Energy and Power subcommittee of the House Commerce Committee. Campaign contributions from energy companies to Congressman Schaefer, for example, went up following introduction of his bill. In 1993-94, Schaefer reported contributions from energy companies and associations of $25,806. They increased by almost $10,000 for 1996-97—once the bill was introduced.

Comprehensive national legislation to reform telecommunications, which passed in early 1996, also attracted substantial donations to congressional campaigns and the national political parties. A 1996 Common Cause study found that "local and long distance telephone companies gave their biggest political donations ever during the last six months of 1995." The bill, which South Dakota Senator Larry Pressler called "the most lobbied bill in history," preempts state authority over the telecommunications industry and sets the conditions for entry of Bell companies into the long distance telephone market.

Certain congressional committees may be popular among members because of the issues with which they deal and their link to campaign contributions. Membership on the House Banking Committee has grown by five since the beginning of the current biennium. The Bureau of National Affairs attributes this to the committee's jurisdiction over financial modernization legislation—proposals that would preempt state authority. "It is a bonanza in terms of PAC funding," says an unnamed source for the BNA story. "The issue before the

Banking Committee pits the banking lobby against the securities lobby, the insurance lobby. It's a committee that naturally attracts major PAC funding. This is one of the richest PAC mines." And apparently a rich source of preemption.

PREEMPTION AND DIVERSITY

In the late 1970s, the National Conference of State Legislatures and the State Government Affairs Council cooperated on a project on "purposeless diversity." Legislators and private sector representatives attempted to identify policy areas in which uniformity among states was desirable. The project's premise was that some kinds of diversity impose costs on the private sector and, therefore, have a dampening effect on the economy. Like many things, though, purposeless diversity is in the eye of the proverbial beholder. Debate in the federal government over preemption often centers on whether uniformity is warranted in order to reduce private sector costs.

For a decade or more, Congress has considered legislation that would preempt state product liability laws. Proponents of preemption in this area argue that a national product liability law would reduce business costs and, therefore, improve the competitive position of American businesses. In testimony before the Senate Commerce Committee in 1993, Alabama Representative Michael Box asserted that these arguments are "specious" and lauded the advantages of a civil justice system that allows states to fine-tune their laws in response to changes within each state. Representative Box summarized by saying that "uniformity has no greater intrinsic value than the value of self- government by states."

In 1996, Congress approved product liability legislation. President Clinton vetoed it, however. During 1997, West Virginia Senator Jay Rockefeller shuttled between the White House and Capitol Hill in an attempt to find a compromise. New product liability legislation could surface again.

PREEMPTION AS A CATCH-22

Some advocates of specific preemption proposals argue that states have not done enough in the area. Proponents of others point out that most states have already acted, so why shouldn't the federal government step in and finish the job? State legislatures are damned if they do, damned if they don't.

In the damned-if-they-do category are some of the federal proposals to regulate managed care. If 41 states already ban the use of so-called gag clauses in communications between managed care doctors and patients, then, proponents ask, what's the harm in having a national law? But federal intrusion precludes additional experimentation and the adjustments that legislatures make as they gain experience with new laws.

In the damned-if-they-don't category this year is child care. President Clinton has made new child care legislation one of his top four or five initiatives for 1998. The administration so far has resisted pleas from some children's advocates to fight for national standards. The advocates argue that these standards are necessary because they believe many current state laws and regulations are inadequate to protect the safety of children.

PREEMPTION AND NATIONAL IMPERATIVES

Occasionally, achieving a national goal overrides concern for state authority. In these instances, preemption is nearly a coincidental effect of the desire to accomplish a compelling national objective. The Voting Rights Act of 1965, for example, substituted federal law for state laws in order to end discrimination. Federal air quality law supplants state laws and regulations because air does not recognize state boundaries, and states, acting on their own, cannot reduce pollution.

The national tobacco settlement and proposals to reform the federal tax system are good current examples. The tobacco agreement, reached among 41 state attorneys general and the tobacco industry, is intended to accomplish several objectives. It would reduce smoking, especially among children and adolescents. It would reimburse states for past and future medical costs for patients with smoking-related illnesses. And it would limit the tobacco companies' liability from at least some financial and legal claims. At the core of the agreement is a trade. The companies agreed to pay $368.5 billion over 25 years, $193.5 billion of which would go directly to the states. States, in turn, would accept federal preemption of state tort law. The attorneys general also agreed, in part to satisfy anti-smoking activists, to preemption in several other areas, including laws regarding smoking in public places, a minimum smoking age, vending machine sales and other retail practices. The settlement must be codified with federal legislation.

Several members of Congress, including Massachusetts Senator Ted Kennedy, Utah Senator Orrin Hatch, North Dakota Senator Kent Conrad and Arizona Senator John McCain, have introduced bills offering their versions of the settlement. Each would preempt state authority.

Proposals to reform the federal tax system have received more attention in the past several months, especially now that it appears the federal budget will be in balance within the year. Some would change elements of the current income tax structure. Others would scrap the income tax in favor of entirely different taxes. Texas Congressman Bill Archer, House Ways and Means chair, and Louisiana Congressman Billy Tauzin have different national sales tax proposals. House Majority Leader Dick Armey advocates a flat tax. The goals of these reformers include simplifying taxes, mitigating inequities and eliminating an unpopular tax. Any of the proposals, however, have consequences for state revenues and state tax codes, including preemption.

THERE ARE SOLUTIONS

State legislators and governors are working to find ways to draw attention to the problems posed by preemption and to minimize the number of federal bills and regulations that supplant state authority. Meeting in November 1997, representatives of NCSL, the National Governors' Association, the American Legislative Exchange Council and the Council of State Governments agreed to a set of "federalism statutory principles and proposals." The proposals are patterned in part after elements of the Unfunded Mandate Reform Act and are designed to place procedural obstacles in the way of attempts at preemption. The groups are now working to generate support in Congress and the administration for such a measure.

Current controversies over preemption and centralization reach back to the drafting of the Constitution, to the early days of the United States, and the debates between Alexander Hamilton and James Madison—differences that led to the formation of the first political parties in this country. They no doubt will continue into the next millennium.

5

YOU SAY YOU WANT A DEVOLUTION

NOAM CHOMSKY

CONTEXT

The drive toward devolution was fueled in part by a deep distrust of the federal government and what the federal government can or cannot do. This deep distrust of the federal government was exemplified by Ronald Reagan's declaration that government is not the solution to many problems but is in fact the problem. Advocates of the decentralization of federal power argue that states, individual entrepreneurs, and businesses can do a better job of solving many of the nation's social and economic problems than can the federal government. They contend that the market will regulate itself by causing unproductive enterprises to close down, whereas the federal government might continue to engage in unproductive activities that are ultimately harmful to the individual and the state.

In this selection, Noam Chomsky, one of America's most prominent political dissenters, argues that right now devolution is harmful for America. He contends that while devolution might be all the rage, it is in fact very harmful for the individual in society and very helpful for big business. Bureaucrats in the business world, he argues, can be as bad as government bureaucrats, but what makes them worse is where their loyalties lie and to whom they answer. In the government, bureaucrats are supposed to be loyal to the people, and theoretically answer to the people's representatives. In the business world, bureaucrats are loyal to their bosses and are concerned only about making profits.

The effects of devolving power and authority from the federal government to the states will be that a layer of protection from business abuses is taken away. The federal government often stands between big business and the individual citizen, protecting the citizen in many instances from the abuses of business. By removing the federal government from the decision-making process, and moving decision making to the states, proponents of devolution are doing nothing more than moving decision making to a level (individual states) where business can much easier control the decisions made. The ultimate losers are the individuals in society.

● *THINK CRITICALLY* ●

1. Chomsky contends that business bureaucrats can be as bad for people as government bureaucrats. Think about the current debates surrounding managed care and HMOs. Is Chomsky right? If not, why not?
2. Why do you think Chomsky trusts the federal government to do a better job of protecting people from business than state governments?

Imagine yourself in the office of a public-relations firm trying to turn people into ideal, manipulatable atoms of consumption who are going to devote their energies to buying things they don't want because you tell them they want those things. They're never going to get together to challenge anything, and they won't have a thought in their heads except doing what they're told. A utopia.

Suppose you're trying to do that. What you do is get them to hate and fear the government, fear the bigness of the government, but not look at the Fortune 500, nor even medium-sized businesses, not ask how they work. You don't want people to see that. You want them to worry about the one thing they might get involved in and that might protect them from the depredations of private power. So you develop a mood of anti-politics.

That's what has happened in America. People hate the government, fear the government, are worried about the bureaucrats.

Take, say, health care. There's a lot of concern that the government bureaucrats will be controlling it, yet there are many more bureaucrats in insurance offices who are already in control. But that's not what people worry about. It's not those pointy-headed bureaucrats in insurance offices who are making us fill out these forms and telling us what to do, and we've got to pay for their lunches and their advertising while they propagandize us. That's not what people's anger is focused on. What it's focused on, after a very conscious manipulation and a perfectly rational design, is this dangerous federal bureaucracy.

What's going on now with the attempt at devolution—the effort to reduce decision-making to the state level—makes great sense if you believe in tyranny. Devolution could be a step toward democracy, but not when you've got private tyrannies around.

General Electric is not influenceable by the population except very indirectly through regulatory mechanisms, which are very weak and which they mostly control anyhow. But you can't vote to decide what GE ought to do, and you can't participate in those decisions.

When you've got private tyrannies around, the only institution that at least in part reflects public involvement, that can cope with them, is the federal government.

Let's say you send block grants down to the states. Even middle-sized businesses have all kinds of ways of pressuring states to make sure that this money ends up in their pockets and not in the pockets of hungry children. Devolution under these circumstances is a great way to increase tyranny and to decrease the threat of democracy as well as to shift resources even more dramatically toward the rich and away from the poor. That's the obvious consequence of the current devolution.

But I've never seen it discussed in the mainstream. What's discussed are complete irrelevancies, like whether we can trust the governors to care for the poor.

What's that got to do with anything? It's totally meaningless. But that kind of absurdity is what's discussed, not the obvious, overwhelming fact that distributing governmental resources to the lower levels will simply make them more susceptible to the influence and control of private power. That's the major fact. And it's part of the same anti-politics: to weaken the federal government.

But not all of the federal government is being weakened. It's just being changed.

The security system is expanding, not only the Pentagon, but even the internal security system—jails, etc. That's not just for control, although it's partly for that. It's also a way of transferring resources to the rich, which is virtually never discussed.

In fact, this manipulation is almost off the agenda, unless you read the business press. But it's overwhelmingly significant. It ought to be a front-page article every day.

By now the sham is so obvious it's hard to miss. The Russians are gone. The Pentagon's budget stays the same; in fact, it's even going up.

It's there for the same reason it always was. How else are Newt Gingrich's rich constituents going to stay rich? You obviously can't subject them to market discipline. They'll be out selling rags! They wouldn't know what it means to exist in a market.

What they know is, the government puts money in their pockets, and the main way it does so is through the whole Pentagon system. In fact, the criminal security system is beginning to take on this character. It's reached, if not the scale of the Pentagon, a sufficient scale so that the big investment firms and even the high-tech industry, the defense industry, are getting intrigued by the prospects of feeding off another public cash cow. So it's not that the government is getting weaker.

But the long and very successful effort over many, many years to get people to focus their fears and angers and hatreds on the government has had its effect.

We all know there's plenty to be upset about. The primary thing to be upset about is that the government is not under popular influence. It is under the influence of private powers. But then to deal with that by giving private, unaccountable interests even more power is just beyond absurdity. It's a real achievement of doctrinal managers to have been able to carry this off.

The new Republicans represent a kind of proto-fascism. There's a real sadism. They want to go for the jugular. Anybody who doesn't meet their standards, they want to kill, not just oppose, but destroy. They are quite willing to try to engender fear and hatred against immigrants and poor people. They are very happy to do that. Their attitudes are extremely vicious. You can see it all over.

Take the governor of Massachusetts, William Weld, who's supposed to be a moderate, nice-guy type. Just last week every day in the newspapers there was another headline about forcing people out of homeless shelters if he didn't like the way they lived.

Some mother took a day off to take care of a mentally retarded child. OK, out of the homeless shelter. He doesn't like that. He thinks she should work, not take care of her child.

Some disabled veteran didn't want to move into a well-known drug den. OK, out in the street.

That's one day. The next day he says state social services have to report to the INS if they think somebody may be an illegal immigrant. Then that person gets deported. Which means that person's child gets deported. The child could well be an American citizen. So American citizens have to be deported, according to the governor, if he doesn't like their parents being here.

This is day after day. Pure sadism. Very self-conscious.

Weld is not a fool. And he's trying to build public support for it by building up fear and hatred. The idea is, there are these teenage kids who are black by implication (although you don't say that in a liberal state) who are just ripping us off by having lots and lots of babies. We don't want to let them do that. So let's hate them and let's kick them in the face. That's real fascism.

And that's the liberal side. It's not the Gingrich shock troops. That's the liberal, moderate, educated side. This aggression runs across the spectrum.

In the long term, I think the centralized political power ought to be eliminated and dissolved and turned down ultimately to the local level, finally, with federalism and associations and so on. On the other hand, right now, I'd like to strengthen the federal government. The reason is, we live in this world, not some other world. And in this world there happen to be huge concentrations of private power that are as close to tyranny and as close to totalitarian as anything humans have devised.

There's only one way of defending rights that have been attained, or of extending their scope in the face of these private powers, and that's to maintain the one form of illegitimate power that happens to be somewhat responsible to the public and which the public can indeed influence.

So you end up supporting centralized state power even though you oppose it.

I would propose a system that is democratic, and you don't have democracy unless people are in control of the major decisions.

And the major decisions, as has long been understood, are fundamentally investment decisions: What do you do with the money? What happens in the country? What's produced? How is it produced? What are working conditions like? Where does it go? How is it distributed? Where is it sold?

Unless that range of decisions is under democratic control, you have one or another form of tyranny. That is as old as the hills and as American as apple pie. You don't have to go to Marxism or anything else. It's straight out of the mainstream American tradition.

That means total dismantling of all the totalitarian systems. The corporations are just as totalitarian as Bolshevism and fascism. They come out of the same intellectual roots, in the early 20th century. So just like other forms of totalitarianism have to go, private tyrannies have to go. And they have to be put under public control.

Then you look at the modalities of public control. Should it be workers' councils, or community organizations, or some integration of them? What kind of federal structure should there be?

At this point you're beginning to think about how a free and democratic society might look and operate. That's worth a lot of thought. But we're a long way from that.

The first thing you've got to do is to recognize the forms of oppression that exist. If slaves don't recognize that slavery is oppression, it doesn't make much sense to ask them why they don't live in a free society. They think they do. This is not a joke.

Take women. Overwhelmingly, and for a long time, they may have sensed oppression, but they didn't see it as oppression. They saw it as life. The fact that you don't see it as oppression doesn't mean that you don't know it at some level. The way in which you know it can take very harmful forms for yourself and everyone else. That's true of every system of oppression.

But unless you sense it, identify it, understand it, you cannot proceed to the next step, which is: How can we change the system?

I think you can figure out how to change the system by reading the newspapers that were produced by twenty-year-old young women in Lowell, Massachusetts, 150 years ago, who came off the farms and were working in the factories. They knew how to change the system. They were strongly opposed to what they called "the new spirit of the age: gain wealth, forgetting all but self." They wanted to retain the high culture they already had, the solidarity, the sympathy, the control. They didn't want to be slaves. They thought that the Civil War was fought to end slavery, not to institute it.

All of these things are perfectly common perceptions, perfectly correct. You can turn them into ways in which a much more free society can function.

SECTION TWO

CIVIL LIBERTIES AND CIVIL RIGHTS

HEAD NOTES/SECTION QUESTIONS

Arguments over how democratic or undemocratic our nation really is, and over how much power the federal government should have in relation to the states, have persisted since the beginning of the nation. Few issues, however, have been more controversial over time than those related to civil liberties and civil rights.

Civil liberties are granted to citizens by the first ten amendments to the Constitution. They are a list of restrictions on the government, protecting people from the government. Government cannot limit speech or religious expression, invade one's privacy, or deprive one of life, liberty, or property without due process. Civil rights are rights that individuals have not to be treated differently (discriminated against, for example) based on classifications of race, religion, gender, or national origin. Civil rights are protection from other people as well as protection from government. Civil liberties have been "on the books" for a long time, while civil rights are more recent.

While the first ten amendments to the Constitution (the Bill of Rights) were ratified in 1791, they were not actually enforced to any great degree early on, and it was only over time that they were enforced at all. In fact, in the previous section we read selections about federalism and how much power the federal government should have in relation to the state governments. We can view the progression toward centralization of power at the federal level in the context of civil liberties and civil rights by looking at what scholars call the "nationalization of the Bill of Rights." The nationalization of the Bill of Rights took a great deal of time. Initially, the Bill of Rights only applied to the federal government, and limited how the federal government could treat citizens. The Bill of Rights did not apply to states.

After the Civil War, the Fourteenth Amendment to the Constitution gave the federal government the responsibility for protecting the rights of former slaves. The Fourteenth Amendment declared that the rights of citizens were not subject to state controls, but rather, federal controls. While the federal government did not use the Fourteenth Amendment to protect the rights of former slaves in the years immediately following the Civil War, the language in the Fourteenth Amendment, especially the second sentence, was very important.

The second sentence to the Fourteenth Amendment says "No State shall make or enforce any law which shall abridge the privileges or immunities of citizens of the United States; nor shall any State deprive any person of life, liberty, or property, without *due process of law*; nor deny to any person within its jurisdiction the *equal protection of the laws*" [italics added].

In the 1940s and 1950s, when the federal courts began to rule such things as segregation unconstitutional, they relied heavily on the second sentence of the Fourteenth Amendment, referring to the due process clause and the equal protection clause often. What the courts did was nationalize the Bill of Rights by incorporating the liberties guaranteed by the Bill of Rights into the Fourteenth Amendment. If the federal government could not limit speech, then based on the Fourteenth Amendment, neither could states. In the 1950s, a political movement began to take shape with the objective of guaranteeing equality for African Americans. The civil rights movement resulted in passage of major federal legislation, including the Civil Rights Act of 1964, which authorized the federal government to end segregation, and the Voting Rights Act of 1965, which authorized the federal government to guarantee the right to vote to all citizens eligible to vote.

While the civil rights movement lost much of its momentum after the mid-1960s, because of its successes several other civil rights movements resulted. In fact, many issues related to civil rights and civil liberties persist today. The readings in this section reflect contemporary civil liberties and civil rights issues related to religious freedom, gender equality, gay and lesbian rights, the right to vote, and the rights of the accused. As you read these selections, think about the following questions:

1. Are the civil rights and civil liberties issues of today as important in your view as the issues of the 1950s and 1960s? Why or why not?
2. Why do you think freedom of thought and expression, and freedom to be free of discrimination, are so important? Could we still progress as a society without civil rights and civil liberties?
3. Is everyone a member of some group that needs or deserves special protection? How do we set boundaries?

LEARN MORE ON THE WEB

American Civil Liberties Union
   http://www.aclu.org/

Center for Technology and Democracy
   http://www.cdt.org/

Civil Rights Division of the Department of Justice
   http://www.usdoj.gov/crt/crt-home.html

Leadership Conference on Civil Rights
   http://www.civilrights.org

⑥

PUTTING THE INNOCENT BEHIND BARS

ANNE MARTINEZ

CONTEXT

In the ideal world, defendants are presumed innocent. According to the Sixth Amendment to the U.S. Constitution, "the accused shall enjoy . . . a speedy and public trial . . . by an impartial jury . . . be informed of the nature and cause of the accusation . . . be confronted with the witness against him . . . [and] have the Assistance of Counsel." The Founders were so worried about a strong central government abusing citizens that they made sure that all citizens accused of a crime have certain rights that the government must guarantee.

The ideal and the reality, however, do not always reflect each other. In a famous discussion of the criminal justice system, Herbert Packer described two competing models of the criminal process in the United States. In the *due process model*, defendants are presumed innocent. Their rights are protected by the criminal justice system, and that very system makes every effort to ensure that innocent people do not go to jail. In this model, cases are argued before a jury, and after each side presents its best arguments, the jury decides the truth.

In reality, however, this ideal world, which sounds very much like what the Founders envisioned the criminal justice system to be, applies to only about 10 percent of all cases. The reality is described by what Packer calls the *crime control model*. In this model, defendants are presumed guilty and are processed in an administrative fashion through the criminal justice system by the actors involved in it. The most fundamental difference between the due process model and the crime control model is the presumption of guilt. If one is presumed guilty, then there is nothing more to do than process him or her through the system.

In this selection, Anne Martinez points out one of the consequences of the crime control model: many innocent people end up in jail. Martinez notes that as many as 10 percent of people convicted of serious crimes are actually innocent. The problem does not lie just with the police, prosecutors, or courts, but rather with the whole criminal justice system. Society is so concerned about crime, and wants so badly for those who have done wrong to face punishment, that the notion of innocent until proven guilty has almost been lost. Rather than innocent until proven guilty, she argues, the criminal justice system seems to be operating on a presumption of "guilty if arrested."

● *THINK CRITICALLY* ●───────────────────────────

1. In your view, is it more important to be "tough on crime" than it is to be protective of the rights of the accused? Is it possible to be both tough and protective of rights at the same time?
2. Is it okay for a few innocent people to suffer wrongly as long as those who are truly guilty do not get off on technicalities?
3. What does it mean to presume someone innocent?

If you don't want to spend time in jail, don't commit a crime. This statement sounds simple enough and widely is accepted as the truth, but in reality it is far from accurate: innocence doesn't protect someone automatically from incarceration, or even from execution.

That is a lesson Marjorie Blaha learned firsthand. When she was charged with a crime she didn't commit, Blaha took comfort in the belief that innocence is the ultimate defense. A veteran of the U.S. Navy, she had great trust in her country and by extension, its system of justice. Blaha mistakenly assumed she would be treated as innocent until proven guilty, not the other way around.

Instead, she spent 116 days in jail, where she was strip-searched, assaulted by another inmate, and confined to a tiny cell. Her life was threatened and her health suffered. Eventually, Blaha received her day in court, and the jury quickly found her innocent. That did not restore her reputation, health, life savings, or the thousands of dollars borrowed from relatives to help pay for her defense.

Others have fared much worse. George De Los Santos, Rene Santana, Charles Dabbs, Nathaniel Walker, V. James Landano, Joyce Ann Brown, Damaso Vega, Clarence Chance, Benny Powell, Clarence Brandley, Matthew Connor, Rubin Carter, Gilbert Alejandro, and Jack W. Davis all faced the death penalty or up to life in prison and spent years behind bars before being exonerated completely.

On May 20, 1992, Roger Coleman was strapped into the electric chair and executed by the state of Virginia, despite a last-minute cover story in *Time* magazine presenting serious questions about his guilt. Once Coleman was convicted, the courts fell deaf to his pleas of innocence, claims of incompetent defense counsel, and lists of evidence never presented. The *Time* article quotes Justice Byron White as writing: "It is hardly good use of scarce judicial resources to duplicate fact finding in federal court merely because a petitioner has negligently failed to take advantage of opportunities in state court proceedings." In other words, sorry, Roger, you missed your chance. We don't have time to listen to you anymore.

The Bureau of Criminal Statistics does not keep count of the number of people initially convicted and later proved innocent of all charges. Thus, it is impossible to pin-point the number wrongfully convicted who never are exonerated and set free.

David Rudovsky, a senior fellow at the University of Pennsylvania Law School, has practiced in a public interest/civil rights firm and spent time as First Assistant Defender with the Defender Association of Philadelphia. In 1986, he received a MacArthur Foundation Award for his criminal justice and civil liberties work. "I've been in the system for about 25 years and seen a lot of cases," Rudovsky notes. "I would say those convicted who are in fact innocent . . . I'd guess between 5 and 10%."

James McCloskey is the founder of Centurion Ministries, an organization that fights to free the wrongfully convicted. Writing in *Criminal Justice Ethics*, he indicates that "it is my perception that at least 10% of those convicted of serious and violent crimes are completely innocent."

How can a justice system adhering to the premise of innocent until proven guilty strip law-abiding citizens of freedom, savings, reputation, and their very lives? Mistakes, outright lies, and incompetence play a part, but it all comes back to attitudes—of the police, judges, jurors, attorneys, and society as a whole. The public wants wrongdoers to be punished and friends, families, and neighbors to be protected. With some exceptions, the people who make up the legal system want the same things, but their zeal to convict the guilty sometimes imprisons the innocent.

The average citizen believes that, for someone to be arrested and, especially, brought to trial, he or she must have done *something* wrong. This simply is not true. A single false accusation is enough to get somebody arrested, and potentially put behind bars.

"If you've got absolutely no corroborating evidence and that person [the accused] has a very firm alibi, there's some chance that [he or she] won't be arrested." Rudovsky points out. What if that individual has no alibi? "Then there's a decent chance that a police officer will swear out a warrant, the person will be arrested, and in terms of serving time, the first question is whether they will be able to make bail before there's a hearing or a trial on the charges. If there's a more serious crime, chances are the bail will be much higher and there's a greater likelihood that someone will spend time in prison or jail pretrial waiting for the case to come to trial. Beyond that, obviously, if you're convincing enough to a jury about your version and the defendant is not, then there's a possibility that the person will be convicted and serve a lot of time, depending on the seriousness of the offense."

It is not the laws themselves that are the problem. "Our protections on paper are strong ones," explains Philadelphia attorney Dennis Cogan, who has been practicing criminal law since 1971, long enough to observe that miscarriages of justice happen frequently. "What can be stronger than the notion, presumption of innocence? And that the defendant doesn't have to prove anything and that the government has to prove guilt beyond a reasonable doubt?" he asks. The answer, Cogan maintains, is that "Human beings are fallible and subject to influences of the outside world like the politicians who are screaming that more criminals should be in jail. When's the last time you ever heard a politician running for office say: 'When I get to the United States Senate and they offer a crime bill, my great concern is that we preserve the protections of the accused. I'm concerned about the survival of the Bill of Rights. I'm concerned about seeing to it that the court system and the process by which we determine guilt or innocence is fair?" According to Cogan, such a candidate never would be elected.

When an accused person arrives in court, he often is met by an overworked prosecutor, a judge who may assume the accused is as guilty as the majority who pass before the bench indeed are, and a jury that, despite being instructed on the presumption of innocence, has trouble applying that concept. Society is fed up with stories of violent criminals getting off on technicalities, offenders released only to harm someone else, and attackers who seemingly have more rights than their victims. It is easy to forget that the person being led before them in shackles well may be a victim himself, a wrongfully accused individual whom it is their job to set free. If the police have arrested this person and collected evidence against him, then he must be guilty.

Not necessarily. The detectives that investigated and arrested him carry large caseloads and are under great pressure to solve cases. They have intimate contact with the violence that sets the public shuddering when it catches a mere 20-second flash on the evening news, and they are charged with uncovering and capturing the guilty party. They don't always do it well. Cogan describes a situation he has seen all too frequently:

> The police start out believing something. They may have gotten incorrect information from an informant they had confidence in: they may be relying on their so-called street smarts and instincts which sometimes do not serve them well at all. And they start off believing something and they close their minds to other possibilities and then they go out and they build their facts, conveniently, sometimes subtly, around the conclusion. And that is what gives rise to the God-awful injustices that we see often.

In August 1994, an Associated Press story reported that a police chemist in Texas is responsible for putting at least three innocent men behind bars, and possibly many more. In one case, he testified that the semen found on the victim matched that of the accused, when it didn't. In another, testimony he gave about blood tests he had performed led an innocent man to come within one juror's vote of the death penalty. Later, the police chemist admitted that the convicted man's blood was not found at the scene at all.

The police don't deserve all the blame. Once someone is arrested, a presumption of guilt takes over. Prosecutors assume that the police got the right person: the judge expects the person the prosecutor brings into court to be guilty; and the jurors "hear the judge's instructions that the defendant is presumed innocent, but they assume, naturally, that if the person didn't do anything wrong the person wouldn't be there." Cogan notes. When an innocent person gets drawn into the legal system, whether through false accusation, official misconduct, or honest mistake, a competent criminal defense attorney often can obtain his or her release quickly. Accused individuals who do not know how to find or can't afford such an attorney are in serious jeopardy. Public defenders, even the most competent, are notoriously overloaded. At the crucial moment when an expert, dedicated defense could save the day, the accused can be served improperly. Once someone is convicted, the chance of exoneration is severely dimmed: if innocence won't keep someone out of jail, it certainly won't get him or her a retrial either. Once a person is wrongly convicted, it takes significant new evidence or determination of material procedural error during the trial to get a new hearing.

IN SEARCH OF JUSTICE

Those who wrongfully languish behind bars are not without champions. The number of people fighting for them is growing. In 1983, McCloskey founded Centurion Ministries to battle for the freedom and vindication of innocent people who have been convicted by the system that was supposed to protect them. The full-time staff of three and volunteers working with the organization have received thousands of petitions for assistance. So far, they have managed to free 12 people from life imprisonment or death sentences in prison.

Cogan has co-founded a committee of the National Association of Criminal Defense Attorneys called Free the Innocent Imprisoned. This nationwide network provides *pro bono* services to aid Centurion Ministries.

In February 1994, a newly formed organization called the Association in Defense of the Wrongly Convicted (AIDWYC) brought together lawyers, activists, and the wrongly convicted for a conference in Toronto, Canada. People from the U.S., Canada, and the United Kingdom told their tales of wrongful imprisonment while judges, attorneys, and laypeople discussed how judicial systems go awry and what can be done about it.

Such organizations face an uphill battle. Those fighting to preserve protections for the accused are charged with being soft on crime because it is impossible to protect the innocent without also protecting the guilty. By and large, the public just doesn't believe that innocent people can be and are arrested, jailed, convicted, and sometimes even sentenced to death.

AIDWYC has proposed the institution of an independent review commission for those who have been convicted wrongly. Sending a case back to the same people who did the convicting in the first place is asking human beings to admit grievous mistakes or own up to malfeasance: this is incompatible with the search for truth. When misconduct rips innocent persons from their families and places them in jail with rapists, murderers, and other felons, those responsible should be held accountable.

Cogan recently attempted to do just that. He sued the city of Philadelphia on behalf of a man wrongly convicted on two counts of first-degree murder and sentenced to die in the electric chair. The suit charged the city and certain named police officers with malicious prosecution, conspiracy to commit official oppression, and other torts. A jury awarded his client $4,500,000, a settlement Cogan says may be the largest ever. The client has yet to see a cent of it, though—the verdict is being appealed.

Winning such cases is difficult, and restitution is uncommon. Crime victims receive compassion, assistance, and, sometimes, restitution. Aren't innocent people who have been stripped of their freedom, bankrupted, and torn from society for years at a time victims as well? At the very least, they should have the money expended for their defense reimbursed. More fairly, compensation for time spent in jail and psychological help in dealing with being arrested and incarcerated for something they didn't do is in order. Their lives never can be restored as they were, but whatever amends that can be made should be.

The following is excerpted from a letter written by Marjorie Blaha as she waited in jail for her day in court: "Arose at 5 a.m. to shower and dress in prison garb—6:30 a.m. eat dead food—7:15 a.m. taken to change into street clothes and subjected to strip search—placed in a 4'×6'×13' high cell with one window view of a wire fence and a door view of another brick wall one foot away. It had all the creature comforts—stainless steel sink toilet (I wasn't sure which hole was for what so I just sat on the 3'×4' metal bench). 9 a.m. I was handcuffed and escorted to a van full of all the male cousins of our mutual knife wielding friend." [This refers to a frightening incident wherein a woman waving a huge carving knife stormed past on a public sidewalk.] On the back of the lined notebook paper, there is a final scribbled sentence: "Started this but just couldn't go on—it made it all too real."

All this occurred as she supposedly was being presumed innocent. The second lawyer she retained expertly defended her, the jury chose to believe her side of the story; and she was exonerated, but that's not enough. Her money is gone, reputation smeared, faith in the government she served shattered, and anger fills her heart—and she is one of the lucky ones!

THE WORST DECISION SINCE "DRED SCOTT"?

WILFRED M. McCLAY

CONTEXT

The First Amendment to the U.S. Constitution says, "Congress shall make no law respecting an establishment of religion, or prohibiting the free exercise thereof . . ." The Founders clearly intended religion to be one area where government could not interfere with the individual, either in a supportive way or a restrictive way. However, separating the church and the state is more difficult than it sounds.

Take, for example, the case discussed by Wilfred M. McClay in this selection. McClay argues that the Religious Freedom Restoration Act (RFRA), a law passed by Congress in 1993, while seeming to be consistent with the separation of church and state, was actually damaging to it. The RFRA was passed by Congress in response to a 1990 Supreme Court case, *Employment Division v. Smith*. In that case, the court ruled that laws that apply to all citizens equally do not violate constitutional protections just because they unintentionally burden particular religious practices. In the Smith case, two members of the Native American Church were dismissed from their state jobs for ingesting peyote (which is an illegal hallucinogen) as part of a religious ceremony. Members of the church claimed that their religious freedoms were violated. The court said their religious freedoms were not violated because any employee, regardless of religious affiliation, would have been dismissed for ingesting peyote.

In response to the court's ruling, which essentially took away any special exemptions that religious organizations had enjoyed from certain state, local, and federal laws, these organizations began to ask Congress to pass a law giving back such exemptions. In 1993 Congress passed the RFRA, which gave religious organizations protection from any laws that "substantially burdened" religious practices. The Supreme Court ruled RFRA unconstitutional saying that only the court could interpret a case or controversy regarding the Constitution, and it had already done that in the *Employment Division v. Smith* case. In this particular debate, the court emphasized the establishment of religion (Congress could not protect religion) and Congress emphasized the freedom of religion (the state could not penalize someone for practicing religion).

McClay argues that although supporters of the RFRA decried the Supreme Court's ruling as an assault on the constitutional right of religious freedom, it was simply a bad law and the court struck it down as such. If the law had passed Supreme Court scrutiny, McClay argues that few government actions would be able to withstand the claims of violating the free exercise of religion. Why? Because the law defined religious freedom in very individualistic terms.

● *THINK CRITICALLY* ●

1. The U.S. Constitution says that "congress shall make no law restricting the establishment of religion." What exactly is "religion"? Could the Church of Marijuana be a religious organization in your view?
2. Based on the Supreme Court's ruling in *City of Boerne v. Flores*, could you envision a situation where in one location a particular activity is considered "religious" while in another location it is not? Explain why or why not.

Few pieces of congressional legislation in recent years have aroused less initial controversy than the Religious Freedom Restoration Act (RFRA), a 1993 bill designed to overturn a Supreme Court ruling that appeared to many to threaten religious liberty. An almost surreal array of leaders from across the full spectrum of American religious institutions and practices—established and novel, liberal and orthodox, mainstream and fringe—endorsed the bill, and some of the bitterest antagonists in today's culture wars, including diehard secularists, were willing to lay down their arms and make common cause in promoting it. RFRA then swept through Congress like a prairie fire, encountering only three nays in the Senate and none in the House. The ever-attuned President Clinton enthusiastically signed it into law.

That RFRA touches upon issues of overwhelming importance to many Americans may help explain the widespread alarm and even outrage this past summer when the Supreme Court, in a 6-3 decision, *City of Boerne v. Flores*, voted to strike it down. The normally staid *Christian Science Monitor*, whose mother church had supported RFRA, editorialized that the Court had "lobbed a figurative bomb into the middle of this nation's already-hot debate over religious rights." "Every church and synagogue, every religious person in America will be hurt by this decision," protested Reverend Oliver Thomas of the National Council of Churches, while David Saperstein of the Union of American Hebrew Congregations declared that the decision would "go down in history with *Dred Scott* and *Korematsu* among the worst mistakes this Court has ever made."

Politicians were not far behind, with Senator Orrin Hatch, the conservative Republican from Utah, declaring that "the Court has once again acted to push religion to the fringes of society" and Representative Charles Schumer, the liberal Democrat from New York, adding heatedly that *Flores* forces citizens "to choose between their government and their God." Most impressive of all, in some ways, was Justice Sandra Day O'Connor's passionate dissent in the case, which she read aloud from the bench to emphasize the strength of her contrary view.

Is *Flores* really as cataclysmic in its implications as the critics say? To answer this question requires a little background.

RFRA was, as I have mentioned, a direct legislative attempt to topple another controversial Court decision, *Employment Division v. Smith* (1990). In that case, the Court rebuffed the claim of two Oregon men who were seeking unemployment benefits; they had been fired from their drug-counseling jobs for using peyote, a hallucinogen, as part of what they maintained were "sacramental" rites. In writing for the majority in *Smith*, Justice Antonin Scalia repudiated the doctrine that government requires a "compelling interest" to burden the free exercise of religion afforded by the First Amendment. (The "compelling-interest" doctrine, itself first established in a 1963 case, had dramatically raised the barrier to any government interference with religious exercise.) Instead, Scalia allowed for the possibility that the free exercise of religion might be legitimately limited by a general law, so long as the limitation was an "incidental effect" rather than the product of a clear intent to target an individual or his faith.

To many observers, particularly those affiliated with some of the more prominent religious communities, Scalia's formulation seemed too dismissive of the claims of religious liberty. Their anger quickly gave rise to the strange-bedfellows' alliance that in turn produced RFRA, a measure explicitly designed to restore the more stringent standard.

Proponents of RFRA claimed at the time that it fell well within Congress's purview to pass this law, since the Fourteenth Amendment gives Congress the right to "enforce" the First Amendment at state and local levels. Yet the language of the Act itself sounded less like an enforcement provision than a proclamation of fundamental law. RFRA stipulated that in the absence of that famous compelling interest, "Government shall not substantially burden a person's exercise of religion even if the burden results from a rule of general applicability." These words, aimed specifically at Scalia's ruling in *Smith*, were a direct legislative rebuke of the Court.

That threw down a gauntlet. Since the task of constitutional interpretation has always belonged to the highest tribune of the judicial branch, it was hardly likely that the Court would submit to such a frontal raid on its powers and perquisites. And indeed the *Flores* decision, written by Justice Anthony Kennedy and joined by both the most liberal and the most conservative members of the Court, scarcely addressed itself to issues of religious liberty at all, focusing instead on RFRA's violation of the constitutional separation of powers, and its damaging effects upon federalism and state power.

In the majority opinion, Kennedy brushed aside any claim that the Act had been designed to correct a serious problem involving repression of religion. Rather, he argued, the law represented a substantive attempt to end-run the Court's decision in *Smith*. From the point of view of the Constitution, Congress had simply exceeded its powers. In the process, it had also begotten a dangerously "sweeping" and disproportionate Act, one likely to have countless unforeseen consequences, "displacing laws and prohibiting official actions of almost every description and regardless of subject matter."

On this last point, Kennedy's view tends to be confirmed by an examination of the facts of *Flores*, a case that arose not out of any state-sponsored persecution of heretics but out of a lowly zoning dispute. St. Peter the Apostle Church, a Roman Catholic parish in Boerne, Texas, wished to expand its 74-year-old church building to accommodate a swelling congregation. But the church building, a mission-style structure of middling charm, was clearly protected by the city's 1991 historic-preservation ordinance. On that basis, Boerne's landmark commission and city council refused to issue a permit to make the desired alterations.

Of such conflicts are local politics made, and normally the conflicts are settled by a process of mutual accommodation that the world little notes nor long remembers. But with RFRA's provisions on the books, the church, and the Catholic Archdiocese which championed it, no longer had to accept even a partial defeat. Instead, it claimed it had been discriminated against, that the historic-preservation ordinance substantially burdened its congregants' free exercise of religion, and that the First Amendment had thereby been traduced.

This was, of course, opportunism of the most naked sort—but precisely the kind of behavior to which RFRA had opened the door. In the wake of the Act's passage, other cases like this one had begun to pop up in jurisdictions across the country. Prison inmates claimed the right to use drugs as part of their religious rituals; an Amish group in Wisconsin claimed, and won, an exemption from a requirement to post orange safety triangles on its members' horse-drawn buggies; a Presbyterian church in Washington, D.C., fought successfully to establish a food program for the homeless over the objections of city zoning officials.

Such cases opened the prospect that state and local governments would be rendered powerless to avert multiplying claims of "burdened" religious expression. Small wonder, then, that sixteen states joined with the city of Boerne in challenging RFRA. All of them faced the possibility of seeing their legal and regulatory structures undermined by religion's imperious claims—and of an ocean of litigation brought by those with sufficient enterprise and brass to try the "sacramental" angle when all else failed. Instead of alleviating public distrust of religion, RFRA was exacerbating it.

In passing RFRA, certainly, Congress seems to have given scant consideration to what it was setting loose. To the contrary, RFRA was one of those carelessly conceived, crowd-pleasing efforts that have become the legislative branch's *spécialité de la maison*. Seizing on a Good Thing and elevating it to an abstract status, sponsors of such legislation blithely ignore the probability that the single-minded pursuit of any Good Thing will inevitably come into conflict with the pursuit of another Good Thing, or foreclose the ability to sustain many other Good Things.

Under RFRA, virtually any local law or regulation could be made vulnerable to the scrutiny of federal courts on the grounds that it unintentionally burdened religious exercise. This makes a potential mockery of American federalism, whose genius is to allow localities to fight these things out themselves. Indeed, after the Supreme Court handed down *Flores*, that is just what happened in the city of Boerne. Deprived of the fuel of RFRA, the Archdiocese and the city council had no choice but to sit down and settle their differences; in August, two months after the Supreme Court ruling, they did so.

But aside from all the practical benefits of relying whenever possible on concrete, local precedents and traditions, there are also other considerations, flowing from the fact that "religion" is such an exceptionally difficult concept to define. Although the First Amendment establishes a rough baseline, it goes no further than that, and there are good grounds for distrusting any particular court's universal formulation—particularly if that formulation is to carry legal weight. Precisely because a satisfactory one-size-fits-all definition cannot be found, there is every reason to prefer the rough diversity of understandings made possible by federal arrangements, which subdivide authority and power in ways that are closer to, and more respectful of, the actual communities and institutions in which genuine, well-established religious faiths are practiced.

RFRA moved matters in the opposite direction, threatening the establishment of a national standard for "religion" and the "burdening" thereof, just as the Department of Agriculture (USDA) does for levels of the *E.-coli* bacillus in the slaughterhouse. In particular, RFRA construed the concept of "burden" strictly in terms of "a *person's* exercise" (emphasis added), thereby leaving the clear impression that the free exercise of religion was primarily an individual matter. Such a presumption virtually ensured that, say, a Church of Marijuana, and any number of ersatz cults and exotic new revelations, could plausibly command an equal standing with established faiths.

Aside from its palpable absurdity, such a development would codify a false understanding of religion, which is not just another word for an individual's collected metaphysical musings. By implicitly defining religion in these terms, RFRA played directly into our pernicious tendency to emphasize the autonomous, unencumbered, and unhistorical self as the building block of social and political reality. This tendency was evinced memorably by the Court itself in its 1992 *Casey* abortion decision, which identified liberty as "the right to define one's own concept of existence, of meaning, of the universe, and of the mystery of human life."

Given such proclivities at the highest levels of our legal culture, it is perhaps understandable that RFRA's drafters chose to couch its claims in the language of self-actualization and individual rights. But what such a formulation leaves utterly out of account is that religion is a social and institutional phenomenon, embodied in historically rooted communities of faith that not only share a highly elaborated and codified system of beliefs but embrace and transmit to others, children in particular, a discipline that reaches into the deepest crevices of their physical, mental, and moral lives. Unless religious communities are free to create and sustain a distinctive moral universe powerful and plausible enough to shape the souls of their adherents, religious liberty will devolve into little more than spiritual consumerism.

Of course, many of our mainstream religious leaders are themselves guilty of encouraging or pandering to just such consumerism, and of failing to transmit their own traditions faithfully. But the greatest *legal* danger to religious freedom in years to come will arise not from that quarter, or, for that matter, from the suppression of peyote-users and aspiring church architects. It will come from the more general erosion of the rights of private association at the hands of the very federal government that RFRA would have made into religion's USDA.

Religious liberty means very little unless religious communities have defensible boundaries. But it is not at all fanciful to imagine, for example, that RFRA could eventually have been invoked by embittered or opportunistic individuals to undermine the authority of their own denominations, on the grounds that these institutions imposed an orthodoxy that "burdened" religious exercise by failing, say, to affirm their life-style, or by prohibiting them from being ordained. By conceiving of religious liberty in strictly individual terms, RFRA contributed to the very problem it sought to solve.

If, in the next round of the battle, defenders of religious liberty raise a different banner, one that respects the integrity and independence of religious groups, and builds upon the unique advantages offered by a federal system, they will have a smaller, less diverse coalition to call upon. They will probably not be joined, as they were in 1993, by People for the American Way and the American Civil Liberties Union. But they will have a far better cause, and they may find a Court that is far more willing to listen to them.

8

DOES ATHLETIC EQUITY GIVE MEN A SPORTING CHANCE?

KAREN GOLDBERG GOFF

CONTEXT

Following the successes of the civil rights movement, as reflected in the passage of the 1964 Civil Rights Act and the 1965 Voting Rights Act, the movement for gender equality gained momentum. In the late 1960s and early 1970s, a newly energized women's movement began to use many of the same tactics, such as demonstrations, rallies, and lobbying, to call for gender equality. While the women's movement was not successful in its ultimate goal, the passage of the Equal Rights Amendment, it was successful in several smaller goals.

One of those smaller goals was the passage of Title IX of the Higher Education Act of 1972. Title IX, as it is commonly referred to today, prohibits federal funding for schools and universities that discriminate against women, including in intercollegiate sports programs. One of the results of Title IX has been a dramatic increase in the amount of money budgeted for women's athletic programs at public colleges and universities, and in the number of women playing college sports. In 1972, about 75,000 women played college sports. Today, nearly 250,000 women play college sports.

In this article from *Insight on the News*, Goldberg Goff points out the difficulties that many colleges and universities are having complying with the 1972 law that requires gender equity in college and university athletic programs. In order to comply with the law, which requires that the number of male and female athletic scholarships be equal to the proportion of male and female students enrolled at the school, many schools have been cutting male sports programs. Critics claim this is unfair to male athletes. Others argue that schools do not have to cut male programs but instead could simply add female programs.

● *THINK CRITICALLY* ●─────────────────────────────

1. In your view, is the federal government doing the right thing or the wrong thing when it tries to enforce gender equality in college sports?

2. In what way is the government able to force colleges and universities to comply with the 1972 law mandating proportionality in athletic programs?
3. Could there be another way other than basing equality on the percentage of males and females at a school to reach gender equality in sports?

Jason Hairston can't recall what emotions he felt most strongly when he heard the news that Providence College in Rhode Island was killing its baseball program. Even after a few weeks, the junior centerfielder could not sort them out.

"I'm past mad, upset and frustrated" says Hairston, a graduate of Good Counsel High School in Wheaton, Md. "What am I going to do? Transfer and sit out a year? Where am I going to go? I've grown up with baseball. It has taken me everywhere in my life. It has kept me motivated to do well in school. I've made sacrifices, missed graduations and funerals because of it. For it not to be there hurts."

Hairston, who hopes to play professional baseball, and his teammates will remain on scholarship through graduation. But with the end of Providence's 80-year-old baseball program, they are the latest victims of gender equity in college sports.

Although Title IX—the 1972 federal law mandating equal scholarships, opportunities and facilities for male and female athletes—has created new chances for women, some athletic departments have had to create those opportunities by subtracting from, and sometimes eliminating, men's programs. The law mandates that the percentages of roster spots in athletic programs be in proportion to the percentages of men and women enrolled at each school—if a school's student body is 55 percent female and 45 percent male, scholarships and roster spots must be appropriated accordingly. Otherwise, the government can deny the school federal funds, a consequence that has colleges searching for ways to add inexpensive women's programs, such as soccer, rowing and softball. But some cash-strapped schools are finding it impossible to add teams for women and still maintain certain non-revenue sports for men.

"If you look at the whole law, it has accomplished a whole lot," says George Washington University Athletic Director Jack Kvancz. "But the proportionality test becomes a real issue. It is the toughest part of Title IX. You sometimes have to rob from Paul to pay Paula, and that is not what most universities want to do."

Kvancz did some creative rearranging recently when GWU purchased all-female Mount Vernon College, adding 300 women to the university's enrollment and changing the male-female ratio by 4 percent. As a consequence, the school will add four women's sports—lacrosse, softball, waterpolo and squash—during the next three years at a cost of $500,000 in scholarships alone, says Kvancz.

Few schools have been able to budget so well. Between 1985–86 (when Title IX first was vigorously enforced) until 1995–96, NCAA Division I schools lost 35 wrestling teams, 19 men's gymnastics teams and 18 men's swimming teams. Meanwhile, 132 women's soccer programs and 83 crew programs were initiated.

At the Olympic level, the effects of 25 years of Title IX were visible at the 1996 Atlanta Summer Games, where women won gold medals in softball, basketball and soccer. Meanwhile, the reduction in men's college sports showed in a more subtle way, with American swimmers winning 12 medals, 15 fewer than they had 20 years earlier in Montreal.

The U.S. Olympic Committee was concerned enough to pledge $8 million in funds from 1997 until the 2000 Sydney Summer Games to help college conferences bolster or restore programs. Last year, men's gymnastics received $4.4 million, and new training centers have been built in San Antonio, Minneapolis and Salt Lake City for youths in sports that no longer are offered at some colleges.

Women's advocates contend that schools need not cut men's nonrevenue sports; rather, they should look at scaling back the excesses of sports such as football, which use a disproportionately large number of roster spots, scholarships and expenses. Most Division I-A football teams are allowed 85 scholarships and an unlimited number of walks-ons, bringing the total to more than 100 spots at some schools. And the average Division I-A program loses about $600,000 annually, according to the Women's Sports Foundation.

"Intercollegiate football and basketball programs have fallen victim to excess," writes Donna Lopiano, executive director of the Women's Sports Foundation, in a recent article titled, "Will Gender Equity Kill the Golden Goose of College Football?" She adds, "The beat-the-Joneses mentality has resulted in an expenditure war that includes country-club locker rooms, indoor practice facilities and first-class hotel accommodations the night before home games."

Meanwhile, male gymnasts, tennis players and wrestlers have found an ally in the Independent Women's Forum, a Washington-based conservative women's group that operates a full-time Play Fair project that examines and addresses gender equity. Kimberly Schuld, director of Play Fair, argues that the root of the problem rests in the law's language.

"The Office of Civil Rights [responsible for enforcing the law] has taken a direction completely at odds with common sense," says Schuld. "There is now discrimination against boys because of it. It is not realistic to expect every woman to be interested in participating in varsity sports."

Schuld notes that a large portion of female students are returning students older than 25 and ineligible by NCAA rules. Another large portion is simply not interested in participating. Play Fair recently surveyed all-female colleges such as Mount Holyoke, Smith and Bryn Mawr. The survey found that only between 10 and 15 percent of the students at those all-female schools play sports.

"If all women are interested in playing varsity sports as men and men hold them back, then wouldn't every student at an all-female school be participating in varsity sports?" asks Schuld. "Wouldn't there be 37 percent participation [equal to total NCAA participation]?"

Leo Kocher, wrestling coach at the University of Chicago, an NCAA Division III school, agrees that there seems to be a double standard. "Look at music and theater—they are dominated by women," Kocher says. "How about student government, nursing and dance? That's probably 90 percent women, and no one seems to have a problem with that. It is accepted that boys just aren't as interested in those things.

"But not in sports—Title IX makes the presumption that the only difference is discrimination. Title IX, the way it is interpreted, is a quota law. As long as you have more males than females, you are subject to a lawsuit. It is about punishing boys for having more interest in sports."

Wrestling programs have been among the hardest hit in the last 20 years. Wrestlers and coaches blame Title IX, but gender-equity advocates say the sport already was dying. Still, non-revenue athletes, coaches and athletic directors are willing to go to great lengths to see that sports such as wrestling remain. At California State University at Bakersfield, nine wrestlers and swimmers have filed sexual-discrimination grievances against the school, which was forced to cut roster spots to try to meet the student population ratio (63 percent female, 37 percent male). At Princeton, the program recently was allowed to become endowed by alumni contributions—at a price of $2.3 million. "In two months, there were enough contributions to fund the program," says Eric Pearson, former Princeton wrestler who coached the ailing program from 1993 to 1996.

George Mason University in Virginia added a $3.50 student-activity fee to its tuition. That enabled the 20,000-student school to keep men's volleyball and men's and women's tennis and still fund a new women's crew team and men's and women's swimming. The University of Maryland has limited roster spots and scholarships—but not entire teams—in men's non-revenue sports. Athletic Director Debbie Yow predicts the university will be in compliance with Title IX by next year, when a women's golf team will begin play. The university also has added women's soccer and softball in recent years.

"We've been as creative as we can get," says Yow, who has eradicated a $7 million athletic-department debt since arriving four years ago. "We sold a [home] football game [and earned $1 million for playing it in Tallahassee, Fla., rather than College Park]. But eventually you run out of ways to find money."

Nevertheless, many schools, facing lawsuits and the withholding of federal dollars, slap together women's programs strictly to meet proportionality standards. At Eastern Illinois, for example, a crew team (and about 60 roster spots for women) was added, even though there are no high-school programs in the state.

"Many schools will hand you a full scholarship if you can sit down at a rowing machine in a gym and go at a certain pace," says Mike Copperthite, executive director of the Washington-based National Coalition for Athletic Equity. "How can we allow the government to take away opportunities from one team and give them to another? It's unfair."

VOTER LOCKDOWN

HAMIL R. HARRIS

CONTEXT

The definition of a democratic society is one in which the people ultimately rule. Of course, in the United States the people do not rule directly, that would be nearly impossible with almost 300 million of us. Instead, in the United States, the people elect representatives to make decisions on their behalf. So, we rule indirectly through our representatives. What this means is that for the average American, the most important way to participate in our democracy is by voting for the representative who will make decisions for him or her.

Yet, we already know that many people simply do not participate in their democracy by voting. In recent presidential elections, for example, only about 60 percent of eligible voters actually turned out to vote. While we should be troubled by these low turnout percentages, many of those people who did not vote made a conscious choice not to vote. Other people, some of whom might have wished to vote, could not because they had been barred from voting by law because they had once been convicted of a crime.

In this selection from *Black Enterprise* magazine, Hamil R. Harris points out that a large number of those barred from voting due to their criminal records are African Americans. He contents that prohibiting someone from voting even after they have served their time and been released is unfair, and particularly damaging to African Americans because they have been disproportionately impacted by the war on drugs. Harris talks about legislation intended to allow felons who are no longer incarcerated to vote in federal elections.

● *THINK CRITICALLY* ●────────────────

1. Does it strike you as fair that someone can be denied the right to vote even after they have paid their debt to society? Why or why not?
2. Is the right to vote a fundamental constitutional guarantee?
3. Why is the legislation that Harris talks about only aimed at federal elections? Do you think states should follow suit if Congress passes such a law?

Nathaniel Mathes seemed like your typical 20-year-old to most observers in 1987. He had recently graduated from Toledo High School in Ohio with a 3.2 grade point average and was in the top 20 of his graduating class. He received a scholarship from the University of Toledo and was coaching high school wrestling to earn some extra money.

But in 1988 he was convicted on federal charges of attempting to sell cocaine. So instead of pursuing his dreams on a college campus, his only claim to fame for the next several years would be that he was in prison with discredited PTL preacher Jim Bakker.

Today, Mathes is out on parole and working as a small business representative for MCI Communications. He's working to restore his family life and actually believes he's a better person now than before his incarceration. But there is one thing keeping Mathes from participating fully in society—like most former convicts, Mathes is barred from the voting booth.

"We've made the transition by rehabilitating ourselves for our families," says Mathes. "Getting the right to vote again would enable us to take advantage of the opportunity to make our voices heard."

With that in mind, Michigan Rep. John Conyers recently introduced the Civic Participation and Rehabilitation Act of 1999, aimed at restoring voting rights to ex-offenders. The legislation would have wide-ranging impact because, as a matter of course, the vast majority of states deny voting rights to those with criminal records.

Why should this matter? Well, unfortunately, this translates into approximately 1.4 million otherwise eligible African Americans barred from the voting booths long after they've served their time and been released.

Forty-seven of the 50 states prohibit former convicts from voting in some measure. Only Maine, Massachusetts, and Vermont have no restrictions on the voting rights of ex-convicts. Thirty-two states prohibit offenders on parole from voting, 29 states prohibit people on probation from voting, and 14 states disqualify offenders for life even after their sentences have been served.

"States put conditions on whether a person can vote again even after they have paid their dues," says Conyers. "At a time when our nation faces record low voter participation, this legislation represents a historic means of both expanding voting rights while helping to reintegrate former felons into our society."

In an Action Alert distributed by the NAACP, President and CEO Kweisi Mfume laid out his case for why the NAACP decided to back the proposed legislation. "The war on drugs has had a disproportionate impact on African Americans. Between 1985 and 1995, there was a 707% increase in the number of African Americans in state prisons for a drug offense, compared to a 306% increase for whites over the same period," Mfume says. "Thus, African Americans are disproportionately losing their right to vote even after they've paid their debt to society. Because voting is such an integral part of being a member of society, the NAACP has worked closely with like-minded groups to develop legislation to allow felons who are no longer incarcerated to vote in federal elections."

The issue also caught the attention of California Rep. Maxine Waters, who co-sponsored the legislation with Conyers. "What we have done is exclude the right for many individuals who have paid the price, who did the time and are now good citizens but can't vote," she says.

Conyers says that while he believes there is a strong need for the legislation, he admits he's facing an uphill battle even getting the legislation to the floor for a vote. Says the Democrat, "Right now, in a Republican Congress, this is a difficult measure, and we are not sure that we can even get it on the calendar." Greg Moore, chief of staff for Conyers says, however, "We have some expectation that there will be a hearing in the fall."

While this bill is unlikely to get out of Congress this year, some ex-offenders like Mathes make a compelling case that someone convicted of a crime deserves a second chance.

"I found God again in prison," says Mathes. "I think if a bill was passed, a lot of individuals who have learned from their mistakes could benefit. You have some bad seeds, but you have a lot of individuals who have learned from their mistakes."

GAY AND LESBIAN RIGHTS

GABRIEL ROTELLO

CONTEXT

Gay rights remain an elusive goal in America. While there are certainly debates taking place about gay rights, particularly within the military, there are no gay rights policies such as federal statutes or major Supreme Court cases. This lack of national policy is due in part to the division in society over gay rights and to the division in the gay rights movement itself.

Gay and lesbian rights have not been incorporated into the 1964 Civil Rights Act, nor have gay rights been addressed in major legislation. For example, in 1995, Congress chose not to incorporate gay rights into an employment rights bill. The Supreme Court has been unclear about its views on gay rights. In 1985, the court held an Oklahoma law that allowed the dismissal of a teacher who advocated homosexual relations unconstitutional. But in 1986, the court refused to hold a Georgia law prohibiting consensual oral and or anal sex unconstitutional. More recently, in 1996, the court held that the equal protection clause makes it unconstitutional to deny rights to homosexuals just because they are homosexuals.

A controversy that is sure to reach the Supreme Court involves the Defense of Marriage Act passed by Congress in 1996. The Defense of Marriage Act says that states will not have to recognize a same-sex marriage, even if the marriage was performed in a state that does allow same-sex marriages. The law was in response to a Hawaii Supreme Court ruling prohibiting discrimination against gay and lesbian marriages. Opponents of same-sex marriages worried that because of the full faith and credit clause of the Constitution, which requires states to recognize laws of other states, same-sex marriages would become legal everywhere if they are legal in Hawaii.

In this selection, Gabriel Rotello discusses the mixed success of the gay and lesbian rights movement and says that the movement itself is ambivalent about its objectives. While all but the most extreme in society now accept that racial minorities should have basic civil rights and that women should receive equal pay for equal work, there is still no broad consensus about the legitimacy of homosexuality. Rotello argues that the gay rights movement itself is divided about its goals, but despite this division, progress is being made and should continue to be made in the future.

● *THINK CRITICALLY* ●────────────────────────────────────

1. In your view, is the gay rights movement similar to the civil rights movement or the women's movement, with the only different being a different group of people, or is it fundamentally different? Does this matter?
2. What do you think it will take for gay rights to be guaranteed in law and by the Supreme Court, and do you think this will ever happen? Why or why not?

For the gay and lesbian movement, these are both the best and the worst of times.

Our key accomplishments in the three decades since the Stonewall Riots, gaydom's most pivotal event, have been mostly in the cultural realm, and concern community building and self-perception.

What was once classified as a mental illness is now considered a source of identity and pride. What was once an almost invisible demimonde is now a vibrant, vocal, and sometimes militant minority. What was once a political movement consisting of two tiny, largely closeted "homophile" organizations—the Mattachine Society and the Daughters of Bilitis—is now a mass movement with literally thousands of openly gay organizations, from large national civil rights groups to local professional societies, health organizations, students groups, community centers, choirs, and softball teams. What was once a culture based on a code of secrecy is now one based on the imperative of openness.

Yet the persistence of anti-gay prejudice in the larger society remains profound, and in some ways our movement appears to have hit a sort of cultural and political glass ceiling. While modern society eventually (if imperfectly) accepted the legitimacy of other social movements—so that today all but the most extreme racists and right-wingers grant that racial minorities should have basic civil rights and that women should receive equal pay—there exists no such broad consensus about the rights of gay men and lesbians to our primary goal, which is the legitimization of homosexuality.

The rights that would flow from such legitimacy—including the rights of gays to marry, adopt, and raise children, be protected by civil rights laws, teach in the schools, serve in the military—have either not yet been acknowledged, or are acknowledged only in some jurisdictions in some cases. They are often frustrated by the deep resistance of the majority of Americans to agree that homosexuality is fully legitimate, and that homosexual people ought to be fully protected.

AN AMBIVALENT MOVEMENT

The failure of the gay rights movement to achieve many of its most basic legal and political objectives—including perhaps the most basic of all, the abolition of sodomy laws that make homosexuality itself a crime in many states—is compounded by deep ambivalence within the gay and lesbian world about what its objectives ought to be and what its identity really is. While traditional civil rights goals are generally pursued by gay legal and lobbying organizations, there is less agreement about them within the larger communities of gay and lesbian people.

Among the gay intelligentsia, for example, a major academic preoccupation is the question of whether homosexuality is, in any essential sense, "real," or is an artificial social construction that ought to be questioned, undermined, and deconstructed. Even among those rank-and-file gay men and lesbians who believe that their sexual identities are in some sense innate, there remains a persistent dispute between so-called "assimilationists" who pursue the social acceptance and normalization of homosexuality and so-called "radicals" who often reject such goals and instead seek the remaking of society along utopian lines, with pleasure and acceptance of diverse lifestyles the key ingredients.

While the basic argument between assimilationists and radicals is longstanding, its lines are not sharply drawn, and many gay people straddle both camps. As a result, the movement is characterized by a deep ambiguity that manifests itself in a thousand ways, often undermining the pursuit of basic civil rights goals. For example, organizational leaders hesitated for many years to press aggressively for same-sex marriage and the rights of gays to serve openly in the military, partly out of a belief that institutions like marriage and the military ought to be undermined, not embraced.

This combination of persistent hostility to homosexuality in the wider society and deep ambivalence among many gay people has produced a mixed political legacy. Gays have met implacable opposition to the two highest profile issues to emerge in the nineties—same-sex marriage and the right to serve openly in the military. We still struggle with mixed results for inclusion in civil rights statutes, and for laws banning employment discrimination, recognizing same-sex domestic partnerships, recognizing gay and lesbian parenting rights, and specifically targeting anti-gay bias crimes. Some cities, counties, and states have enacted such laws, and some courts have recognized such rights, but most still do not. Nor, in most cases, does the federal government.

CHALLENGES: GROWING UP AND FIGHTING AIDS

Perhaps the two issues that have the greatest bearing on the future of gay life are the state of gay and lesbian youth and the perpetuation of the AIDS epidemic.

The psychic wounds inflicted upon young gay people by social anti-gay prejudice tend to produce major negative consequences later in life, and an increasing concern of the movement is the effort to reach out to young gay people with support and positive role models. Yet homophobic fears of the "recruitment" of youth, and many gay people's fears of being perceived as pedophiles, have placed severe limits on this project, and much remains to be done.

In the AIDS arena, the transmission of HIV among gay men continues at tragically high levels. More effective drugs have been developed, but even that good news appears to have potentially negative consequences. HIV has now mutated and produced multiple drug-resistant strains in up to 50 percent of those taking the drugs, strains that can be transmitted to others. At the same time, the hopeful news about treatments appears to have resulted in an increase in unsafe sex. Many epidemiologists fear that a rise in unsafe sex, combined with the emergence of multiple drug-resistant strains of HIV, may produce a more intractable AIDS epidemic in the future. In matters of pure self-protection and physical survival, AIDS prevention is unquestionably the most pressing item on the agenda of gay men, and yet even here tremendous disagreement exists about goals, methods, and ideology.

Despite these deeply troubling problems, gay men and lesbians have shown remarkable resilience, determination, and organizational ability. The wide array of political, legal, social, and public health groups we have created continues to grow. There are now more openly gay public officials. The gay press is more vibrant than ever, and the mainstream media's long black-out of gay issues has effectively ended. Attacks on gay rights are increasingly met with effective political and legal opposition.

Perhaps our greatest successes have come in the cultural realm. More people than ever are out of the closet in all walks of life, and open gay culture is spreading from urban enclaves to Mainstreet, USA. Lesbian and gay celebrities, journalists, teachers, politicians, and sports figures increasingly are declaring themselves and providing positive social role models. There has been an explosion of openly gay characters on television and in films, challenging and altering negative stereotypes.

In the next five years, the movement will probably remain preoccupied with the issues that have dominated the past decade: employment discrimination, same-sex marriage and domestic partnership, gay parenting rights, youth issues, AIDS prevention and treatment, and the state-by-state fight over gay inclusion in civil rights statutes. There will undoubtedly be both progress and setbacks in all these realms, but the social world of openly gay and lesbian culture will continue to expand.

It is upon that cultural foundation—openness, the dissipation of negative stereotypes, the creation of positive role models, the personal interaction between straight and openly gay Americans—that the future of the gay and lesbian movement ultimately rests. If so, our ultimate success seems reasonably assured. AIDS aside, time is on our side.

PART II
INSTITUTIONS/
STRUCTURE OF
GOVERNMENT

THE PRESIDENCY, CONGRESS, AND THE JUDICIARY

HEAD NOTES/SECTION QUESTIONS

In establishing a governmental system, the Founders created a strong national government with three separate branches: legislative, executive, and judicial. Each branch was given specified powers; however, each branch was also made dependent on the other two as well. In the *Federalist No. 51*, James Madison sums up the problem the Founders were facing. Madison wrote, "In framing a government, which is to be administered by men over men, the great difficulty lies in this: you must first enable the government to control the governed, and in the next place, oblige it to control itself." The independent/dependent nature of the governmental system that the Constitution established is known as the separation of powers and checks and balances.

The separated powers and checks and balances are spelled out in the first three articles of the Constitution. Article I establishes the legislative branch of government with two houses, a House and a Senate. The legislative branch is given several specific powers. They include the power to regulate commerce with foreign nations and among states and Indian tribes, to declare war, to raise and regulate a military, to lay and collect taxes, and to make all laws necessary and proper for carrying into execution the other powers given to the legislative branch. Yet, the Constitution also places a check on the legislative branch by giving the president the power to veto laws passed by Congress and by giving the Supreme Court the right to declare anything Congress does unconstitutional.

Article II establishes executive power and places that power in a President of the United States. The constitution makes the President the commander-in-chief of the armed forces; however, since Congress has the power to declare war and regulate the army and navy, the president's power as commander-in-chief is not whole. The president also has the power to appoint various federal officers, including federal judges. A check is placed on this power by having the president seek the advice and consent of the Senate with some appointments. Additionally, the president is supposed to take care that the laws passed by Congress are executed faithfully, which means the president must be faithful about doing what Congress intended.

Article III places all judicial power in one Supreme Court, and in such inferior courts as Congress establishes. By giving Congress the authority to establish the federal courts, the constitution checks the powers of the Supreme Court. In addition, since the constitution gives the president the authority to appoint federal judges, with the advice and consent of the Senate, the power of the Supreme Court is checked even further.

The Founders created a governmental system with a very elaborate combination of separated powers and checks and balances. How well has the governmental system worked? Since the United States has survived great turmoil and even prospered over the past 200 years, it is safe to say that the governmental system has worked as well as it could. However, tension between the branches continues to this day, as was the intention of the farmers. In the readings in this section, we examine some of that tension. We look at how difficult the president's job is, and how that job can be even more difficult if the president does not understand the separated nature of power within the political system. We also look at conflict between the executive and legislative branch over the power to make war, a conflict that the Founders clearly intended.

We then look at the legislative branch and consider where work has traditionally been conducted in Congress, in committees, and how that is changing. We look at the potential problems that a loss of civility can cause in the legislative arena, and we examine the method of voting used to elect members of Congress. We also examine judicial review and look at whether Congress should take steps to curb it. Finally, we look at the Supreme Court and the politics involved in nominations to the Supreme Court. As you read these selections, think about the governmental system as one with separated powers and checks and balances and think about the following questions:

1. Does the system of separated powers and checks and balances work?
2. Which of the three branches has gained the most power in relation to the other branches over the last 200 years? Which has lost the most power during that time?
3. If you could make one change to the Constitution related to separated powers and checks and balances, what would it be?

LEARN MORE ON THE WEB

President of the United States
  http://www.ipl.org/ref/POTUS/

White House
  http://www.whitehouse.gov/

Presidential Elections
  http://www.multied.com/elections/index.html

Presidential Inaugural Addresses
  http://www.bartleby.com/124/index.html

THOMAS
  http://thomas.loc.gov/

U.S. House of Representatives
  http://www.house.gov/

U.S. Senate
  http://www.senate.gov/

The Library of Congress
  http://www.lcweb.loc.gov/global/legislative/congress.html

Federal Judiciary Homepage
  http://www.uscourts.gov/

Supreme Court Decisions
  http://supct.law.cornell.edu/supct/

Justices of the Supreme Court
  http://supct.law.cornell.edu/supct/justices/fullcourt.html

American Bar Association
  http://www.abanet.org

THE WORLD'S HARDEST JOB

JOHN DiCONSIGLIO

CONTEXT

The president gets far less attention in the Constitution than does the Congress. In fact, the Founders spent a great deal of time in Article I of the Constitution detailing the powers, duties, and responsibilities of the legislative branch and spent comparatively less time detailing the powers, duties, and responsibilities of the president. The reason for their vagueness was their fear of a strong executive. They simply did not want another monarch. In addition to being somewhat vague about the president's job description, many of the powers that they did spell out require the president to seek the advice and consent of the Senate.

The president's powers include the power to make appointments to the Supreme Court and other important posts, with the advice and consent of the

Senate. In addition, the president has the power to convene Congress and inform Congress periodically of the "State of the Union." The president has the power to make treaties, so long as the Senate approves the treaties by a two-thirds vote. The president has the power to veto legislation passed by Congress, and the power to grant reprieves and pardons. Both of these powers are checks on the legislative and judicial branches. Finally, the Constitution makes the president "Commander-in-Chief of the Army and Navy of the United States."

In addition to these formal, or constitutional, powers, political scientist Richard E. Neustadt argues in his classic study *Presidential Power*, that the president's own personal leadership style and ability to persuade add greatly to the president's power. Presidents have used their ability to persuade, their personal reputation, and their public prestige to enhance what little actual authority the Constitution gives them. Today, the president is considered the most powerful person in the world, and the job can be rather difficult.

In this selection, John DiConsiglio asks the question, is the presidency too much for one person to handle? He notes that the president's job has become much more demanding since George Washington was president nearly 215 years ago. While the Constitution assigns the president relatively few formal powers, over time the president's actual power has increased dramatically, and with the increase, the job has become much more demanding.

● *THINK CRITICALLY* ●───────────────────────────────

1. In your view, what kind of person does it take to be a successful president these days?
2. Given the inherently political nature of the job, is it possible to please everyone? If not, would it be possible for anyone to live up to the expectations placed on the president?
3. In your view, should the president have some privacy, or should everything about the president be open to the press and the public?

It's 6 a.m. in the White House, and there's no time for breakfast. Your National Security Adviser is waiting in the West Wing to brief you on the crisis in Bosnia. You guzzle a cup of coffee and sign off on a budget proposal to be sent to Congress, before an aide reminds you that the Israeli ambassador is on his way for a meeting. While you wait, you put the finishing touches on a speech. Then you check your schedule: You have a meeting with the Speaker of the House at 11 a.m. And members of the U.S. Olympic team will be on the White House lawn at noon for a ceremony. And that's just before lunch.

Welcome to a typical day in the life of the President of the United States—the man with the hardest job in the world. He's Commander in Chief of the armed forces, the country's top legislator, and the leader of his political party.

His decisions can trigger war, inspire peace, and change the fate of every nation on earth. All for an annual salary of $200,000—a fraction of what a top athlete makes.

What is it like to stand in the President's shoes?

"No one can experience with the President of the United States the glory and agony of his office," said President Lyndon Johnson. "No one can share the burden of his responsibilities, or the scope of his duties."

CONSTITUTIONAL ROLE

Is this what our Founding Fathers had in mind when they created the post of President in 1787? Not exactly. The only roles the Constitution assigns to the President are those of Commander in Chief and chief executive of the federal government. The rest of the job description was left blank. But as the nation grew and experienced wars and economic crises, Americans increasingly looked to the President for leadership. And strong Presidents—from Abraham Lincoln to Woodrow Wilson to Franklin Roosevelt—answered the call, overcoming grave national emergencies by expanding the power of their office.

Now, some critics wonder if the world's toughest job has become too tough. Pointing to scandals and policy failures that have marred the record of recent Presidents, they say the Presidency has become too demanding for any one person to handle.

"Each Presidency of the last 30 years began with optimism and enthusiasm, and ended on a down note," says Theodore Lowi, government professor at Cornell University. "Recent Presidents are remembered more for what they couldn't accomplish, than for what they did."

Other analysts say that while the Presidency has had it ups and downs, it remains the most effective elected office in the world. The job's growing responsibility, they say, has only heightened its prestige. "George Washington was called on to lead 13 fractious states," says Dom Bonafede, an expert on the Presidency at American University. Today, "Bill Clinton is the leader of the entire world."

Below, we examine four key factors that have shaped the modern Presidency. As you read, ask yourself: Has the office become too powerful and complex?

What kind of person can handle such pressure and responsibility? What qualities should we look for in electing the most powerful person in the world?

THE IMPERIAL PRESIDENCY

Although the Presidency is more than 200 years old, the greatest changes in the office have occurred in just the last 60 years.

Much of the growth in Presidential power is the work of one man: Franklin D. Roosevelt. Roosevelt became President during the Great Depression of the

1930s, one of the worst crises in American history. With half the country out of work, and millions of people on the verge of starvation, Roosevelt took bold action. His New Deal programs gave the government responsibility for providing Americans with work, welfare, food, and health care, areas the federal government had never been involved in before. These new programs vastly expanded the federal government—and the power of the President who ran them.

"Our idea of the modern active President is Roosevelt," Lowi says. "He stretched his power to unprecedented lengths."

Roosevelt's successors took on even greater power. Both John Kennedy and Lyndon Johnson used the office to champion civil rights. Johnson and his successor, Richard Nixon, dramatically increased the President's foreign-policy role by sending troops to fight in the Vietnam War (1964–1975) without consulting Congress.

Critics say this continual growth of power has created an "imperial Presidency," an office with greater powers than the Constitution allows. Many of these powers rightfully belong to state and local governments, they charge. Others worry that so much power in the hands of one person can lead to abuse. President Nixon, for example, conducted illegal spying and other criminal activities out of the White House with little restraint.

But this same power can be the key to a successful Presidency. "We applaud leaders who get things done," says Bonafede.

Even though the President has grown stronger, he still faces a major obstacle to having his way—Congress.

The Constitution says that only Congress can pass laws. So the President depends on Congress to pass his program. "This isn't easy," says historian Paul Boller. "Even the strongest President can't run the country on his own."

THE RISE OF GRIDLOCK

Sometimes the relationship between Congress and the President works smoothly. Strong Presidents like Roosevelt and Johnson were able to steamroll legislation through Congress.

But today, especially when Congress and the President come from different parties, Congress is less likely to let the President have his way. "Congress is trying to put the brakes on," says Richard Byers of George Washington University. "It's not that the President suddenly has any less power. It's just harder for him to use it."

No one knows this better than President Clinton. Clinton, a Democrat, came to office with ambitious plans, like reforming the nation's health-care system. But Congress delayed, altered, or watered down his plans—and killed his health-care proposal outright. Since the Republicans gained control of Congress in 1995, the problem has gotten worse: Every major proposal has turned into a fierce tug of war, with neither side giving an inch.

This kind of gridlock cuts both ways: at worst, it can make it impossible for the President to get things done; but it also prevents either branch from gaining too much power. The Constitution "almost mandates conflict," Lowi says. "It's not pretty, but it's checks and balances at work."

THE CHARACTER ISSUE

The hardest part of the President's job may be getting elected in the first place. Today, anyone who makes it to the Oval Office must first endure a grinding Presidential campaign. A candidate's character may be attacked, his personal life placed under a microscope, and his every utterance ruthlessly analyzed.

Every President since Washington has weathered criticism. But the unrelenting personal scrutiny Presidents face today dates from the 1970s, when reporters helped uncover President Nixon's role in the Watergate scandal. Since then, everything about a President—from his family life to his high school report card—is fair game. "Anyone who thinks about running for President these days must prepare for the likelihood of personal attacks," says Joan Hoff, of the Center for the Study of the Presidency. "Nothing is out-of-bounds."

President Clinton, for example, faced intense scrutiny of his personal life, involving everything from rumors of extramarital affairs to questions about old business deals.

This media "feeding frenzy" may discourage qualified people from seeking the Presidency. "Even a Jefferson or a Lincoln would not campaign for the office today," says David Herbert Donald, a biographer of Lincoln. A case in point is General Colin Powell, former Chairman of the Joint Chiefs of Staff. Powell considered running for President, but decided against it—primarily, many believe, to avoid putting his family through the rigors of a Presidential campaign.

This process, though unforgiving, does have the advantage of weeding out those who aren't up to the task. "The leaders who make a difference are the ones who are determined to hang in there, with stamina and grit," says *New York Times* political writer William Safire. "They must be willing to take the abuse in return for the opportunity to serve."

WOULD YOU WANT THIS JOB?

Do we expect too much from the President? "We know he's human, but we expect him to be Superman," says James David Barber of Duke University. Indeed, one reason we think of the last few Presidents as failures, Barber says, may be because they could never live up to our unrealistic expectations. "We ask him to be all things to all people. Of course he can't fulfill that role."

On the other hand, being the world's most powerful leader is an awesome job. Why shouldn't he be held to the highest standards? "This isn't a job that just anybody can do," says Lowi. "When you run for President, you know what you're getting into. These guys aren't wimps. The greats get hit with the slings and arrows, but we remember them as still standing at the end of the day."

Still, as President Clinton puts it: "This job looks a lot easier when you're not sitting where I am."

THE SEPARATED SYSTEM

CHARLES O. JONES

CONTEXT

Checks and balances force the different branches of government, especially the legislative and executive branches, to cooperate with each other in order to accomplish their duties and goals. The Constitution gives each branch just enough power to block the other branches, but not enough power to dominate them. In this way, the Founders actually institutionalized conflict among the branches of government, but the purpose was to encourage compromise.

For example, the Congress cannot pass a law unless both houses agree to the same language, and then the president can veto it, thus checking the power of the legislative branch. The Congress can check the power of the executive branch by overriding the president's veto, impeaching the president, or refusing to confirm the president's appointments. However, in an age where the president often proposes legislation to the Congress, another check on presidential power that the Congress has is simply to refuse to pass the president's legislative agenda.

In this selection, Charles O. Jones discusses the separated system as it relates to the first Clinton administration, and President Clinton's legislative agenda. He contends that President Clinton's failure to enact his much vaunted health care reform program was due in part to the president's failure to understand the separated nature of the political system, especially the checks and balances. Governing is not so much about what one branch of government (in this case the executive) can do alone, but about what can be accomplished by building cross-partisan coalitions between the elected branches (compromising). In short, governing is all about the different branches (especially the executive and legislative branches) working together.

● *THINK CRITICALLY* ●────────────────────────────

1. Who do you think would make a more effective president, one who has little in the way of grand visions but understands the workings of government (an insider), or one who has grand visions but does not understand the workings of government (an outsider)? Why?
2. Although there is pressure to compromise, what are some of the advantages that the president has in dealing with Congress?

Shortly after his inauguration, President Bill Clinton reiterated an extravagant campaign promise, accompanied by a dramatic announcement:

> As a first step in responding to the demands of literally millions of Americans, today I am announcing the formation of the President's Task Force on National Health Reform. Although the issue is complex, the task force's mission is simple: Build on the work of the campaign and the transition, listen to all parties, and prepare health care reform legislation to be submitted to Congress within 100 days of our taking office. This task force will be chaired by the First Lady, Hillary Rodham Clinton.

The effect was to draw accountability clearly and unmistakably to the White House, indeed, into the residence itself. The president and his partner by marriage would be held directly accountable for what happened. Yet as political scientist Hugh Heclo observed, "Never in the modern history of major social reform efforts had a president with so few political resources tried to do so much."

Ours is not a unified political and governmental system. Setting ambitious goals, promising swift action, and assuming complete management for dramatic change, taken together, represent a huge political gamble for a leader in a government of truly separated institutions. To do so having won 43 percent of the popular vote is surely an instance of derring-do. By drawing accountability to himself, Clinton accentuated a problem inherent in a separated system. A prime challenge to presidents is to manage the often-lavish expectations of their accountability under conditions of distributed power. A necessary background for my assessment of the Clinton presidency, therefore, is an understanding of the diffused accountability inherent in our system.

ACCOUNTABILITY IN A SEPARATED SYSTEM

Though a government of separated institutions sharing or competing for powers has many virtues, focused responsibility is not one of them. Accountability is highly diffused by dint of the dispersal that is characteristic of separationism. And though some observers argue that to have accountability everywhere is to have it nowhere, that is not so. A system like ours has substantial individual accountability but limited collective accountability. The reasons why are clear enough to those familiar with constitutional history.

Operationally, formal accountability for presidents is primarily rhetorical. Presidents speak of representing the public. The media often act as enforcers, holding presidents accountable to an inexact public-interest standard. Presidents are held answerable for actions within the government, and yet the precise manner of holding them to account is rather indistinct. This reality is central to the governing strategy of modern presidents. They should be aware that they will be held responsible for that over which they have only limited control. At the very least, they must avoid contributing further to this tendency by guaranteeing grand results.

In brief, the White House cannot depend for support on what happened in the last election but must account for how the members' policy preferences relate to the next election. The president must develop and redevelop policy strategies that acknowledge the ever-shifting coalitional base. Serious and continuous in-party and cross-party coalition building thus typifies policy making in the separated system.

The defining challenge for a new president is to capitalize on his freshness without elevating further the lofty expectations of his position. The president is well advised to resist the efforts by others, or himself, to assign him the heady charge of being the commander of government.

MANAGING HIGH EXPECTATIONS

Imagine that the fires of ambition burn so strongly that sleep is your enemy. Success by most measures comes easily, but it does not provide solace. The need to do more is all-consuming. There is no reward great enough; an obstacle overcome is less valued than the identification of a new challenge.

Conceive, if you can, the challenge involved in making everyone happy, then in getting credit for having done so and you will understand why there is little time or patience for sleep. Meet Bill Clinton, "first in his class"; bound to be president.

Bill Clinton's ambition is for a kind of greatness that is defined by approval. He wants to do good things for many people. He is a talker, engaged in a game-like process of exploration. As such, he is puzzled by listeners who hear the talk as commitment. Talkers find satisfaction in the immediate response. They are unlikely to make a strong distinction between campaigning and governing. Nor are they likely to be intrigued by the intricacies of the lawmaking process. Bill Clinton is the quintessential campaigner as president. He most assuredly is not a lawmaker president in the Lyndon Johnson mold; had he been so, he may have had more successful years. What follows, then, is a description and analysis of a presidency increasingly at risk, one persistently "on the edge," as Elizabeth Drew entitled her book on the Clinton administration, yet one prepared as few have been to seek reelection.

The 1992 campaign and election were bound to encourage a parliamentary-style accounting. A new-generation Democrat won after twelve years of Republican dominance of the White House. He promised to work hardest at economic recovery, as well as acting on a number of other issues generally acknowledged to form the contemporary agenda. One party would now be in charge of both ends of Pennsylvania Avenue. The gridlock that was presumed by many to have prevented the proper functioning of government was judged to be over.

Additionally, there was the sheer energy and excitement conveyed by the youthful Clinton-Gore team. It would require a substantial degree of self-discipline to ensure that postelection enthusiasm did not overreach and contribute to inflated expectations as to what could be achieved by the 103rd Congress.

Contributing to high expectations were political analysts, especially those who adhere to the perspective on national elections that I term "unitarian" (as opposed to "separationist"). At root, the unitarians disagree with the separation of powers concept. They propose reforms designed to ensure one-party government so as to achieve collective accountability. For the unitarian the best possible election result is that in which one political party wins the White House and majority control of both houses of Congress. That party is then expected to display unity on policy issues and to produce a record for which it can be held responsible at the next election. Though I cannot produce an exact count, I would wager that most political analysts are unitarians.

In contrast, the general voting public and most members of Congress are practicing "separationists." For the separationist the best possible election result is one that reinforces the legitimacy of independent participation by each branch. Party leaders, including presidents, are then expected to build cross-partisan support within and between the elected branches whether or not one party has majorities in Congress and a president in the White House. A separationist perspective of the 1992 election would have stressed the rejection of George Bush without identifying a mandate for Clinton. By this view, voters continued to split their tickets, albeit in new and interesting ways, making it difficult to spot a "mandate."

Evidence for this separationist interpretation abounds. There is the substantial vote garnered by Ross Perot, the most for an independent or third-party candidate since Theodore Roosevelt ran in 1912. A president won in a three-way contest by designating a credible agenda and projecting a sufficiently moderate policy posture as to be reassuring to just over half of the Ronald Reagan (1984) and Bush (1988) voters who were disillusioned with the Bush presidency. Clinton's campaign strategy was, by William Schneider's view, to "convince middle-class voters that Democrats could work within the Reagan-Bush consensus." Moreover, House Republicans had a net gain of ten seats and received 46 percent of the national vote for the House, compared to Bush's 37 percent of the national vote for president.

It follows from these assertions that a partisan, unitarian approach was unlikely to succeed. Yet that is the approach Clinton employed. Not only that, but Clinton's activist style drew accountability to himself. A book of promises, entitled *Putting People First*, was published during the campaign; it was bound to raise hopes while defining awesome challenges and providing a scorecard for the media. In reading from this text of pledges, little was to be left untouched by a Clinton-Gore administration—it included 35 proposals for the "national economic strategy" and 577 proposals for "other crucial issues."

Lacking was an understanding of how ours is truly the most elaborated lawmaking system in the world. It does not submit to enthusiasm alone. Effective leadership starts with knowing how the system works. The 1992 election produced exceptionally challenging conditions for lawmaking, requiring extraordinarily sensitive strategies for producing cross-party majorities on Capitol Hill. Bill Clinton lacked the skills for devising these strategies and therefore had to learn them or, like Reagan, rely on those who did have that competence.

It is with the understanding of the centrist underpinnings of Clinton's electoral and preinaugural support that one comes to understand the problems the new president faced during the first two years of his presidency. For the actions that could be taken early in order to demonstrate momentum—executive orders regarding abortions performed in military hospitals, federal funding of fetal tissue transplant research, the importation of abortion pill RU-486, and ending the ban on gays in the military—were likely to project a substantially more liberal cast than could be justified by public opinion as expressed either in the election or in subsequent polls.

Moreover, actions that were more moderate-to-conservative in nature—reducing the federal workforce, terminating advisory committees, seeking to make government more efficient—were overshadowed at the start by the more liberal actions cited above. Why? They were noncontroversial, not newsworthy, and therefore unavailable as ballast to the liberal tilt on controversial issues.

As if these developments were not sufficient to ensure Republican unity, Democrats in the House of Representatives used the rules of that chamber to prevent Republicans from effective participation in the amending process. Senate Republicans were in a substantially stronger position than their colleagues in the House due to the fact that they had sufficient numbers to prevent the closing of debates, an advantage used early against the president's economic stimulus package and late in 1994 to kill much of the president's program.

With all of these problems and miscalculations, Clinton's first year was moderately productive under contentious political circumstances in which partisan lines hardened substantially. Several bills vetoed by Bush were passed again and signed by the president, a deficit-reduction package was enacted by Vice President Gore's tie-breaking vote in the Senate and two votes in the House, NAFTA was approved with the crucial support of Republicans, and the president got a modified version of his National Service Program.

However, many of the most contentious issues were carried over to the second session. As a result, the second year was among the least productive of major legislation in the post–World War II period. Of the ten presidential priorities mentioned in the State of the Union Message, four became law—the GATT (again with Republican support in a special session), Goals 2000, an anticrime package, and community development loans. Each was important, but none was as important for the president as the proposal to reform the health care system—a matter that dominated the politics of the year. "We will make history by reforming the health care system," was the president's promise in his January 1994 State of the Union Address. Yet by September 26, 1994, Senate Majority Leader George Mitchell had issued the last rites.

Perhaps most stunning as a measure of political mismanagement was the fact that by raising expectations, inviting responsibility, and yet failing to produce, the president and his leaders in Congress deflected criticism of Republicans for having obstructed much of the president's legislative program. As was noted in a *New York Times* editorial, Republican cooperation "was never part of the original promise." Democratic leaders had informed the president that they could deliver without Republican support. Republicans were content to be excluded. In the end it permitted them to avoid the accountability that was solicited by the administration.

Clinton's personal strengths are many. He is a superb campaigner—an effective and empathetic communicator with the public and a man with an "upbeat personality." He is, unquestionably, highly intelligent, possessed of an extraordinary capacity to identify and explore public policy issues. We also know from David Maraniss's fine biography, *First in His Class*, that he knows how to cram for an exam—a characteristic displayed in playing his role in lawmaking, as he often waits to the last minute to engage the issue to the extent of making a choice.

THE MIDTERM EARTHQUAKE

But Bill Clinton also has a number of weaknesses. He had never held a position in the federal government. While governor, he worked with a Democratic legislature, seldom having to take Republicans into account or to display the kind of lawmaking prowess of a governor from a state with a more competitive two-party government. As with most governors, he lacked direct experience in foreign and national security policy. He is an admitted "policy talk wonk" who finds it difficult to concentrate on a limited agenda. And there is ample evidence that Bill Clinton lacks direct experience in forming and accommodating to an effective staff. Clinton's strengths are more intellectual than managerial.

Moreover, instead of compensating for his weaknesses, Clinton preferred to capitalize on his strengths. He sought to govern by campaigning, not lawmaking, virtually melding the two in his own mind and in his behavior. In his first two years the president visited 194 places, making 264 appearances (excluding foreign travel, visits to Arkansas, and vacations). Bill Clinton is the most traveled president in history, exceeding even President George Bush. One effect was to reinforce the distorted view of the president as the government, with the effect of holding him accountable for what is and has ever been a separated system of diffused accountability. As a consequence, Bill Clinton became a major issue in the midterm election. The result was to produce a very different presidency for his second two years in office.

It is standard wisdom that congressional elections are state and local events, albeit with important national effects. In 1994, however, there were two bids to nationalize the midterm elections: one by the president, who seemingly could not resist joining the fray, and one by Newt Gingrich, the House Republican Leader in waiting, who had national, crusadelike ambitions.

As the election approached, the president might well have followed the advice given Harry Truman by the Democratic National Committee Chairman in 1946—that is, stay out of midterm politics! Truman, whose standing in the polls was at 40 percent, accepted this advice. "He kept silent on politics." Few, if any, Democratic candidates invoked his name.

Clinton was in a similar situation, with approximately the same poll results. And in fact his pollster, Stanley Greenberg, issued a memorandum to Democratic candidates advising that they run on their own accomplishments, not on those of the president. "There is no reason to highlight these as Clinton or Democratic proposals. Voters want to know that you are fighting to get things done for them, not that you are advancing some national agenda."

A flurry of foreign and national security policy decisions on North Korea, Haiti, and Iraq—all judged to be successful—resulted in a boost in the president's approval rating to 50 percent, exceeding his disapproval rating for the first time in six months. That was the good news; the bad news was that the good news encouraged him to reenter the campaign. He launched a last-minute, furious schedule of appearances, drawing attention to his record and attacking the Republican "Contract on America," as he called it. By campaigning so energetically in the last week, the president naturally attracted press attention to himself as an issue. The effect was to ensure that dramatic Republican gains would be interpreted as a rejection of Clinton's presidency, whether or not that conclusion was merited in terms of actual voting behavior.

The other half, or more, of the nationalization of the 1994 elections is explained by what the Republicans did. As political scientist Gary C. Jacobson pointed out: "All politics was not local in 1994. Republicans succeeded in framing the local choice in national terms, making taxes, social discipline, big government, and the Clinton presidency the dominant issues." The Republicans tied "congressional Democrats to Clinton, a discredited government establishment, and a deplorable status quo."

Gingrich, too, deserves notice for his daring strategy of committing Republican candidates to a bold midterm party platform, the "Contract with America." It is true that most voters knew little or nothing about the contract. But the act of getting over three hundred Republican candidates to commit themselves in a media show at the Capitol on September 27 had profound effects on how the election results would then be interpreted.

The new Republican leaders were also not in the least bothered by Democratic claims that the contract tied "Republican candidates back into their congressional leadership." That was precisely the point. Gingrich and company would be strengthened in their effort to establish firm control of the agenda if the new members supported them. Meanwhile, the Democrats were in considerable disarray. Bill Clinton was still president, but he was not leader of the Democrats in any serious or meaningful sense. One study concluded that "the more the Democratic incumbent voted to support the president's policies, the more likely he or she was to be defeated."

Justified or not in terms of what the voters actually wanted, a new agenda had been created. "Change isn't Bill Clinton's friend anymore," is how two reporters put it. A Washington Post editorial referred to a "sea change," pointing out that "this was not just an 'anti-incumbent' vote. The incumbents who were defeated this year were Democrats—and in particular Democrats in Congress. . . . the change called for went almost uniformly in one direction, and that was against liberalism and toward the right." A mandate had been declared, centered in just one of the three elected branches—the House of Representatives. Meanwhile, defeated or not, Bill Clinton remained in office, now freed from the responsibilities of leading Congress, for which he seemed ill-suited anyway.

RECLAIMING LEADERSHIP

How then did this policy-ambitious president—one who wanted government to do more, not less, and to do it better, not worse—how did he respond to dramatically new political conditions? I have made the point that Bill Clinton is not a lawmaker president. Yet there are functions that cannot be avoided, choices that have to be made—notably whether to sign or to veto a bill, to let it become law or to let it die without his signature. How did the president cope? He altered his governing style from that of a campaigner to that of a prospector, searching for a role compatible with the unusual politics of the time. The strategy devised in 1995 contained these tenets:

- Associate the president with the change seemingly demanded by the voters.
- Remind the public that the president was there first with many of the issues in the Contract with America.
- Argue that the Republicans are going too far. It is not necessary to destroy programs to improve government. Be the voice of moderation against the extremist Republicans. "I'm for that, but not so much."
- Search for high-profile issues subject to executive order, pushing the limits of that power (as with the anti-teenage smoking measures and barring government contracts with firms replacing strikers).
- Await the completion of lawmaking, then exercise the veto while imploring Republicans to meet on "common ground." Avoid specifics in favor of a "no, that's not it" response.
- Travel, taking your presidency to the people, posturing as the voice of reason, the interpreter of change, the preserver of values.
- Take full advantage of the uniquely presidential status in foreign and national security issues and disasters.

Taken as a whole, this strategy was defensible and rational given the president's political status. It permitted him to turn full attention to raising money and creating an organization for reelection while Republicans were absorbed with the difficult and often unrewarding exercises of balancing the budget and reforming social programs. Lacking an opponent, the president was able to rise above the fray, even calling for a moratorium on politics as usual. Republicans, on the other hand, were engaged in a hotly contested nomination battle in the early months of 1996, with the winner, Bob Dole, then held responsible for leading the Congress that was taken from the president in 1994. Until he announced his resignation from the Senate, Dole found himself battling surrogate campaigners—Tom Daschle, Ted Kennedy, and Chris Dodd—rather than the president.

CLINTON IN HISTORICAL PERSPECTIVE

Bill Clinton joins others whose presidencies have been at risk. Indeed, the imbalance between expectations and authority perpetuates political peril for presidents.

I stressed earlier that Bill Clinton amplified the inherent risk for the president by raising expectations despite weak political advantages. He invited accountability for the failures that, given the overreaching that characterized his early months in office, were likely to come. A dramatically new politics was created as a result.

Freed from the exacting demands of his original ambitious agenda by the 1994 elections, the president settled into the role of moderating the striking, even threatening, policy changes proposed by Republicans. Though not a leadership role, it is a mode that becomes him. As the nation's moderator in the serious policy debates at hand, he can justify the travel and public exposure that he finds personally and intellectually rewarding. He displayed patience in 1995, permitting Republicans to dominate the agenda and awaiting the time when his veto power would inevitably attract their lawmaking efforts—inexorably drawing them into the public arena where he excels. At last the campaigner could reinsert himself into the policy process. But having been more an observer than participant during the active congressional session, it was no simple matter for President Clinton to reconnect with the lawmaking process. Therefore, negotiations with congressional leaders have been protracted and disorderly, with the Republicans of the 104th Congress having drawn to themselves precisely the large measure of accountability that the White House invited in the 103rd Congress. Given his experience, President Clinton was more than happy to oblige in holding Republicans responsible for, among other things, shutting down the government.

Control of his political destiny was taken from the president in the 1994 elections, and so he positioned himself to take advantage of what others did or failed to do. The reports of his political demise were premature. Once more, Bill Clinton demonstrated his capacity for political regeneration. Perhaps even he would agree, however, that the separated system works best when success is measured less by recovery than by effective participation by the president throughout. It is exceptional to be the "Come Back Kid" over and over again. Yet it is substantially more imposing as president not to require recuperation.

THE HISTORICAL BATTLE OVER DISPATCHING AMERICAN TROOPS

STEPHEN M. LEAHY

CONTEXT

In the previous selection, we read about the separate powers of each branch, and how presidents can fail to achieve their legislative objectives if they do not clearly understand the separated nature of those powers. In this selection, we read about one area of policy where the Constitution is less than clear about which branch of government, the executive or the legislative branch, should dominate.

The Constitution makes the president commander-in-chief of the armed forces, but gives Congress the authority to declare war. Some argue that what the Founders intended was for sole leadership of the military during time of war to be in the hands of a civilian leader, the president. In order for the president to make decisions about war and war making, though, Congress must first have declared a war. However, the Constitution is just vague enough that there is disagreement. In addition, the power of the president to make discretionary decisions about war expanded during the 20th century when the United States became a major military power.

This increased presidential power has not come without debate. In 1972 Richard Nixon ordered a massive bombing campaign of North Vietnam, known as the "Christmas bombing," after peace negotiations failed. He did not seek congressional approval for this war-making action, and the extent of the military action shocked many people, including many members of Congress. In response to this event, and the Vietnam conflict in general, Congress passed the War Powers Resolution over President Nixon's veto in 1973. The War Powers Resolution was supposed to limit the president's war-making ability absent a formal declaration of war by Congress.

The War Powers Resolution, however, did not put an end to the debate over the president's power to wage war. In this article, Stephen M. Leahy summarizes the conflict between the president and Congress over the right to dispatch American troops. He notes that while the Constitution rests some war powers in Congress and some in the president, since World War II, the president has largely ignored Congress' constitutional role. The Vietnam conflict exposed the hazards in the presidential domination of war-making abilities, and in response, Congress attempted to take back some of its constitutional powers. Presidents have continued to insist, however, that they have the ability to dispatch troops even if they do not consult with Congress when doing so. The debate thus continues, and so far, the president continues to have the upper hand.

● *THINK CRITICALLY* ●───

1. Based on your reading of the Constitution, where do you think the power to dispatch troops and wage war lies, with the president or the Congress?
2. While there is at times conflict over the president's decision to dispatch troops, do you feel that presidents abuse this power? If so, cite a recent example. If not, why the disagreement?

Under the war powers clauses of the Constitution, who has the power to dictate when American soldiers should fight—and die? Since the creation of the Republic, presidents and Congress have fought over who should control the power to involve the nation in war. This debate assumed a new form after World War II. Increasingly after 1950, politicians endorsed a bipartisan foreign policy which, in effect, ceded the leadership role to the president and a consultative role to Congress.

This relationship first was challenged directly during the Vietnam War era. As did his predecessors—Pres. Harry Truman (in 1950 concerning Korea) and Pres. Lyndon Johnson (in 1965 about Vietnam)—when ordering the 1970 invasion of Cambodia, Pres. Richard Nixon argued that, as Commander-in-Chief, he possessed the authority to commit troops into combat. Nixon's action motivated Congress to enact the War Powers Resolution in 1973 to assert its formerly dominant foreign policy role. While the courts have not ruled on the constitutionality of its proposed limits, the law effectively has institutionalized the bipartisan foreign policy.

The War Powers Resolution inevitably involved a debate over the meaning of two complementary (if not conflicting) provisions of the Constitution. Under it, Congress is empowered "To declare War, grant Letters of Marque and Reprisal, and make Rules concerning Captures on Land and Water" and "To make rules for the Government and Regulation of the land and naval forces," while the president "shall be Commander-in-Chief of the Army and Navy of the United States." These seemingly complementary provisions have provoked debate over the scope of presidential prerogative, and specifically whether presidents unilaterally can commit troops into military conflicts ostensibly to preserve the nation.

Complicating this debate, the *Federalist Papers*—and many Supreme Court rulings—seem to support three contradictory interpretations on this claimed prerogative. One is that the Constitution supports the president's right to commit troops into combat. Another view denies any such ability to involve U.S. armed forces in any conflict without a Congressional declaration of war. A final view argues that the Constitution forbids any unqualified presidential power, but practicality dictates that the president must act during emergencies.

World War II and the Cold War eventually led to acceptance of the third interpretation. Because of revolutions in communications and armaments, crises and wars could break out at a moment's notice. Consequently, American legislators adopted what Sen. Arthur Vandenberg (R.-Mich.) called "the bipartisan foreign policy." In theory, a president informally should consult with Congress before considering military action. During a crisis, the president should act and Congress uncritically should support the nation's leader. The U.S. needed to demonstrate its determination to prevail in any situation. Opposition would undermine confidence in the president and thereby harm the national security. According to this way of thinking, politics had to "stop at the water's edge."

In practice, the bipartisan foreign policy for a time reduced Congress to rubber-stamping presidential decisions. In 1954–55, the People's Republic of China shelled two offshore islands. Quemoy and Matsu, occupied by the Republic of China (Nationalist China, or Taiwan). As Congress went into session in 1955, Pres. Dwight Eisenhower asked for a "fight if we must" resolution. After one day of hearings, Congress quickly authorized the President to use force to defend those islands.

When Great Britain abandoned its historic role in the Middle East after 1956, Eisenhower asked for a similar resolution to fight any future communist subversion in that region. Several Democratic representatives suggested that Congress should hold the President accountable for money spent in the Middle East. Their proposal did not command support; indeed, House Democratic leaders criticized them for undermining confidence in the President. The Eisenhower administration's proposed Middle East Resolution passed, although an amendment was added in the Senate requiring the President to seek additional authority to fight a war. During the 1962 Berlin crisis. Congress authorized Pres. John F. Kennedy to fight there as well.

The 1964 Gulf of Tonkin crisis exposed the flaws of this evolving uncritical Congressional support of the president. On Aug. 2, 1964, two American destroyers providing communications assistance for a South Vietnamese commando raid in North Vietnam were attacked by North Vietnamese ships. Two days later, one of those American destroyers reported another suspected attack. Seeking another "fight if we must" resolution, Pres. Johnson portrayed these incidents as unprovoked attacks by North Vietnam and sought legislation authorizing future military operations. After one day of hearings, the House unanimously endorsed the proposed Gulf of Tonkin Resolution. The Senate also quickly passed the bill.

The Gulf of Tonkin incident proved to be a limited military engagement. In 1965, however, Johnson unilaterally authorized continued bombing attacks on North Vietnam and dispatched U.S. troops to South Vietnam. When Congress later that year approved an appropriation bill to finance war measures, Johnson announced that he had sufficient legal authority to conduct military operations in Vietnam. He did not seek a Congressional declaration of war.

From 1966 until 1970, as the Vietnam War became controversial, anti-war activists sought to repeal the Gulf of Tonkin Resolution. While succeeding in thwarting, Johnson's reelection bid in 1968, they could not get Congress to repeal the resolution. As Nixon's initial attempts to end the war on his terms failed, anti-war activists began a series of so-called moratorium protests in late 1969.

Despite increases in dissent and as part of strategy pressuring North Vietnam to negotiate an end to the war, Nixon ordered American troops to invade Cambodia in April, 1970. He did not inform Congress in advance of this decision and only consulted with one sympathetic senator, John Stennis (D.-Miss.). To many in Congress and in the public, the Cambodian invasion proved troubling. Many feared that Nixon planned to escalate, rather than end, what by then had become an extremely unpopular war.

In response to these fears, Congress banned funding for combat operations in Cambodia and began to debate whether to repeal the Gulf of Tonkin Resolution. Nixon denied that his actions were governed by that resolution. His close supporter, Senator Robert Dole (R.-Kans.), sponsored the resolution's successful repeal. Nixon then announced his intention to continue the war under his authority as Commander-in-Chief.

While Congress continued funding the Vietnam War, pro- and anti-war members from both parties challenged Nixon's broad assertions. In May, 1970, for example, Rep. Dante Fascell (D.-Fla.) introduced a bill intended to define the president's war powers. Rep. Paul Findley (R.-Ill.) earlier had introduced a bill requiring the president to report military actions to Congress. After holding hearings on these measures, the House retreated from enacting legislation that would strictly limit presidential war-making powers. Instead, it passed a bill that tried to institutionalize the bipartisan foreign policy. This bill recognized the president's duty to act in "certain extraordinary and emergency circumstances." A second section stipulated that the president should consult with Congress. Other sections required presidents to notify Congress after committing troops into military conflict. The House passed this bill in late 1970, but the measure died when the Senate took no action.

In the interim, Sen. Jacob Javits (R.-N.Y.) had introduced another proposal, which was endorsed by both influential pro-war Sen. Stennis and anti-war Sen. Thomas Eagleton (D.-Mo.). Their backing seemed to ensure Senate passage of Javits approach. This bill, introduced in December, 1971, rejected the claim of presidential prerogative and defined the sole four situations whereby presidents could act without specific Congressional authorization: to protect U.S. territory and its possessions; to repel or forestall attacks on American armed forces stationed overseas; to protect American citizens abroad during an evacuation; or as part of a treaty commitment ratified by Congress. Other sections limited any presidential commitment of troops to 30 days, unless Congress authorized or ended such action by concurrent resolution. (Such a resolution does not require the signature of the president.) The Vietnam War specifically was exempted from the bill's stipulations. Like the House bill, the Senate approach contained a reporting provision.

Though the Vietnam War lurked in the background, the resultant debate over war powers legislation paralleled the almost 200-year-old question of prerogative. Nixon claimed the right of prerogative, while the Senate proposal denied it. The House bill, in contrast, conceded that a president may act in emergencies, but must involve Congress in decision-making. The Nixon White House saw each bill as a threat to its prerogatives. To prevent their passage, the Nixon Administration decided to endorse tacitly the House approach. This encouraged the House managers, led by Rep. Clement Zablocki (D.-Wis.), to refuse any compromise with the Senate. Despite their differences, House and Senate managers decided to hold a conference committee meeting in 1972. The Nixon Administration, hoping to stymie the committee's work, announced that it only could support the unamended House bill.

In his book, *No More Vietnams*, Nixon recalled his thinking about the war powers bills. He thought these proposals simply were a manifestation of anti-war feeling and that, should he succeed in defeating them in 1972. Congress would not revive the issue after the end of the war in January, 1973. Nixon's assessment was wrong. Instead, supporters of the Vietnam War no longer feared that Congress retroactively would apply the law to that conflict. Thus, the imminent end of the war increased Congressional support for war powers legislation.

The ensuing Watergate scandal and Nixon's claims of executive privilege to justify his noncompliance with requests for information relating to it intensified public distrust of the presidency. About the same time, Nixon ordered the continued bombing of Cambodia. Confident of passage, House managers added a section empowering Congress to end military hostilities by concurrent resolution.

By the summer of 1973, Congress was deadlocked over these differing proposals to define the scope of and limits to presidential powers. Because the House had embraced the termination-of-hostilities section, Javits decided to accept a non-binding "purpose and policy" section, which stated that presidents exercised their Commander-in-Chief powers pursuant to declaration of war, a specific statutory authorization, or an attack on the U.S., its territories, or the nation's armed forces. Other sections required the president to consult "in every possible instance" with Congress. The president also had to report whenever U.S. forces were introduced into combat or hostile situations. Any inserted forces would have to be removed within 60 days, unless necessity required that 30 more days were needed to effect withdrawal. Moreover, Congress could direct the president by concurrent resolution to end a military commitment.

Despite opposition from senators demanding the definition of presidential powers, the revised Javits-Zablocki bill passed Congress in October, 1973. The House vote, however, fell eight votes short of the necessary two-thirds vote to override an expected presidential veto. Nixon's actions during the Watergate crisis revived a dying bill. In response to the demand of Special Prosecutor Archibald Cox for the release of specified White House tapes, Nixon refused, citing executive privilege. Nixon then fired Cox. Simultaneously, the President had placed the country on war footing in response to Egypt's invasion of Israel to begin the so-called Yom Kippur War.

The burgeoning Watergate scandal emboldened Congress, now faced by a weakened president preoccupied with a potential war. Only in the wake of these events did the House override the presidential veto by seven votes on Nov. 7, 1973. Later that day, the Senate overrode the veto by a wide margin. Passage of the War Powers Resolution seemingly marked a historic turning point against "the Imperial Presidency." In reality, though, this law has had a quite different result.

The first significant controversy over its use occurred in the aftermath of the 1975 U.S. troop evacuations from Southeast Asia. On March 5, the *Washington Post* reported that U.S. armed forces were prepared to evacuate Americans from Cambodia, causing members of Congress to demand consultation. On the advice of Secretary of State Henry Kissinger, Pres. Gerald Ford knowingly disobeyed the consultation requirements of the law. During the subsequent evacuation of South Vietnam and the rescue of the *Mayaguez*-crew held hostage in Cambodia, Ford merely notified key members of Congress of the commencement of those military operations. Afterward, members of Congress criticized the President for his failure to have consulted with legislators.

In effect, the evacuations from Southeast Asia created a precedent accepting the premise that the War Powers Resolution did not apply to rescue efforts. Later presidents have cited their powers as Commander-in-Chief when authorizing military operations to free Americans during the Iranian hostage rescue mission (1980) and the invasions of Grenada (1983) and Panama (1989).

PRESIDENTIAL ACTIONS

Unilateral presidential military actions, moreover, were not confined to rescue missions. In September, 1982, Pres. Ronald Reagan ordered U.S. armed forces to Lebanon to help reestablish order in that nation. On Aug. 29, 1983, those forces, under orders from Reagan, shelled artillery batteries in Lebanon. These artillery barrages were offensive operations—not acts of self-defense—and this decision precipitated a month-long constitutional crisis.

Reagan and Congress eventually reached a compromise with the passage of the Multinational Force in Lebanon Resolution, which allowed the President to base U.S. armed forces in Lebanon for 18 months. This resolution contained another section which declared that the War Powers Resolution became operative on Aug. 29. During the signing ceremony, Reagan praised Congress for granting him the authority, but repudiated the assertions that the War Powers Resolution became operative on Aug. 29 and that Congress unilaterally could end a military commitment.

In contrast, the War Powers Resolution seemed to have worked during the initial stage of the 1990–91 Gulf War crisis. At its onset following the Iraqi invasion of Kuwait, Bush extensively consulted with members of Congress and praised them for the "Vandenbergian" support of his policies. Throughout the fall of 1990, Bush invited Congress to legislate, but only if endorsing a resolution effectively authorizing the use of force to liberate Kuwait. When it appeared that Congress might not pass such a resolution, Bush made a bold assertion of prerogative. He claimed that he already had sufficient authority to conduct offensive operations. Congress averted a crisis by passing the Gulf War Resolution in January, 1991.

The Haitian crisis of 1994 offered another potential challenge to claimed presidential powers. Clinton skirted the law as he bullied the Haitian dictatorship to step down. Had he followed through with his threatened invasion, he effectively would have challenged the War Powers Resolution (and the Constitution). Congress conceivably could have voted to terminate the unauthorized invasion or might have voted to end funding for it. Nothing was done, and Clinton succeeded in forcing the withdrawal of the Haitian military dictator and dispatched American troops for peacekeeping objectives.

Throughout its history, the War Powers Resolution has encountered many criticisms, including from key legislative authors. Eagleton, a strong opponent of presidents claimed war-making prerogative, subtitled his study of the issue, *A Chronicle of Congressional Surrender*. Javits complained that Congress lacked the will to enforce the resolution. Strong supporters of presidential prerogative have attacked the law as unconstitutional and dangerous. No president has recognized the validity of the termination of hostilities by concurrent resolution.

There are several reasons why the law has not been challenged. For a president to do so, he would have to show an injury to the nation from the resolution. During military crises, presidents have preferred to act, rather than claim injury. Presidents also have not challenged the law because they tacitly endorse its provisions. Ford Administration counsel Philip Buchen described the resolution as "realistic" and "neither cumbersome nor unseemly." While Pres. Jimmy Carter frequently complained of Congressional restrictions, he often reiterated his support for the law. Even Reagan stated in 1987, "There's a part of it that I think is fine." Finally, a court challenge would require a president to argue that he alone possessed the power to send troops into combat.

For the future, the War Powers Resolution most likely will remain unchanged. Most politicians—both presidents and members of Congress—ignore it until the onset of military crises. Even when Republicans, who heretofore had been the sharpest critics of the law, won control of Congress in 1994, they could not muster a majority to amend it. A prolonged constitutional crisis, like the environment that led to its passage in 1973, could create a situation leading to changes, but at that point, Congress and the president inevitably would prefer a negotiated settlement, rather than testing the War Powers Resolution in court. A final reason for the law's resilience is that it reflects the bipartisan ideal advocated by Vandenberg and continues to influence the executive-legislative relations in the foreign policy area.

A new consensus has evolved. In effect, presidents consult Congress and, for the most part, Congress supports presidents during crises. In this modified form, and reflecting this altered consensus, the War Powers Resolution will continue to frame the debate over war and peace.

THE CHANGING ROLE
OF THE COMMITTEE

GORDON S. JONES

CONTEXT

Woodrow Wilson, who studied Congress as a student at Johns Hopkins University, once said that Congress in committee is Congress at work. Wilson's observation about where the real work of Congress takes place, made in the late 1800s, was right on target. Political scientists who study Congress have long held that the real work of Congress is that which takes place in the committees. The committee is where public policy is made.

For example, before a bill ever makes it onto the House or Senate floor for a vote, it must first pass through a committee or several committees. While at the committee, hearings are held about the bill, reports written about it, negotiations between the political parties are held on it, and a final vote cast on it. By all measures, if a bill can make it out of committee, then it can probably get passed on the House or Senate floor because all of the real work was done in the committee. At least, that is what we have always thought.

In this selection, Gordon S. Jones argues that the committee system that has historically anchored work in Congress is becoming irrelevant when it comes to passing legislation. Whereas committees used to be the place where legislation was negotiated and written, he contends, today much of the legislative work in both houses of Congress takes place on the floor, after the committees have completed their work. In addition, due to the budget constraints of the last couple of decades, budget committees and conference committees have become much more powerful than most other standing committees. So, what role do committees play today? Increasingly, Jones asserts, they serve as a partisan tool of the majority party rather than as work chambers.

● *THINK CRITICALLY* ●

1. If work that used to be conducted in committee is increasingly being conducted on the House and Senate floors, isn't this better for democracy because it makes law making more open to the public? Why or why not?
2. Can you think of any changes in the rules that could help strengthen the committees again?

A congressman elected in 1974 was asked by his local newspaper what committees he wanted to serve on in Washington. He replied that he had seen committees in action before, and they never got anything done, so he wouldn't serve on any. At the time, his view was a mark of naivete, but if he were to make the same remark today, he would be much closer to the truth.

Historically critical to the legislative process, the role of standing committees as part of the operations of the modern Congress is changing. The changes are not abrupt and are incomplete, but they are part of an identifiable trend. Committees are likely to remain important, but they will become increasingly irrelevant from the standpoint of legislation.

In the recent history of Congress, one can identify a number of factors that lead to this conclusion.

First, there is the fact that the trend toward legislative irrelevancy has been under way for 20 years or more. While the number of committees (and subcommittees) is up, overall attendance is down, and committees undertake more and more tasks that do not result in legislation.

Second, committee chairmen in the House are now term limited. Under a rule change adopted by the Republican majority at the beginning of the 104th Congress, no committee chairman can serve longer than three terms.

Chairmen in office at the beginning of the 104th Congress, in 1995, will have to step down at the beginning of the 107th Congress, in January 2001, assuming Republicans keep control. Should the Democrats regain control of Congress [in the fall of 1998, or in 2000], they might possibly reverse this rules change, but there would be serious political costs to doing so.

CHAIRMANSHIPS ARE STILL DESIRABLE

And yet, the chairmanship of committees remains very desirable. We can tell just how desirable by how upset current chairmen are about this limitation. Some (such as Gerald Solomon of New York, chairman of the powerful Rules Committee) have announced their intention not to run again. Some are talking about exercising their seniority on other committees of which they are members, becoming chairmen of a different committee.

There is also a move afoot to abandon the rule, or at least to modify it so that chairmanship terms would expire on a rolling basis, one-third in each Congress. There would be heavy political costs involved in abandoning the rule and a lot of resistance to the committee-switching ploy. The rolling expiration makes some sense, but there are practical difficulties with implementation.

Which committees would go first? That could be determined by lot, but what happens when a chairmanship is set to expire in [2004] and the chairman loses the election of [2002]. Does his successor serve only one term, or does he get three, which would upset the one-third, one-third, one-third progression.

The explanation for the desirability of chairmanships is obvious: Committee chairmen dispose of substantial resources in the form of positions and money. These assets in turn give a member great opportunities for news coverage, coalition building, and political advancement. They might even allow him to legislate, though that point is secondary.

With the House closely divided between the two major parties, legislation written in committee is often dead on arrival on the floor. Committees report bills and then are tasked by the leadership with building a coalition that can pass them.

Often, the leadership takes an active role in modifying the committee bill, or even in crafting a bill from scratch. The leadership is often more attuned to the nuances of what the House or Senate will accept than is a committee chairman, who may have cultivated a compliant committee membership, at least on his side of the aisle, a compliance that does not prevail in the body as a whole.

LEGISLATION REWRITTEN ON THE FLOOR

Particularly in the more loosely organized Senate, important legislation is often written, or rewritten, on the floor. Historically, a bill that could command a substantial majority in committee was virtually untouched on the floor. Amendments would be offered, usually to establish that a given senator was defending the interests of his constituency.

Many of these amendments would be withdrawn after debate, in exchange for a promise of some future action. But even when they went to a final vote, without the support of the committee chairman, very few of them would pass, and the final bill would not differ much from the bill reported.

That has changed now, as political entrepreneurs work with outside groups to get major modifications in reported bills. A determined senator with a particular interest could always use the Senate's rules to influence bills, but it was the exception when one did so. Now it is the rule.

Many senators have been elected under self-imposed term limits, and they cannot wait until they rise to the top of the hierarchy to have an impact on bills. Sen. John Ashcroft of Missouri, for example, freely admits that he will never be around long enough to be a committee chairman. If he is to have a major impact on bills, he must act as an entrepreneur and work on bills on the floor, whether they come from committees he sits on or not.

Or consider the recent appointment of a select committee to consider the possibility of Chinese influence in technology-transfer waivers. This is a matter that could easily have been made to fit under the scope of one of the existing committees of the House.

But with the Government Reform and Oversight Committee, under the chairmanship of Dan Burton of Indiana, bogged down in endless squabbling over campaign irregularities, the leadership reached for the able and popular (not to mention ambitious) Chris Cox of California to chair a more flexible and responsive special "committee."

The importance of committees in the legislative process is further attenuated by the rise of the Budget Committees and the attendant reconciliation process. In an era of constrained resources, the Budget Committees assume a position of superiority in the allocation of spending and taxing. The legislative committees are given "reconciliation instructions," told, in effect, to cut spending by so much or raise taxes to this level.

Failure to abide by these instructions invokes points of order, requiring supermajorities (60 votes) to overcome in the Senate. There is also the matter of the recent growth in importance of the conference committee, which has the final say over the content of every important bill that reaches the final legislative stages.

House and Senate leaders appoint conferees and thus have enormous say over the actions of the conference. When Democrats were last in power in the House, they adopted a rules change allowing the Speaker to remove members of a conference committee and appoint new ones. Speaker Tom Foley never used this power (he had it only for a short time), but Speaker Newt Gingrich has used it to get results from a conference that he wanted.

LEGISLATIVE PROCESS A CHARADE

The result is that the whole legislative process—from committee action to passage of bills on the floor of the House and Senate—becomes a charade, having little to do with the final shape of important legislation.

Consider the tobacco legislation that was before the Senate. Its supporters did not much care what was in the bill they were going to pass. They just wanted to pass something.

If it had, that would have virtually forced the House to act, and once both bodies had passed something, the real work would get done in a conference. That conference would be dominated by conferees from the Commerce Committee, which approved, 19-1, a bill that could not pass the Senate.

Until recently, the conference was limited in its scope to the provisions passed by the two bodies. Things that had passed both bodies had to be in the final bill, and things that had passed neither body were outside the scope of the conference and could not be added.

It was Republicans, in the wake of the Gramm-Rudman-Hollings budget legislation, who voted to override the ruling of the chair and establish the precedent that the conference can do anything it wants. Or more accurately, whatever the leadership wants. Thus conferees now routinely drop from bills provisions passed by both bodies, which used to be a violation of the rules. Or they add new provisions passed by neither body; again, a violation of the old rules.

As long as the committee has an important budget and staff complement, there is little likelihood that it will disappear as an institution. But there is also little likelihood of any resurrection in its importance to the legislative process.

The sharp increase in partisanship further undermines the committee system. When I came to Washington in the 1960s, only the House Education and Labor Committee saw bitter partisan battles. Indeed, both parties chose members of that committee for their ideological rigor and uncompromising natures.

Now, virtually every committee has that same kind of head-butting political friction. The days when the chairman and the ranking member got together for a few drinks and laid out the work of the committee—and then delivered on their agreement—are gone. There are too many younger members, thirsting after the chairman's job, to let him get away with excessive coziness with the other party.

GENERATIONAL FACTORS

The generational factors work in other ways to undermine the committee system. Although the seniority system has been done away with in both houses, it remains the de facto rule, with few exceptions, particularly in the Senate. The result is the elevation to committee chairmanships of old bulls who are out of touch with the younger members of the party.

Legislation that moves through a committee chaired by Ted Stevens of Alaska (in his sixth six-year term) or Pete Domenici of New Mexico (fifth term) is unlikely to be well received by a Republican caucus averaging two terms. The difficulty is not always a matter of tenure.

An ideological maverick such as Jim Jeffords of Vermont has almost no chance of securing the support of a majority of his caucus, though by cooperating with Democrats he may be able to get majorities within his Labor and Human Resources Committee.

Committees today do not engage in actual fact-finding. To a large extent, they are charades with a prearranged slate of witnesses making points known in advance. The majority party controls the witness list and makes certain that its point of view is disproportionately represented. The hearing itself begins with a series of opening statements from members that are little more than posturing for the news media. Often there will be no more than the chairman and ranking minority member in attendance.

Witnesses appear in panels after the opening statement, and they deliver testimony whose contents are known in advance. Indeed, it must be submitted in 75 copies at least 24 hours ahead of time. Members rarely engage witnesses in any extended dialogue, eliciting real information. Hearing proceedings are published and forgotten. They are never read by members and rarely even by staff. One Supreme Court justice has declared the hearing record irrelevant to a proper interpretation of the legislative intent.

Examples of hearings that actually elicited information include a series conducted by Sen. Orrin Hatch in the Judiciary Committee, on abortion in 1982, and on the Equal Rights Amendment in 1984. In these hearings, Hatch had only one witness at a time and left the witness before the committee for the whole day, following lines of inquiry wherever they led, with ample time for follow-up and exchange of views. Those attending, or taking the time to read the proceedings, actually learned something about the issues.

The attenuation of legislative impact in committee is taking place unevenly. In some committees, it is well advanced, in others, not much more than beginning. In a few instances, such as the labor law hearings now under way in the House under the chairmanship of Pete Hoekstra of Michigan, the trend may be reversed for a while. But in the long run, I believe that the institution of the congressional committee will develop along the lines I have sketched out. Committees will finish by being bases of political support for ambitious politicians but will remain largely irrelevant to the legislative process.

Civil Discourse Is Crucial for Democracy to Work

Claiborne Pell

CONTEXT

The Congress of the United States exists to solve the problems of the nation. Those people who occupy seats in the Congress, men and women of great (self) importance, get there by waging fierce battles against opponents of equal (self) importance. Often these battles, called election campaigns, are ugly, involving questionable practices, mud slinging, and personal attacks. Once one candidate wins, however, all of that conflict and emotion must be put aside so that the process of governing can take its place. As an institution, Congress could not function with the kind of behavior that takes place in an election campaign.

There are certain informal norms that guide behavior in Congress to ensure that the same kind of behavior that is common in a campaign does not filter into the legislative arena. Among those informal norms, members of Congress are expected to be honest with one another, courteous to one another, and engage in reciprocity with one another. There have been times in the history of Congress when emotions ran over and civility took a back seat. For example, in 1985 California Representative Bob Dornan and New York Representative Thomas Downey nearly came to blows on the House Floor because Dornan called Downey a "draft-dodging wimp."

While members of Congress seldom engage in fisticuffs these days, some say that manners are changing on Capitol Hill and that the result is the institution's ability to solve the nation's problems is suffering. In this selection, former Rhode Island Senator Claiborne Pell warns that a loss of civility both in the Congress and in the larger society is dangerous for democracy. Pell argues that the warning George Washington gave when he left office about the perils of excessive partisanship are as relevant today as they were in 1786.

● *THINK CRITICALLY* ●

1. Why is it so important for political debate, both in Congress and in the larger society, to remain civil? Are there ever times when debate should not necessarily remain civil? If so, when?
2. In your view, is there a relationship between reasoned debate and compromise? Explain why or why not.

If upon completing six terms in the Senate I could have one wish for the future of our country in the new millennium, it would be that we not abandon the traditional norms of good behavior that are the underpinning of our democratic system.

Comity and civility, transcending differences of party and ideology, always have been crucial elements in making government an effective and constructive instrument of public will. But in times such as these, when the pendulum of history seems to be reversing its swing and there is so much fundamental disagreement about the role of government, it is all the more essential that we preserve the spirit of civil discourse.

It has been distressing of late to hear the complaints of those who would abandon public service because they find the atmosphere mean-spirited. They seem to suggest that the basic rules of civilized behavior have been stifled by an opportunistic system. They make a good point, although I hasten to say that this was not a consideration in my own decision to retire at the end of my present term.

After more than 35 years, I have come to expect a certain amount of rancor in the legislative process. But I certainly agree that it is threatening to get out of bounds. I say this with great respect for my colleagues in the Senate. They are a wonderfully talented group of men and women, dedicated to serving their constituents and to improving the quality of our national life. Even this exceptional group, however, sometimes yields to the virus of discontent which has infected the American body politic.

Before retiring from the Senate to become president of the University of Oklahoma, David Boren sent a letter to his colleagues lamenting the fact that "we have become so partisan and so personal in our attacks upon each other that we can no longer effectively work together in the national interest." It was a thoughtful warning that has meaning far beyond the Senate and applies to our whole national political dialogue.

The fact is that the democratic process depends on respectful disagreement. As soon as we confuse civil debate with reckless disparagement, we have crippled the process. A breakdown of civility reinforces extremism and discourages the hard process of negotiating across party lines to reach a broad-based consensus.

The Founding Fathers who prescribed the ground rules for debate in Congress certainly had all these considerations in mind. We address one another in the third person with what seems like elaborate courtesy. The purpose, of course, is to remind us constantly that whatever the depth of our disagreements, we are all common instruments of the democratic process.

Some of that spirit, I believe, needs to be infused into the continuing national debate outside the halls of Congress. It should be absorbed by our political parties and respected by the media, particularly in this era of electronic information. The democratic process is not well-served by spin doctors and sound bites.

Nor is it well-served by blustering assertions of no compromise. Boren had the temerity—and wisdom—to suggest that instead of holding weekly meetings to plot how to outsmart each other, the party caucuses in the Senate should hold two meetings a month to explore bipartisan solutions to pending issues. Again, it's another good idea which could apply to the national dialogue.

It is interesting to note that George Washington in his farewell address on Sept. 19, 1786, warned about excessive partisanship in terms that still have relevance:

> The spirit of party serves always to distract the public councils and enfeeble the public administration. It agitates the community with ill-founded jealousies and false alarms; kindles animosity of one part against another; foments occasional riots and insurrection.

Of course, Washington's words were addressed to a struggling new nation striving for stability, so they seem somewhat quaint and a bit alarmist. But 200 years later we are well reminded that the survival of our democratic republic always has depended upon reasoned deliberation that avoids partisan extremes.

ALICE DOESN'T VOTE HERE ANYMORE

MICHAEL LIND

CONTEXT

In the United States, members of the House of Representatives are elected from districts whereby a plurality of the vote determines who wins. This means the candidate who receives the most votes wins, even if the most votes is only 40 percent of the total. The result of this plurality system of voting and electioneering is that the two major parties, Democrats and Republicans, are nearly always assured of a win, and minority parties, Greens, Reform, Libertarians, etc., are nearly always assured not to win.

Some argue that the plurality voting system discriminates against minority parties. For instance, if seats in the House of Representatives were to have been allocated proportionally after the 1992 presidential election, the Reform Party would have been able to fill 19 percent of the seats. That is the percentage of the vote that Reform Party candidate Ross Perot received in the election. One of the reasons that we do not have a tradition of third parties in the United States is because our electoral system makes it very difficult for third-party candidates to win seats in Congress.

In this selection, Michael Lind describes the current plurality voting method for electing members of Congress. Lind argues that as a result of the plurality voting method, many people (the majority in some congressional districts) are not represented by the candidate (or party) they supported in the election. He argues that the United States should abandon the plurality method for a proportional representation method. With a proportional representation method, seats in the House would be allocated based on the proportion of support a particular party has in a district (or group of districts).

● *THINK CRITICALLY* ●

1. In your view, is the current plurality voting method problematic, as Lind says it is? Why or why not?
2. If a proportional representation method for electing members of the House of Representatives were instituted, which third or fourth party in your area would gain seats? Would the Democratic and Republican parties lose representation? Explain how.

When it comes to the way we elect Congress, we're on the wrong side of the looking glass.

"Oh, my," said Alice, "is it really true that there are elections in Wonderland?"

"Of course, you foolish girl," the Queen of Hearts replied. "This is a constitutional monarchy. The Single Member of the Congress of Wonderland is elected by democratic means. Come, I shall introduce you to the electorate."

Alice followed the Queen to a field, in the middle of which was a table where the Mad Hatter and three of his friends were feasting. "The Mad Hatter's Party, with its four members, is one of the three political parties here in Wonderland," the Queen told Alice. "The other two parties, Tweedledum's Party and Tweedledee's Party, have three members apiece." Sure enough, Tweedledum and Tweedledee stood nearby, each with two followers.

"The electoral system of Wonderland," the Queen continued, "is based on the method of Plurality Voting by Single-Member Districts, sometimes known as Winner Takes All. You understand how that works, of course."

"No," said Alice sorrowfully, "I am afraid I do not."

The Queen shouted, "Off with her head!"

"Please," Alice begged, "I'll do my best to learn about the electoral system of Wonderland, if only you will explain it."

"Very well," the Queen said. "But I must warn you, the more I explain about Plurality Voting, the less you will understand it. For example, the most important part of our system of Plurality Voting by Single-Member Districts is the shape of the district."

"I cannot imagine why," Alice said.

The Queen was shocked. "Have you never heard of the Gerrymander?" At the mention of its name, the Gerrymander, a large and rather fearsome creature somewhat like a cross between a salamander and a Jabberwock, shambled forth. "Go on," the Queen ordered the beast, "draw the Single-Member District for the forthcoming congressional election."

Alice watched as the Gerrymander, dipping its brush in the pot of red paint hanging from its neck, began to outline a square in the grass. Soon the square's borders included the three members of the Tweedledum Party and the three members of the Tweedledee Party. But when it came to the four supporters of the Mad Hatter's Party, the Gerrymander painted a red stripe right down the middle of their banquet table.

"There," the Queen said with satisfaction. "Thanks to the Gerrymander, we now have a Single-Member District with two large parties, those of Tweedledum and Tweedledee, with three voters apiece, and one small party, the Mad Hatter's Party, with only two voters."

"But that isn't right!" cried Alice. She rushed to the Mad Hatter. "Aren't you going to do something?"

"Why on earth should I?" he asked.

"You have the biggest party," Alice replied. "Your party has four members, and the other two parties have only three voters apiece."

"Oh, you silly girl," said the Mad Hatter, pointing to the red stripe bisecting the table. "Can't you see that my party has only two voters eligible to vote in the Single-Member District?"

Alice noticed Tweedledum and Tweedledee handing purses full of coins to the Gerrymander. "Don't you see what they've done to you? They've drawn the Single-Member District to minimize the power of your voters!"

"Of course they have," the Mad Hatter chuckled. "We'd have done the same to them, if we could afford to pay the Gerrymander."

"But it isn't fair to your party! Why don't you protest?"

"Protest!" All four members of his party, the two inside the Single-Member District and the two outside, burst into laughter. "Protest? Why, our elections have always been held this way. To protest would be unpatriotic and vulgar." At this, the Mad Hatter and his friends resumed their banquet.

Alice was thinking very deeply. At length she said, "I have devised a strategy by which your party can maximize its influence, even though the Gerrymander has turned you into a minority party."

The Mad Hatter looked up from the table in annoyance. "Are you still here?"

Alice explained her plan. "The Queen of Hearts said that Wonderland has a Plurality Voting System. Therefore, it is all very puzzling, I admit, the winner needs either a simple majority in a two-party race or less than a majority, a mere plurality, in a three-party race. In a plurality election, the greater the number of parties, the smaller the plurality that is necessary to win."

"Yes, yes, yes," the Mad Hatter said, drumming his fingers on the table. "Is there a point to this tedious lesson in political science?"

"Who can get that plurality is very, very important," Alice insisted. "Your two-person party is too small to win. Therefore you must decide which of the other two parties you prefer."

"Oh, that is easy," replied the Mad Hatter. "The positions of the Tweedledee Party are nearest our own positions, whereas we find the Tweedledum platform positively hateful."

"Well, then," Alice responded, "you must vote for the Tweedledee Party, not for your own."

"Not vote for our own party!" the Mad Hatter exclaimed.

Alice explained: "If you vote for the Tweedledee Party, then it will defeat the Tweedledum Party, by five votes to three. But if you vote for your own party, then you increase the chances that the Tweedledum Party will win. It's only rational."

"It may be rational, but this is Wonderland, and I'll have none of it!" the Mad Hatter declared.

There was no time for further argument, for at that very moment the Queen ordered, "Let the ballasting begin!"

A large balloon appeared above the treetops and drifted over the field. The balloonist shouted down to the Mad Hatter's Party: "How do you want your ballast cast?"

"Two for the Mad Hatter's Party!"

The balloonist tossed down two bags of ballast, which crashed in the midst of the table. Following the instructions of the other parties' voters, he cast three bags of ballast at the feet of Tweedledum and three at the feet of Tweedledee.

"The ballasting is complete," the Queen announced, as the balloon, deprived of ballast, drifted up into the sky and disappeared, taking the panicked balloonist with it.

"The election is a tie," Alice observed. "Tweedledum and Tweedledee each have three votes."

"No matter," said the Queen. "Under our Single-Member District Plurality Voting System, the outcome in a close race is often decided by the way the Swing Vote breaks."

"Who casts the Swing Vote?" Alice asked.

"Why, you do, little girl. Guards!"

Two guards appeared and forced poor Alice to climb up a tree containing an old, rotten, and very unsafe swing. With a great deal of anxiety, Alice sat in the swing and hung on for dear life as the guards gave it a push.

Back and forth Alice swung. As she passed overhead, first the Tweedledum Party and then the Tweedledee Party reached up, promising concessions in return for her support. Finally, on the third pass, the Swing Vote broke. Screaming, Alice was hurtled into the arms of Tweedledum.

"I got the Swing Vote!" Tweedledum exclaimed. "I won the election! I won the election!"

"But that isn't fair!" Alice cried. "It isn't fair three ways! It isn't fair the first way because the district was Gerrymandered, so the biggest party, the Mad Hatter's, was turned into a minority. And it isn't fair the second way because the plurality method of voting ensured that either the Tweedledum Party or the Tweedledee Party would win, even though a majority of the voters in the district voted against each party. And it isn't fair the third way because the election was so close that its outcome was settled by a Swing Voter, me, whose views may have nothing in common with what all of the other voters in the district want. It isn't fair at all! It's a travesty of democracy, which means nothing if it does not mean majority rule!"

The Queen gasped. "Little girl, what does democracy have to do with majority rule? In Wonderland, democracy means the Rule of the Largest Minority, helped out by a minuscule Swing Vote, in a Gerrymandered Single-Member District. Majority rule, indeed! Off with her head!"

The electoral system of Wonderland, as described above (with apologies to Lewis Carroll), is, as Alice rightly insists, unjust and perverse. Unfortunately, that electoral system is our own. (Coincidentally, it is one that Carroll himself would not have approved of. A mathematician by training, he was fascinated by voting systems and produced important work on voting theory, including developing elaborate alternative voting procedures that would eliminate bizarre distortions like those in Wonderland, that went completely unnoticed until the 1950s. He used to pass out pamphlets explaining his obscure theories to his Oxford colleagues, none of whom had an inkling as to what he was talking about.)

Plurality voting by single-member districts is how we elect the House, state legislatures, city councils, and other legislative bodies. Our method produces the same undemocratic effects identified by Alice, but they are somewhat less humorous when we tally their political consequences:

Gerrymandering

Under the Constitution, state legislatures are permitted to redraw the lines of U.S. House districts every 10 years, following the census. If the Republicans gain control of the statehouses in the midterm elections next November (32 states currently have Republican governors; 18 have GOP-controlled legislatures), this could spell disaster for the Democrats. As Republican National Chairman Jim Nicholson predicts: "The winners are going to determine the political landscape in at least the first decade of the next millennium, because they are the people who are going to preside over the process of reapportionment and redistricting of their respective states as a result of the 2000 census." Because the party of the president usually loses seats in midterm elections, this is an ominous prospect. And Democrats have good reasons to fear a Republican gerrymander: The current [15-seat] Republican majority in the House is largely due to cynical GOP efforts during the last round of redistricting in 1991 to forge what some Democrats have called an "unholy alliance" with black and Hispanic Democrats to carve up racially mixed liberal districts into "safe" black and Hispanic seats and equally "safe" Republican seats. The GOP even went so far as to make expensive redistricting software available to minority activist groups as part of its plan to split up the white liberal vote and ghettoize the nonwhite liberal vote.

As a result, there are only four white Democrats in the House from South Carolina, Georgia, Alabama, Mississippi, and Louisiana combined. In Newt Gingrich's Georgia, before racial gerrymandering, there were nine Democrats (eight white and one black) and only one Republican. Today the Georgia delegation numbers eight Republicans, all white, and three Democrats, all black.

Swing Vote

A relatively modest swing vote breaking rightward has helped make the South a solidly Republican stronghold. A shift of only a few percentage points can move divided districts from the Democratic to the Republican camp. Where the districts themselves are swing districts, holding the balance of power between the two parties in Congress, the votes of a tiny minority of swing voters in a few districts can create a revolution in national politics. Morton Kondracke, a columnist for *Roll Call*, estimates that less than 12,000 voters nationwide, or six-hundredths of 1 percent of the eligible voting population, swung the vote to the House Republicans in 1996.

Plurality Winners

The recent rise of third-party politics threatens to strengthen the hold of the two dominant parties in Congress, rather than weaken it. For instance, in a special House election in New Mexico last year, Carol Miller won 17 percent of the vote as the Green Party candidate, splitting the Democratic vote and sending a Republican to Washington to represent a district in which only 42 percent of the voters supported him. She intends to run again in 1998 and is unlikely to fare any better. With more and more Reform, Green, New, and Libertarian party candidates running for congressional seats, perverse results are inevitable: Minuscule returns for a Green Party candidate can throw an overwhelmingly progressive district to the Republicans, just as a spoiler Libertarian Party candidate can ensure the election of a Democrat in predominantly conservative districts. The third-party candidate loses, and the wrong major party candidate wins.

Plurality voting by single-member districts may be crooked, but it's the only game in town, isn't it?

No, as a matter of fact it isn't. Most liberal democracies have rejected plurality voting because of its unfair and paradoxical results. Instead, they elect their legislatures by some version of proportional representation by district.

Here's how proportional representation works: Imagine a region with five adjacent single-member congressional districts. In each district, the electorate is divided between Republicans (60 percent), Democrats (20 percent), and Greens (20 percent). Under plurality voting, even though Republicans are only a slight majority of the electorate, they will get 100 percent of the vote. The region will send five Republicans to Congress, no Democrats, and no Greens. Under proportional representation, the five adjacent districts would be consolidated into one five-member delegation, which would send three Republicans, one Democrat, and one Green. This distribution of seats would more accurately reflect the distribution of sentiments in the electorate. In politics, who wins depends upon the rules.

Note that under proportional representation, the Alice-in-Wonderland results of our system, gerrymandering, plurality winners, and swing votes, simply disappear. State legislatures would abandon partisan gerrymandering, because it could no longer effectively prevent the minority from picking up at least a few seats. Racial gerrymandering would no longer be necessary, either. If people wanted to vote along racial or ethnic lines (which is far from a good idea in principle), then members of significant racial or ethnic minorities would be sure to elect one or two members of a multimember district, even if the white majority itself voted along racial lines.

The plurality winner problem would also vanish. A party with 60 percent of the votes couldn't win 100 percent of the seats in a district, only 60 percent of the delegation.

What about the swing vote? It is most troubling in two-party systems, in which the swing voters hold the balance between the parties. The democracies that use proportional representation tend to have multiparty systems, and it is likely that the United States would as well if proportional representation were adopted here. English-speaking populations are not innately more likely to be divided into two parties than are German-speaking populations. A two-party system is an unintended but almost inevitable byproduct of the plurality electoral system.

Such a multiparty system might also help reduce the polarization of American politics. Because a coalition of two or more parties, not just a single majority party, would probably hold power in the House and Senate, a party would gain little political capital by attempting to demonize the president, or to vilify potential coalition partners in the other parties. The rigid connection between lobbies and parties would dissolve as lobbies found it more useful to try to influence two or more parties instead of identifying themselves wholly with one.

Another benefit of proportional representation is that it could abort the otherwise inevitable emergence of a solid Republican South, or any other region that is "solidly" one party or the other. Right-wing Republicans in Cambridge,

Berkeley, or New York's Upper West Side might be able to elect at least one or two members of Congress from their own area. Right now, in many districts, the minority party does not even bother to run a candidate. With five-member districts, any party with a chance at winning one-fifth of the vote could run candidates. It would no longer make sense for parties to write off whole districts, or even whole states. All of America would become politically competitive for the first time in history.

At this point, the defender of the status quo is certain to introduce a parade of horribles: for example, the fractionalization of the electorate into too many ineffectual parties, or the tyranny of small, fanatical parties in the multiparty legislature. The first can easily be dismissed: Under proportional representation, interests tend to coagulate into a handful of substantial parties. And we can eliminate the problem of tiny fanatical parties, which has bedeviled Israel, by insisting that no party can get seats in the legislature unless it wins a certain threshold, say, 5 percent, of the national vote. Thus, even if neo-Nazis win a district in Louisiana, they won't be seated in Congress unless they pass the national threshold.

Proportional representation tends to have a stabilizing effect on democracies, usually because a centrist party, such as the Free Democrats in Germany, moderates the extremist tendencies of its coalition partners. By contrast, elections in plurality democracies such as Britain and the United States tend to produce wild shifts in public policy, even though only a small number of swing voters may have changed their votes.

In the United States, the political history of the last quarter-century probably would have been far less turbulent had we adopted proportional representation to elect the House in, say, the 1950s. What would have happened is, of course, anybody's guess. Mine is that three major parties would have emerged from the wreckage of the Democrats and Republicans: An upscale progressive party based in New England and the Pacific Northwest, a conservative party based in the South, and a working-class populist party, with members who were socially conservative but fiscally liberal. On social issues, the House might have had a populist-conservative majority; on economic issues, a populist-progressive majority. The destruction of federal welfare programs and the balancing of the budget through regressive policies, the work of a centrist Democratic president and a right-wing Republican congressional majority, might never have taken place. The far left would have been just as thwarted, but New Deal liberalism, based on an alliance of Northern progressives, Southern populists, and working-class Catholics, might have endured.

What about the executive branch and the Senate? Proportional representation works only with multicandidate districts. For single-candidate offices, a system known as preference voting (also called the "instant runoff") could thwart Wonderland democracy. Where three or more candidates ran for an office such as the presidency, the voter would be instructed to rank the candidates in order of preference. Thus a voter in our imaginary three-party America who prefers the progressive to the populist candidate on social issues, while preferring the populist to the conservative one on economic issues, would assign the following ranking on the ballot: Progressive (1), Populist (2), Conservative (3). If no candidate wins a majority, the second-choice votes are redistributed among the top two candidates. In extreme cases, it might be possible for a candidate who got the most first-preference votes to lose to a candidate who won an overwhelming majority of second-preference votes.

Preference voting makes it almost impossible for a candidate strongly opposed by most voters to get elected in a three- or four-way race. Even more important, the adoption of preference voting for senatorial and presidential races would give candidates an incentive to seek support beyond their own parties. While elections under the plurality system tend to produce rival moderates exaggerating their differences, elections under the preference voting system would encourage candidates from genuinely different parties to reach out to members of other parties. The candidates would campaign not only for the first-preference votes of their party but for the second-preference votes of the parties that were nearest to their positions on particular issues. There might be coalition cabinets and even fusion tickets, with a president from one party and a vice president from another.

Preference voting can also eliminate two potential problems that multiple parties might pose to the American constitutional system. In a separation-of-powers political system like ours, conflict is endemic, particularly when different parties control the branches. If Congress were divided among multiple parties, it could severely weaken its power relative to the presidency. The president could claim to represent "the people," using that as a pretext to get around a Congress split among a number of squabbling parties. Preference voting in presidential elections might reduce that danger by encouraging the candidates, in campaigning for second-choice votes, to promise a multiparty coalition Cabinet.

Second, preference voting might also decrease the likelihood of another catastrophe that can occur from the collision of multiple parties with a plurality electoral system, the minoritarian president. In some countries with presidential systems, political chaos and even civil wars have erupted when a president supported by only a small minority has won election in a multiple-party race. Preference voting would guarantee that the winning candidate would always receive a majority of second-choice (and perhaps third-choice) votes, meaning that voters would never be stuck with their least favorite candidate.

Can proportional representation ever be more than a fantasy in the United States? It's already used to elect the city council of Cambridge and it was used for many years by the Cincinnati City Council (it was scrapped in the 1950s because it allowed blacks a chance to be elected).

There are no constitutional obstacles to changing our method of voting. The Constitution is silent about electoral systems. Our plurality system was established by statute; it can be replaced by statute. Alternatively, Congress, which has the ultimate say over how its members are elected, might give the states the right to determine how their congressional delegations are chosen. In 1995, Rep. Cynthia McKinney (D-Ga.) introduced the Voters' Choice Act, which would allow states to use proportional representation to elect their congressional delegations.

A supporter of the status quo might argue that our system is somehow uniquely suited to the American character or to our political culture, or that two centuries of tradition have sanctified it. But the Founding Fathers did not actually choose the plurality system in any meaningful sense; they simply adopted the British electoral system they grew up with. No real alternative existed until the 1850s, when an Englishman named John Hare devised one of the first influential versions of proportional representation.

Far from being alien to American society, proportional representation is arguably the only appropriate electoral system for a society as diverse as ours. It encourages social peace by giving every major segment of the population a piece of the action. Proportional representation has proved most successful in ethnically divided societies, such as the Baltic states and South Africa, since it permits every significant minority to elect at least some representatives. The traditional American theory of democracy, majority rule with minority rights, has always been questionable. We cannot count on the federal judiciary to protect the rights of minorities, because its composition, over time, will reflect the partisan majority in the other two branches. Properly understood, democracy means majority rule with minority representation. Under proportional representation, the black or Hispanic or libertarian or socialist or populist minority would have the opportunity to elect the occasional member of Congress, state legislator, or city council member, instead of having to cast a doomed vote.

If the traditionalist argument in support of plurality voting were valid, it ought to be most powerful in Britain, from which the U.S. inherited its archaic electoral method. There, however, Prime Minister Tony Blair made a national referendum on the replacement of plurality voting by proportional representation an important part of his campaign. Australia, New Zealand, and Ireland already have forms of proportional representation in some elections, and Canada recently considered the idea when it attempted to redesign its senate (the plan failed for reasons that had nothing to do with the issue of proportional representation). If Britain and Canada scrap plurality voting, the United States, in a generation or two, might find itself alone among advanced democratic countries in clinging to an electoral procedure rejected as unfair and primitive everywhere else. The "world's greatest democracy" may end up having the least democratic electoral law.

Needless to say, politicians elected under a given voting system are unlikely to change it. In the United States, the best way to force the political class to undertake electoral reform may be to sponsor initiatives in states, such as California, whose constitutions permit this method of direct action. Most electoral reforms, such as the extension of suffrage to women and blacks, were adopted by progressive states before they were enacted by congressional statute or constitutional amendment.

In the 1996 election, less than half of the electorate voted. Under the current electoral system, choosing not to vote is a rational decision by people who do not identify with either of the two parties, or who live in congressional districts or states in which one party has an overwhelming majority. When the system is rigged against you, a boycott makes perfect sense (international comparisons demonstrate, to nobody's surprise, that voter turnout is far lower in democracies with plurality voting than in multiparty democracies using proportional representation).

Though it may be justified, popular alienation threatens democracy itself in the long run. If people believe, correctly, that they are not represented by the

American political elite, they will be drawn to the kind of antipolitics represented on left, right, and center by Jerry Brown, Pat Buchanan, and Ross Perot, respectively. At its worst, antipolitics is the opposite of political reform; its goal is to smash constitutional, representative democracy, not to improve it. As Americans grow more alienated from the two-party system that our antiquated voting scheme encourages, they may be tempted to support a charismatic president who, claiming a popular mandate, promises to get things done, with little regard for constitutional niceties or those crooks in Congress. Only a few years ago, a majority of Americans polled said that they would support Colin Powell for president, knowing almost nothing about his political views. That he wore a uniform was apparently sufficient recommendation. A North American version of Latin American–style Peronism or French-style Bonapartism, disguised as presidential prerogative or direct democracy, is all too conceivable in the 21st century.

Time is running out. Soon, we will have to prove to ourselves that the American political system has not discredited democracy itself, only the democracy of Wonderland.

THE IMPERIAL JUDICIARY AND WHAT CONGRESS CAN DO ABOUT IT

EDWIN MEESE III AND RHETT DEHART

CONTEXT

Early in the nation's history, the Supreme Court was thought of as a rather lowly place to work by many. In fact, within a couple of years of the establishment of the Supreme Court, one justice left to join the Supreme Court of South Carolina, which was considered a much more prestigious job. What made the court so meaningless was in part that nobody knew exactly how the Supreme Court would function within the three branches of government. It was not clear that the Supreme Court would ever have much power, or be considered as important as the other two branches.

What in part changed the fortunes of the Supreme Court was John Marshall, the fourth Chief Justice, who served from 1801 to 1835. Marshall was determined when he became Chief Justice to bring respect and honor to the high court. Within a couple of years, a case came before the court that gave him the opportunity to define exactly what role the court would play in the new democracy. In *Marbury v. Madison*, John Marshall wrote that only the Supreme Court had the authority to interpret what the law is according to the Constitution. Through what became known as judicial review (or the Doctrine of Judicial Review), the Supreme Court held that only it had the power to review acts of Congress, the president, or the states to determine whether their acts were constitutional or not. Thus the court reserved for itself the right to determine what the Constitution means.

In this selection, former U.S. Attorney General Edwin Meese III and Rhett DeHart argue that the Supreme Court has taken the Doctrine of Judicial Review too far and is today an imperial body operating outside of the democratic process. As evidence of the excesses of judicial activism, they cite Supreme Court cases that allowed racial preferences and quotas, created a right to public welfare assistance, hampered criminal prosecution, lowered hiring standards for the U.S. workforce, discovered a right to abortion, and overturned state referenda. Meese and Rhett argue that Congress has at its disposal the ability to confine the judiciary to its proper constitutional role, and outline five steps that Congress can take to do so.

● *THINK CRITICALLY* ●

1. Do you agree that judicial activism has been bad for democracy? Why or why not?
2. Does "activist judge" mean liberal judge?
3. Of the five ways that Meese and DeHart claim that Congress can confine the judiciary to its proper role, which if any seem possible in the current political climate?

Under the modern doctrine of judicial review, the federal judiciary can invalidate any state or federal law or policy it considers inconsistent with the U.S. Constitution. This doctrine gives unelected federal judges awesome power. Whenever these judges exceed their constitutional prerogative to interpret law and instead read their personal views and prejudices into the Constitution, the least democratic branch of government becomes its most powerful as well.

America's Founding Fathers created a democratic republic in which elected representatives were to decide the important issues of the day. In their view, the role of the judiciary, although crucial, was to interpret and clarify the law—not to make law. The Framers recognized the necessity of judicial restraint and the dangers of judicial activism. James Madison wrote in *The Federalist Papers* that to combine judicial power with executive and legislative authority was "the very definition of tyranny," and Thomas Jefferson believed that allowing only the unelected judiciary to interpret the Constitution would lead to judicial supremacy. "It is a very dangerous doctrine to consider the judges as the ultimate arbiters of all constitutional questions," said Jefferson. "It is one which would place us under the despotism of an oligarchy."

Unfortunately, the federal judiciary has strayed far beyond its proper functions, in many ways validating Jefferson's warnings about judicial power. In no other democracy in the world do unelected judges decide as many vital political issues as they do in America. We will never return the federal government to its proper role in our society until we return the federal judiciary to its proper role in our government.

Supreme Court decisions based on the Constitution cannot be reversed or altered, except by a constitutional amendment. Such decisions are virtually immune from presidential vetoes or congressional legislation. Abraham Lincoln warned of this in his First Inaugural Address when he said:

> "[T]he candid citizen must confess that if the policy of the government, upon vital questions, affecting the whole people, is to be irrevocably fixed by decisions of the Supreme Court . . . the people will have ceased to be their own rulers, having, to that extent, practically resigned their government into the hands of that eminent tribunal."

When the most important social and moral issues are removed from the democratic process, citizens lose the political experience and moral education that come from resolving difficult issues and reaching a social consensus. President Reagan explained how judicial activism is incompatible with popular government:

> "The Founding Fathers were clear on this issue. For them, the question involved in judicial restraint was not—as it is not—will we have liberal courts or conservative courts? They knew that the courts, like the Constitution itself, must not be liberal or conservative. *The question was and is, will we have government by the people?*" [Emphasis added.]

JUDICIAL EXCESSES

When federal judges exceed their proper interpretive role, the result is not only infidelity to the Constitution, but very often poor public policy. Numerous cases illustrate the consequences of judicial activism and the harm it has caused our society. Activist court decisions have undermined nearly every aspect of public policy. Among the most egregious examples:

Allowing Racial Preferences and Quotas

In *United Steelworkers of America v. Weber* (1979), the Supreme Court held for the first time that the Civil Rights Act of 1964 permits private employers to establish racial preferences and quotas in employment, despite the clear language of the statute: "It shall be an unlawful employment practice for any employer . . . to discriminate against any individual because of his race, color, religion, sex, or national origin." Had the Court decided *Weber* differently, racial preferences would not exist in the private sector today. The *Weber* decision is a classic example of how unelected government regulators and federal judges have diverted our civil-rights laws from a color-blind ideal to a complex and unfair system of racial and ethnic preferences and quotas that perpetuate bias and discrimination.

Creating a "Right" to Public Welfare Assistance

In *Goldberg v. Kelly* (1970), the Supreme Court sanctioned the idea that welfare entitlements are a form of "property" under the Fourteenth Amendment. The Court's conclusion: Before a government can terminate benefits on the grounds that the recipient is not eligible, the recipient is entitled to an extensive and costly appeals process akin to a trial. Thanks to the Court, welfare recipients now have a "right" to receive benefits fraudulently throughout lengthy legal proceedings, and never have to reimburse the government if their ineligibility is confirmed. The decision has tied up thousands of welfare workers in judicial hearings and deprived the truly needy of benefits. By 1974, for example, New York City alone needed a staff of 3,000 to conduct *Goldberg* hearings.

Hampering Criminal Prosecution

In *Mapp v. Ohio* (1961), the Supreme Court began a revolution in criminal procedure by requiring state courts to exclude from criminal cases any evidence found during an "unreasonable" search or seizure. In so holding, the Court overruled a previous case, *Wolf v. Colorado* (1949), which had allowed each state to devise its own methods for deterring unreasonable searches and seizures. The Supreme Court in effect acted like a legislature rather than a judicial body. As a dissenting justice noted, the *Mapp* decision unjustifiably infringed upon the states' sovereign judicial systems and forced them to adopt a uniform, federal procedural remedy ill-suited to serve states with "their own peculiar problems in criminal law enforcement."

In fact, nothing in the Fourth Amendment or any other provision of the Constitution mentions the exclusion of evidence, nor does the legislative history of the Constitution indicate that the Framers intended to require such exclusion. Instead we ought to explore other means of deterring police misconduct without acquitting criminals, such as permitting civil lawsuits against reckless government officials and enforcing internal police sanctions against offending officers with fines and demotions.

Since *Mapp v. Ohio*, the exclusionary rule has had a devastating impact on law enforcement in America. One recent study estimated that 150,000 criminal cases, including 30,000 cases of violence, are dropped or dismissed *every year* because the exclusionary rule excluded valid, probative evidence needed for prosecution.

Lowering Hiring Standards for the U.S. Workforce

In *Griggs v. Duke Power Co.* (1971), a plaintiff challenged a company's requirement that job applicants possess a high-school diploma and pass a general aptitude test as a condition of employment. The lawsuit argued that because the diploma and test requirements disqualified a disproportionate number of minorities, those requirements were unlawful under the Civil Rights Act of 1964 unless shown to be related to the job in question.

The Court ruled that under the Act, employment requirements that dispro-portionately exclude minorities must be shown to be related to job perfor-mance, and it rejected the employer's argument that the diploma and testing requirements were implemented to improve the overall quality of its work-force. Moreover, the Court held that "Congress has placed on the employer the burden of showing that any given requirement must have a manifest rela-tionship to the employment in question."

In fact, the Act explicitly authorizes an employer to use aptitude tests like the one challenged in *Griggs*. This insidious court decision has lowered the quality of the U.S. workforce by making it difficult for employers to require high-school diplomas and other neutral job requirements. It also forced employers to adopt racial quotas in order to avoid the expense of defending hiring prac-tices that happen to produce disparate outcomes for different ethnic groups.

"Discovering" a Right to Abortion

In *Roe v. Wade* (1973), the Court considered the constitutionality of a Texas statute that prohibited abortion except to save the life of the mother. Although the Court acknowledged that the Constitution does not explicitly mention a right of privacy, it held that the Constitution protects rights "implicit in the concept of ordered liberty." The Court ruled that "the right of personal privacy includes the abortion decision," and it struck down the Texas statute under the Due Process Clause of the Fourteenth Amendment. The Court then went on, in a blatantly legislative fashion, to proclaim a precise framework limiting the states ability to regulate abortion procedures.

The dissenting opinion in *Roe* pointed out that, in order to justify its ruling, the majority had to somehow "find" within the Fourteenth Amendment a right that was unknown to the drafters of the Amendment. When the Fourteenth Amendment was adopted in 1868, there were at least 36 state or territorial laws limiting abortion, and the passage of the Amendment raised no questions at the time about the validity of those laws. "The only conclusion possible from this history," wrote the dissenting justices, "is that the Drafters did not in-tend to have the Fourteenth Amendment withdraw from the States the power to legislate with respect to this matter."

One of the most pernicious aspects of the *Roe* decision is that it removed one of the most profound social and moral issues from the democratic process with-out any constitutional authority. For the first two centuries of America's exis-tence, the abortion issue had been decided by state legislatures, with substantially less violence and conflict than has attended the issue since the *Roe* decision.

Overturning State Referenda

In *Romer v. Evans* (1996), the U.S. Supreme Court actually negated a direct vote of the people. This case concerned an amendment to the Colorado constitution enacted in 1992 by a statewide referendum. "Amendment 2" prohibited the state or any political subdivisions therein from adopting any policy that grants homo-sexuals "any minority status, quota preference, protected status, or claim of discrimination." The Court ruled that the amendment was unconstitutional because it did not bear a "rational relationship" to a legitimate government purpose and thus violated the Equal Protection Clause of the Fourteenth Amendment.

The state of Colorado contended that this amendment protected freedom of association, particularly for landlords and employers who have religious objections to homosexuality, and that it only prohibited *preferential treatment* for homosexuals. But the Court rejected these arguments and offered its own interpretation of what motivated the citizens of Colorado, claiming that "laws of the kind now before us raise the inevitable inference that the disadvantage imposed is born of animosity toward the class of persons affected."

The dissenting opinion argued that Amendment 2 denies equal treatment only in the sense that homosexuals may not obtain "preferential treatment without amending the state constitution." Noting that under *Bowers v. Hardwick* (1986), states are permitted to outlaw homosexual sodomy, the dissent reasoned that if it is constitutionally permissible for a state to criminalize homosexual conduct, it is surely constitutionally permissible for a state to deny special favor and protection to homosexuals. The Court's decision, the dissent charged, "is an act not of judicial judgment, but of political will."

It is hard not to regard the *Romer* decision as the pinnacle of judicial arrogance: Six appointed justices struck down a law passed by 54 percent of a state's voters in a direct election, the most democratic of all procedures. In one of the most egregious usurpations of power in constitutional history, the Court not only desecrated the principle of self-government, but appointed itself the moral arbiter of the nation's values.

TURNING THE TIDE

Fortunately, Congress has a number of strategies at its disposal to confine the judiciary to its proper constitutional role:

1. The Senate should use its confirmation authority to block the appointment of activist federal judges.

When a president appoints judges who exceed their constitutional authority and usurp the other branches of government, the Senate can properly restrain the judiciary by carefully exercising its responsibilities under the "advise and consent" clause of Article II. Section 2 of the Constitution.

Normally, the Senate Judiciary Committee conducts a hearing on the president's nominees. Those nominees who are approved by the committee or submitted without recommendation go to the full Senate for a confirmation vote.

Unfortunately, the confirmation process in recent years has been relatively perfunctory. The Senate has been reluctant to closely question a nominee to ascertain the candidate's understanding of the proper role of the judiciary. The Senate committee hearing provides an excellent opportunity to discern a judicial candidate's understanding of a constitutionally limited judiciary. It also provides a public opportunity for judicial watchdog organizations to testify in support of or against a particular nominee.

The Constitution established Senate confirmation to ensure that unqualified nominees were not given lifelong judgeships. In carrying out this important responsibility, senators should ascertain a prospective judge's commitment to a philosophy of judicial restraint and fidelity to the Constitution. In so doing, they should carefully review all the opinions, legal articles, and other materials authored by the candidate, the personal background report prepared by the Federal Bureau of Investigation, and the testimony of judges and other attorneys who have had ample opportunities to view a candidate's work.

In the name of efficiency, the full Senate sometimes votes to confirm judicial nominees in bundles. This practice should cease. Senators should vote on each nominee individually, in order to remind the prospective judge and the public of the awesome responsibility of each new member of the judiciary and to hold themselves accountable for every judge they confirm to the federal bench.

2. Congress should strip the American Bar Association of its special role in the judicial selection process.

The American Bar Association (ABA) has shown itself to be a special-interest group, every bit as politicized as the American Civil Liberties Union or the National Rifle Association. In the 104th Congress, for example, the ABA officially supported federal funding for abortion services for the poor, racial and ethnic preferences, and a ban on assault weapons; and it opposed a ban on flag-burning, reform of the exclusionary rule and of death-penalty appeals, and a proposal to restrict AFDC payments for welfare mothers who have additional children. Hence it should be removed from any official role in evaluating judicial nominees. It would still be free to testify before the Senate Judiciary Committee concerning potential judges, but it would not have any special status or authority.

The Senate will always need the impartial assessment of judges and lawyers who have a detailed knowledge of the work and background of a judicial candidate. In place of the ABA, the Senate should appoint a special fact-finding committee in each of the 94 federal judicial districts. These lawyers would be selected for their objectivity, ideological neutrality, and understanding of the constitutional role of the judiciary. They would obtain the detailed information the Senate needs to evaluate a candidate, and would give that information directly to the Judiciary Committee without subjective comments or evaluation.

3. Congress should exercise its power to limit the jurisdiction of the federal courts.

Congress has great control over the jurisdiction of the lower federal courts. Article III, Section 1, of the Constitution provides that "[t]he judicial power of the United States, shall be vested in one supreme Court, *and in such inferior Courts as the Congress may from time to time ordain and establish.*" [Emphasis added.] It is well-established that since Congress has total discretion over whether to create the lower federal courts, it also has great discretion over the jurisdiction of those courts it chooses to create. In fact, Congress has in the past withdrawn jurisdiction from the lower federal courts when it became dissatisfied with their performance or concluded that state courts were the better forum for certain types of cases. The Supreme Court has repeatedly upheld Congress's power to do so.

Congress also has some authority to limit the jurisdiction of the Supreme Court and to regulate its activities. Article III of the Constitution states that the Supreme Court "shall have appellate jurisdiction, both as to law and fact, *with such Exceptions, and under such Regulations as the Congress shall make."* [Emphasis added.] Although we recognize that the scope of Congress's power to regulate and restrict the Supreme Court's jurisdiction over particular types of cases is under debate, there is a constitutional basis for this authority.

In the only case that directly addressed this issue, the Supreme Court upheld Congress's power to restrict the Court's appellate jurisdiction. In *Ex Parte Mc-Cardle* (1869), the Court unanimously upheld Congress's power to limit its jurisdiction, stating:

"We are not at liberty to inquire into the motives of the legislature. We can only examine into its power under the Constitution; *and the power to make exceptions to the appellate jurisdiction of this court is given by express words.* What, then, is the effect of the repealing act upon the case before us? We cannot doubt as to this. Without jurisdiction, the court cannot proceed at all in any case." [Emphasis added.]

Although some respected constitutional scholars argue that Congress cannot restrict the Supreme Court's jurisdiction to the extent that it intrudes upon the Court's "core functions," there is no question that Congress has more authority under the Constitution to act than it has recently exercised.

The 104th Congress displayed an encouraging willingness to assert its authority over the jurisdiction of the lower federal courts. For example, the Prison Litigation Reform Act of 1995 reduced the discretion of the federal courts to micromanage state prisons and to force the early release of prisoners. The Act also makes it more difficult for prisoners to file frivolous lawsuits. (An incredible 63,550 prisoner lawsuits were filed in federal court in 1995 alone.) Congress also passed the Effective Death Penalty Act of 1995. This Act limited the power of the federal courts to entertain endless habeas corpus appeals filed by prisoners on death row, significantly expediting the death-penalty process.

Other issues are due for some congressional muscle-flexing to restrain an activist judiciary:

Private-School Choice

Some radical groups like the American Civil Liberties Union argue that the government would violate the First Amendment's Establishment Clause if it gave a tuition voucher to a family who uses it at a religious school. Under current Supreme Court precedents, school vouchers are almost certainly constitutional. Nevertheless, some federal judges have indicated that they would invalidate private school choice plans under the Establishment Clause. Moreover, if more activist justices are named to the Supreme Court, a liberal majority could crush one of the most promising educational initiatives in recent years by judicial fiat. To ensure that the issue of private-school choice is decided through the democratic process, Congress should consider restricting the Court's jurisdiction over this issue.

Judicial Taxation

"Judicial taxation" refers to federal court orders that require a state or local government to make significant expenditures to pay for court-ordered injunctions. For example, one federal judge ordered the state of Missouri to pay for approximately $2.6 billion in capital improvements and other costs to "desegregate" the school districts of St. Louis and Kansas City, which in recent years had lost many white students. To attract white students back into the system, a federal judge required Kansas City to maintain the most lavish schools in the nation, and actually ordered the city to raise property taxes to pay for his court-ordered remedies.

There's a name for tax increases imposed by appointed, life-tenured federal judges: taxation without representation. Under the Constitution, only Congress can lay and collect taxes: our Founding Fathers would be appalled at the thought of federal judges doing so. In *Federalist No. 48*, James Madison explained that in our democratic system, "the legislative branch alone has access to the pockets of the people." To codify this principle, Congress should consider restricting the federal courts' authority to order any government at any level to raise taxes under any circumstance.

Use of Special Masters

Federal judges sometimes appoint "special masters" to micromanage prisons, mental hospitals, and school districts. In the past, these special masters have been appointed to carry out the illegitimate excursions of judges into the province of the legislative and executive branches. Moreover, the use of special masters has been a form of taxation, in that state and local governments are required to pay their salaries and expenses—which have often been extravagant. In some cases, special masters have hired large staffs to help execute the court order. Congress should outlaw special masters; without them, federal judges would be constrained by the limits on their time and resources from managing prisons or other institutions.

Same-Sex Marriage

No area of the law has been more firmly reserved to the states than domestic relations. Nevertheless, the Court's reasoning in *Romer v. Evans* suggests the possibility that some federal judges will "discover" a constitutional right to homosexual marriage, and thus remove the issue from the democratic process.

The Hawaii Supreme Court recently indicated that it would soon recognize homosexual marriages, which all other states would then have to recognize under the Full Faith and Credit Clause of the Constitution (Article IV). This possibility motivated Congress to pass the Defense of Marriage Act, which authorized any state to refuse to recognize a same-sex marriage performed in another state. The Act does not, however, prevent the federal judiciary from usurping this issue. Congress should consider going one step further to remove the jurisdiction of the lower federal courts over same-sex marriages to ensure that this cultural issue is decided by the legislative process in each state.

4. The states should press Congress to amend the Constitution in a way that will allow the states to ratify constitutional amendments in the future without the approval of Congress.

One reason judicial activism is so dangerous and undemocratic is that reversing or amending federal court decisions is so difficult. When a decision by the

Supreme Court or a lower federal court is based on the Constitution, the decision cannot be reversed or altered except by a constitutional amendment. Such constitutional decisions are immune from presidential vetoes or congressional legislation.

The existing means of amending the Constitution, however, are seldom effective in halting judicial activism. The amendment procedure set forth in Article V of the Constitution is difficult and lengthy for good reason: to avoid hasty changes spurred by the passions of the moment. But history has shown that even the most egregious court decisions—particularly those that affect the balance of power between the national government and the states—have been impervious to correction by constitutional amendment. One reason for this is that Congress, which must initiate such amendments, is loath to give up federal power.

The amendment procedure of the U.S. Constitution led Lord Bryce to conclude in his 1888 study, *The American Commonwealth*, that "[t]he Constitution which is the most difficult to change is that of the United States." This difficulty has encouraged judicial activism and allowed the unelected federal courts to "twist and shape" the Constitution, as Jefferson predicted, as an "artist shapes a ball of wax." The reason that the difficult amendment procedure encourages judicial activism is simple: Life-tenured judges are less likely to show restraint when the possibility that their rulings will be rejected is slight.

Consequently, one strategy to rein in the federal judiciary is to revise the amendment procedure in Article V of the Constitution to allow the states to amend the Constitution without Congress's approval and without a constitutional convention.

Here's how it would work: When two-thirds of state legislatures pass resolutions in support of a proposed amendment to the Constitution. Congress would have to submit it to all the states for ratification. The proposal would then become part of the Constitution once the legislatures of three-fourths of the states ratify it. Congress's role would be purely ministerial. This process would give the states equal power with Congress to initiate an amendment and would further check the power of the federal courts and of Congress.

5. Congress should stop the federalization of crime and the expansion of litigation in federal court.

Whenever Congress enacts a new federal criminal statute or a statute creating a cause-of-action in federal court, it enlarges the power and authority of the federal courts and provides more opportunities for judicial activism. At the same time, the federalization of crimes that have traditionally concerned state and local governments upsets the balance between the national government and the states. The following steps can help reduce the federalization of the law and once again restore balance to the federal-state relationship.

Recodify the U.S. Code

In the present federal criminal code, important offenses like treason are commingled with insignificant offenses like the unauthorized interstate transport of water hyacinths. The Federal Courts Study Committee found that the current federal code is "hard to find, hard to understand, redundant, and conflicting." Ideally, Congress would start with a blank slate, recodifying only those offenses that truly belong under federal jurisdiction. Due to the highly political nature of crime, such an undertaking might require the creation of an independent commission, modeled after the recent commission for closing unneeded military bases.

Require a "Federalism Assessment" for Legislation

This idea would require that all federal legislation offer a justification for a national solution to the issue in question, acknowledge any efforts the states have taken to address the problem, explain the legislation's effect on state experimentation, and cite Congress's constitutional authority to enact the proposed legislation.

Create a Federalism Subcommittee Within the Judiciary Committees of the House and Senate

First proposed by President Reagan's Working Group on Federalism, federalism subcommittees would attempt to ensure compliance with federalism principles in all proposed legislation.

Judicial activism has harmed virtually every aspect of public policy in America. Liberalism has accomplished much of its agenda in the last 30 years not through the electoral process, but instead in the federal courts. Conservatives will never be able to shape public policy until they can curb activist judges. Congress can and should move to do so.

SEEKING A SUPREME COURT SEAT

JEFF SIMMONS

CONTEXT

How does one become a Supreme Court judge? Unlike it does for the president and for members of Congress, the Constitution sets no formal qualifications for federal judges, including Supreme Court judges. Instead, Article II, Section 2 says that the president should nominate judges with the advice and consent of the Senate.

Since the Constitution establishes no formal qualifications to be a federal judge, informal qualifications have developed over time. Among the most important of these informal qualifications is competence and exceptional legal qualifications. The American Bar Association (ABA) has for several years rated nominees as to their legal qualification. Among the criteria that the ABA looks at are things such as where the nominee attended law school and the amount of judicial or governmental experience the nominee has had. Clearly, competence is important. Only the most competent get the chance to serve on the Supreme Court.

However, other criteria are important as well. Presidents often seek out nominees who have similar policy goals and share a similar political ideology. They often seek out nominees who will gain the president some political support. For instance, Ronald Reagan announced even before he was president that he would nominate a woman to the Supreme Court if elected. His purpose was to gain political support from women. Thus, we see that gender plays a role in choosing a nominee, as does race. In fact, groups interested in gender and/or racial diversity often lobby for seats on the federal bench, and the Supreme Court.

In this article from *Hispanic Outlook*, Jeff Simmons discusses the National Hispanic Bar Association's efforts to encourage the appointment of a Hispanic American to the Supreme Court. Simmons argues that despite the fact that the Hispanic community is 27 million and growing, Latino representation on the federal court in general is very low. A list of possible Hispanic candidates to fill a vacancy on the Supreme Court is discussed. In the end, Simmons contends that America draws strength and wisdom from its diversity, and it is now time for Hispanic Americans to have the opportunity to contribute on the Supreme Court.

● *THINK CRITICALLY* ●

1. In your view, is it proper for groups such as the National Hispanic Bar Association to advocate for a spot on the Supreme Court? Why or why not?
2. With the Hispanic community comprising nearly 30 million people, is it fair to say that the Supreme Court should include a Hispanic member?
3. Does greater diversity on the Supreme Court represent more tolerance for racial and ethnic diversity in America?

On the anniversary of the historic equal opportunity ruling of *Brown vs. Board of Education*, a group gathered on the steps of the United States Supreme Court. Roughly a dozen leaders from across the nation assembled, the court's massive columns towering above them.

But these were not leaders in the African American community. They were congressional representatives, civil rights advocates, and prominent attorneys, and all men and women of Latino heritage. Portraying a united front on this important anniversary, the group championed another landmark change: a change in the face of the Supreme Court.

"It was 220 years ago that our nation was founded on the principle that all men were created equal, and while this concept was true, opportunities for Hispanic Americans have not been equal," José Gaitan, then-president of the National Hispanic Bar Association, said on that day in May 1996.

"It is because of this that we find ourselves today, despite the fact that we've had 220 years of history in this country, we find ourselves without a Hispanic American on the United States Supreme Court."

That half-hour on the courthouse steps was a remarkable moment for those who gathered, not only because it provided a forum to voice their concerns but because it dispelled any perceptions that the Hispanic community was not unified and could not rally behind any potential candidates to sit on the governing body.

"I don't think it was a perception. I think it was a manufactured excuse," says Carlos Ortíz, general counsel for Goya Foods in New Jersey and HNBA's liaison to the White House.

"We have been as united as anyone in this country. No group, not the African American community, not the Jewish community, not the Jewish and Catholic communities, has ever been more united than we are in expressing the urgent need for more diversity on that court.

"And yet, for some reason, because one or two individuals had expressed some minor reservations, that was used as an excuse, and many believed it was used as a divisive tactic—to divide the community," says Ortíz.

Nevertheless, despite that impressive and unified front—congressional representatives from Illinois, California, and New Jersey, and leaders of groups such as La Raza and the Puerto Rican Legal Defense and Education Fund—the face of the nine-member court remains the same. Another justice has yet to publicly announce an intention to retire, though last spring rumors about the next vacancy were still alive.

The campaign to appoint a Latino to the court is largely being driven by the HNBA, in collaboration with groups and leaders across the nation. It is part of the organization's efforts to expand the number of minorities in the judicial system, from clerks to magistrates.

The HNBA reports, for instance, that only four of the 970 law clerks who have served the current justices have been Latino. An analysis of Hispanic American federal court appointees by administration also shows little progress during President Clinton's tenure.

Overall, Clinton is responsible for 12 Latino appointments, comprised of nine to the federal courts and three to the circuit courts of appeal. That outpaces President George Bush, who appointed eight. But President Ronald Reagan had appointed 15, and President Jimmy Carter, 16.

Only 3.3 percent of the nation's federal magistrates are Latino. The number of Latino attorneys in the nation is similarly disheartening: only 2.8 percent of the 880,000 lawyers. These are rates that have remained generally stagnant or inched upward at a snail's pace, a growth significantly outpaced by the Hispanic population explosion in America.

"As we approach the millennium, the Hispanic community in this country has grown. It's 27 million and growing," notes Martin Castro, a commercial litigator with the Chicago firm of Baker & Mackenzie who chairs the HNBA's United States Supreme Court Committee. "You cannot have the highest tribunal in our nation not reflect that portion of our diverse nation."

The court's history has seen demographics, race, and religion play a role, with historic actions guiding the first African American—the late Thurgood Marshall—and the first woman—Sandra Day O'Connor—onto the bench, ground tread upon once again with the confirmations of Clarence Thomas and Ruth Bader Ginsburg.

It was during the 1992 presidential campaign that the HNBA intensified its efforts to encourage Latino representation on the court. Then-Governor Clinton, the HNBA reports, had promised that the judiciary would "look like America."

The HNBA even compiled—after extensive background research and interviews—a list dubbed the Magnificent Seven: well-regarded potential nominees to the court. The group presented those names to President Clinton upon the retirement of Justice Byron White, but Clinton subsequently nominated Ginsburg (whom the HNBA voted unanimously to endorse).

One year later, Justice Harry Blackmun announced his retirement, and again the HNBA stepped up its lobbying efforts. But President Clinton nominated Judge Stephen Breyer (and despite any dismay, the HNBA endorsed Breyer as well).

It was during this time that the perception of a "lack of unity" in the Latino community surfaced. But two years later there appeared to be progress.

Ortíz, in a recent article titled "Hispanic American Representation in the Federal Judiciary: Better Than Before—But Still Not Good Enough," cited a private meeting with Clinton's closest advisors, in which they assured the HNBA that the "unity in the Hispanic community was no longer an issue."

The Magnificent Seven has since been amended; it now contains six names, potential candidates that the group is poised to pitch at a moment's notice.

"We have always been of the opinion that it's necessary for us to be prepared in the event that there's a vacancy," said Castro. "This is not a cyclical issue for us; this is something that is on the front burner for the Hispanic community."

The most recent list is comprised of:

• **Joseph E. Baca,** a justice on the New Mexico Supreme Court. Baca was elected to the court in January 1989. He was previously an assistant district attorney in Santa Fe and a district court judge in Albuquerque. In 1994, President Clinton appointed Baca as director of the State Justice Institute, a private nonprofit corporation established by Congress to provide grants to assist State court systems.

• **Fortunato "Pete" Benavides,** a judge with the United States Court of Appeals for the Fifth Circuit in Austin, Texas. Benavides was appointed by Clinton to the court in 1994, and he previously served as a trial and appellate court judge for 15 years.

• **José Cabranes,** a judge with the United States Court of Appeals for the Second Circuit in New Haven, Connecticut. President Jimmy Carter appointed

Cabranes to the federal bench in 1979, distinguishing him as the first Puerto Rican appointed to the bench in the continental United States. He previously had served as general counsel of Yale University, and was chief judge of the U.S. District Court in Connecticut when President Clinton appointed him to the second circuit bench in 1994.

• **Gilbert Casellas,** chairman of the United States Equal Employment Opportunity Commission in Washington, D.C. Clinton named Casellas—who was then confirmed by the U.S. Senate—as chairman in 1994. Previously, Casellas practiced law since 1980 with the Philadelphia firm of Montomery, McCracken, Walker & Rhoads.

• **Vilma S. Martínez,** a litigation partner with Munger, Tolles & Olson in Los Angeles, California. Martínez previously had been a staff attorney with the NAACP, Legal Defense and Educational Fund, and served as the Equal Employment Opportunity counsel with the New York State Division of Human Rights. She also served on President Clinton's Advisory Committee on Trade Policy and Negotiations from 1994 to 1996.

• **Cruz Reynoso,** a law professor with the University of California in Los Angeles. Reynoso previously was in private practice for a decade in El Centro, California, and since 1993, served as vice chairman of the U.S. Commission on Civil Rights. He also had been appointed by President Jimmy Carter as the United States delegate to the United Nations Commission on Human Rights and was a member of the Select Commission on Immigration and Refugee Policy.

Castro, the Chicago attorney, said that it is important to remain vigilant in the campaign, and to remind the nation's leaders that "this historic lack of representation must be remedied."

The reasons go beyond just statistics, pointing also to diversity and respect. Castro said that the appointment of a Latino justice would acknowledge that "finally, we as Latinos have made it to the table."

"It would also send a strong message to Americans across the country that Americans of Hispanic descent are one and the same, that we have contributed greatly to the building of this nation and we continue to contribute greatly."

If a retirement does occur in the coming months, Castro said, "it would be a great legacy for the Clinton administration to finally open the doors of the Supreme Court, which have been closed for so long to Latinos."

But if the current judicial makeup appears to stretch into the next presidential term, expect the issue of minority representation to be propelled to the fore by HNBA and other organizations.

"I hope we have an appointment before the next presidential election," Castro said. "I don't see it as being anything but a positive issue regardless of the political campaign. We have been lucky to have bipartisan support on this issue. This is not a Democratic-Republican issue. This is an American issue."

But Ortíz said that political considerations most likely will be taken into account when making the appointment.

"Whichever political party is the first one to appoint the first Hispanic American, that's going to give them an extra feather in their cap, extra points, extra credit. It would behoove each party," Ortíz said. "The Hispanic American vote cannot be taken for granted anymore."

These were words often repeated on that May day on the courthouse steps two years ago. Speaker after speaker weighed in on the Supreme Court's vital role in history, and on the future of the country.

Congressman Robert Menéndez (D-New Jersey), the fifth to address reporters, eloquently stated: "As a nation, we have worked best when we've worked together. We've drawn strength and wisdom from our diversity, and the slowly unfolding history of tolerance and diversity can be charted by appointments to the Supreme Court."

"The Supreme Court in many ways is a treasury of our society, and appointments to the court have a tradition of reflecting tolerance in our society."

THE BUREAUCRACY

HEAD NOTES/SECTION QUESTIONS

The word "bureaucracy" never appears in the Constitution. The Founders simply never thought to establish a branch of government called the bureaucracy, probably because they could not envision the need for it. However, as the size of government has grown and as the amount of work government does has increased, the need for a permanent staff of people to do the work has also increased. In fact, today some people call the bureaucracy the fourth branch of government, despite the fact that the Constitution only stipulates three branches.

Technically, the bureaucracy is part of the executive branch. Why? Because the Constitution makes the president chief executive, and directs the president to "take Care that the Laws be faithfully executed." The Constitution makes the president responsible for all of the bureaucracy because, all the bureaucracy is really doing is helping the president faithfully execute the laws passed by Congress. As the chief executive, the president has nearly 2 million employees who are busy executing these laws.

As we know, everyone likes to pick on the bureaucracy. However, it has a tough job. When Congress passes a vaguely written law, the bureaucracy is required by the Constitution to execute it, which means the bureaucracy often has to interpret it. This makes the bureaucracy open to all kinds of criticism for how it is interpreting the laws passed by Congress. In this brief section, we read two selections, one about a bureaucratic agency trying to redefine itself in the midst of change, and another about a bureaucratic agency often in hot water for the way it does its job. As you read these selections, think about the following questions:

1. If you could add a section to the Constitution creating a fourth branch of government called the bureaucracy, what two powers would you give it? What two checks would you impose on it?
2. Is the bureaucracy destined to be disliked by people because of the very nature of its job, or can you think of a situation in which people might begin to think more highly of the bureaucracy?
3. Make the argument that the bureaucracy is undemocratic. Make the argument that the bureaucracy is democratic.

LEARN MORE ON THE WEB

U.S. Federal Government Agencies Page
  http://www.lib.lsu.edu/gov/fedgov.html

National Performance Review
  http://www.npr.gov/

THE FOREST SERVICE UNDER FIRE

SUSAN ZAKIN

CONTEXT

Among the several duties that the Constitution gives the president, one is to "take Care that the Laws be faithfully executed." This means the president is responsible for carrying out the laws passed by Congress. If you think about it, this is an enormous task because the president is only one person. Every time Congress passes a new law, and it passes many, the president is constitutionally bound to make sure the law is executed as Congress wants it to be executed.

Over time, presidents have gone to Congress and asked for help. The result has been the growth of a portion of government that we call the bureaucracy, whose job it is to take the laws passed by Congress and execute them. Indeed, the way that Congress writes laws gives the president, and by extension the bureaucracy, great leeway in applying the laws to real cases. Instead of writing very detailed laws that might take an enormous amount of their time and effort, members of Congress write very general laws, and leave it up to the president and the bureaucracy to apply the laws to individual cases.

The result of this is that the bureaucracy has great freedom to apply the law, and often finds itself blamed for doing things that people do not like. Sometimes, even the president and Congress are critical of the way the bureaucracy has applied the law. Take, for example, the U.S. Forest Service, whose job it is to manage the nation's timber supply. In the process of managing the nation's timber supply, the Forest Service often finds itself caught in the middle of a struggle between the timber industry and recreational enthusiasts.

In this article from *Sports Afield,* Susan Zakin talks about the pressures on the U.S. Forest Service brought about by these conflicting parties. Although the Forest Service was established by Congress to manage the nation's timber supply, fewer board feet of wood are currently being cut and the national forests are increasingly used for outdoor recreation rather than for wood harvesting. These two uses, cutting timber and outdoor recreation, are often in conflict. In the end, Zakin notes, the Forest Service may need to try to redefine itself and its mission in the face of these conflicting demands.

● *THINK CRITICALLY* ●────────────────────────────

1. Are the pressures that the Forest Service faces a result of political forces in Washington, or the demands of people throughout the country? Would it make a difference where the pressure comes from as to the reform the Forest Service undertakes? Why or why not?
2. If its original mission is no longer relevant, should the Forest Service be shut down? Why or why not?

Michael P. Dombeck may be the least colorful chief in the history of the U.S. Forest Service. But his methodical nature could be the best thing to happen to an agency facing a major mid-life crisis. More than a century after legislation mandated its creation, the Forest Service is torn between its old role as the nation's timber supplier and today's growing demand for recreation on the public's 191 million acres of mountains, trout streams and hiking trails.

Controlled by a tradition-bound old guard, the Service faces court challenges across the country and a steady loss of disillusioned biologists.

CALL TO REFORM

Change isn't coming easily to an organization that has been characterized by its bureaucrats as a collection of fiefdoms so decentralized they rival the murderous factions of Macbeth. That's where Dombeck's low-key personality, or "nerdiness," as one colleague put it—comes in. A fisheries biologist with a knack for low-profile but effective politicking, Dombeck, 49, has mastered the art of moderation. But is he tough enough to make the cut?

"The process of reforming the Forest Service has just begun," says Steve Holmer, of the Western Ancient Forest Campaign, an environmental group based in Washington, DC. "They've still got a bureaucracy built to cut 12 billion board-feet a year and they're cutting 3 billion. There's a huge amount of deadwood, and biologists are nonexistent on many forests. Having some heads roll would be appropriate, given the abuses."

No one is more aware of the debate over the agency's mission than Dombeck, a man more comfortable talking about growing up just outside the

Chequamegon National Forest in northern Wisconsin than he is answering tough questions about disenchanted scientists or lawsuits over endangered species.

Dombeck knows recreation is key to the agency's future. "People are increasingly using national forests for recreation," he said in an interview early this year. "In 1980, we had 560 million visits to national forests. In 1996, we had 860 million. We expect to exceed a billion during the first decade of the 21st century."

But the national forest's history leaves managers ill-prepared to run a playground rather than a lumber mill. Dombeck often points out that the Organic Act of 1897 listed watershed protection and timber harvesting as the twin missions of the agency. But the mandate to protect rivers was soon drowned out by cash registers ringing up logging profits. By the 1980s, logging on the national forests reached levels that even Dombeck calls unsustainable.

Last November, the Forest Service admitted for the first time that its timber program was losing $15 million a year. The General Accounting Office previously placed losses much higher, at $1 billion between 1992 and 1994.

While recreation currently generates income for the Service only through a pilot user-permit program, Dombeck announced in late February that hunting, fishing and other wildlife-related recreation on national forests generated more than $12 billion for local communities in 1996. By the year 2000, agency projections indicate that more than 77 percent of jobs in the national forests will be related to recreation, compared to about 15 percent for resource exploitation.

RESOURCE DEBATE

Like Forest Service chiefs before him, Dombeck finds himself attacked on one side by timber, mining and grazing advocates; on the other, environmentalists who say reform isn't coming fast enough. But his worst problem may be agency bureaucrats accustomed to running their own empires. Logging is down, but timber bureaucrats spawned by the go-go years of the Bush and Reagan administrations are loaded for bear—or biologists.

Ironically, Dombeck hails from the old-guard culture. After a stint as a fishing guide during his student years, Dombeck worked his way up the Forest Service ladder. He switched to the U.S. Bureau of Land Management in 1989, becoming the agency's acting director in 1994, and chief of the embattled U.S. Forest Service on January 6, 1997.

Jim Cooper, a former U.S. Forest Service biologist who worked with Dombeck in the '80s and counts himself a friend, believes Dombeck's long tenure in the agency may allow him to understand both sides well enough to effect change. "Mike's upbringing has been in a multiple-use agency," he says. "You learn over time that you need to cut timber if you want to do certain things. He'll come from a point of moderation."

Dombeck's reforms have indeed been incremental and well thought out, concedes Steve Holmer. In the 1999 budget, Dombeck wants to freeze at 1997 levels the compensation payments the Government makes to counties for tax revenue that's lost on federal land within their boundaries. He is also calling for a 50 percent funding increase to enhance opportunities for fishing, hunting, wildlife viewing and conservation education within the national forests and a $20 million hike in resource management funds. At the same time, he's proposing a 10 percent reduction in the timber cut, although the timber budget would drop by only 5 percent.

His most controversial reform is a proposed 18-month moratorium on road building in roadless areas larger than 5000 acres. With 373,000 miles of roads in the national forests, conservationists say he should close existing roads as well. And those who favor continued resource extraction, such as Idaho Republican congresswoman Helen Chenoweth, are targeting the proposal, and Dombeck, for attack. On January 15, Chenoweth sent a letter to members of Congress stating that Dombeck's proposal would be "devastating to people and the environment."

"The Forest Service roads program has been under attack for 15 years," Dombeck says. He claims the moratorium is a commonsense measure, not a disguised bid for more wilderness. As budgets have dropped, Dombeck says, the agency hasn't maintained its current roads. He wants time to assess and maintain these roads before building more.

Dombeck has also liberalized the agency's policy on whistleblowers. He's willing to say, "We can't abrogate our legal responsibilities to enforce the laws passed by Congress and signed by the President." But he's shown little willingness to discipline high-ranking staff who consistently manage national forests in ways that leave them vulnerable to lawsuits.

Nowhere has this come into sharper relief than the forests of the Southwest, where logging was shut down for 18 months after a federal judge required the Service to do additional planning to protect the endangered Mexican spotted owl. More recently, the agency has been barraged by lawsuits alleging it is failing to protect rivers from damage linked to cattle grazing. In despair over the agency's failure to protect wildlife, four veteran biologists took early retirement last fall. An April 1, 1997, status report by fisheries biologists leaked to the media found that existing laws weren't being followed and species were becoming endangered as a result.

And still, most of the region's top officials deny that there's a problem.

SCIENCE VS. POLITICS

Dombeck may be leery of the old guard due to the abbreviated tenure of his predecessor, Jack Ward Thomas, who was supposed to bring science into an agency dominated by commodities. But while Steve Holmer says Thomas never really got control of the agency, Dombeck, with his imported cadre of loyalists and the continued support of the Administration, may be able to fulfill President Clinton's promise to manage America's roadless areas by science, not politics.

According to Leon Fager, a biologist who managed the southwest region's threatened and endangered species program before leaving the agency in protest, even managing the forests as a business would be an improvement: a business, at least, would meet the public's demand for water, wildlife and recreation.

"We've always operated on the multiple-use principle, but that doesn't mean we have to do everything on the same acre," says Fager. "I'd rather see us work under appropriate use. That would be more a 21st-century approach."

Mike Dombeck won't say the same thing out loud, but many people who plan to be around in the 21st century hope he's thinking it.

20

WARNING: CUTTING THE FDA COULD BE HAZARDOUS TO YOUR HEALTH

JOSHUA WOLF SHENK

CONTEXT

One thing that Republicans in Washington and throughout the country have complained about for many years is the size of the federal bureaucracy and the feeling that the bureaucracy is not accountable enough. They have claimed that the federal bureaucracy is too large and out of control. Advocates of downsizing the federal bureaucracy want more than anything else for the bureaucracy to be more accountable, both to Congress and to the president.

In recent years, Republicans in Congress have talked about and have actually tried to downsize several agencies, including the Department of Education, the National Endowment for the Humanities, the Department of Commerce, and the Environmental Protection Agency. Recognizing the real concerns about the cost and size of the federal bureaucracy, the Clinton administration launched the National Performance Review (NPR) in 1993, an initiative to make the government (read: bureaucracy) work better and cost less. Has it worked? Some say that the NPR has actually helped streamline government and cut costs, while others contend that the program has not been as successful as it could have been.

Still others argue that cutting bureaucracy can be harmful to Americans. Defenders of the bureaucracy argue, rightly, that the bureaucracy does real things for real people. In this article from *The Washington Monthly*, Joshua Wolf Shenk discusses the Food and Drug Administration (FDA) and the difficulty the agency has doing its job. Critics of the FDA claim that the agency takes too long in approving new products, thus hurting industry. However, advocates of the FDA point out that the agency has been given increased responsibilities by Congress with little additional money to fund the new responsibilities. Shenk argues that the FDA does a good job of regulating the nation's food supply but could improve its evaluation of product safety.

● *THINK CRITICALLY* ●

1. Some conservative critics, such as the Washington Legal Foundation, claim that the FDA hurts business by being so slow in its approval process. What is your view of this type of criticism, is it valid or not?
2. In your view, what is the bigger problem for the FDA, not doing an adequate job, or not getting credit for the job it does do?
3. Can you think of ways the FDA could do its job better? Explain how.

It was the first time Don Vasbinder had seen a body in a bag of cocoa beans. In late 1993, inspectors from the Food and Drug Administration (FDA) sniffed something wrong in a shipment of beans from Brazil. Inside, they found a rotting corpse. "That was a first for me," says Vasbinder, the director of imports for the Baltimore district office of the FDA. "But the old-time food inspectors say that's not uncommon. In fact, they found another body shortly thereafter in Philadelphia."

If Vasbinder, a slight man with big block glasses and a Ph.D. in chemistry, is unfazed by this story, it's because in his 20 years with the FDA he has seen just about everything. Rusted surgical knives. Rotted mud fish from Singapore. Condoms with holes in them. And those are just the imports. Including the multi-billion dollar domestic market in pharmaceuticals, medical devices, and food, the FDA regulates products that account for 25 cents of every dollar spent in this country. A tour of FDA facilities in Baltimore, where scores of inspectors and scientists are only a small part of the 9,000-person, $980 million agency, yields a quick understanding of the FDA's importance. In the pesticide group, chemists have found dangerous levels of DDT in grain intended for breakfast cereal. In the drug lab, chemists have caught at-home tests for pregnancy and glucose that do not work as claimed. Stories of impure food and drugs—laced with unsafe chemicals, insect parts, rusted metal, even cigarette butts—are common.

Of course, as inspector Dean Cook points out while we walk through a spice plant filled to the roof with sacks of cola nuts, black pepper, and oregano, the vast majority of the goods he checks are safe. Reviewers of drugs and medical devices at FDA headquarters in Rockville, Maryland also attest that most manufacturers want to make money by producing good products, not by scamming the system. But it is equally obvious that bad apples (so to speak) abound, both in this country and abroad. Keeping the food supply clean and the marketplace of drugs and medical devices safe and effective often takes more than a strong sense of smell. With chemical compounds and complicated medical devices, it takes years of careful study.

The FDA has always been controversial. Industry lobbied hard against the original Food and Drug Act in 1906, and the agency has been granted more power only when scandals shocked Congress into action. In 1996, though, the agency's waters are particularly choppy. Besides Republican hostility, the FDA also faces pressure to move more quickly from liberals in Congress such as Representative Ron Wyden and Senator Barbara Mikulski.

With the FDA's very existence called into question, you might expect the Washington press corps, congressional auditors, and the executive branch to be scrambling to evaluate the agency. In what way are the critics correct? What are the FDA's strong suits? What is the agency trying to do—and what is it actually doing where the rubber meets the road (or where the tablet meets the mouth)?

In a town often scandalously blithe about matters vital to the lives of Americans, the FDA has gotten no such treatment. The watchdogs are napping. If they woke up, they'd find an agency with a clear mission, dedicated staff and leadership, and the best safety record and reputation of any health agency in the world—an agency that is often wrongly maligned. The FDA isn't perfect, and its imperfections aren't pretty. But only through tough, fair scrutiny and analysis, of which this piece is a modest effort, can it be improved.

DRUGSTORE COWBOYS

The purpose of a business is simple: to provide a desired good or service and make a profit. In government, purpose is sometimes more difficult to discern. What is an agency's mission? In what way does it improve citizens' lives?

FDA Commissioner David Kessler sums up the FDA's mission in three words: "safeguarding America's health." More specifically, the FDA ensures the safety of the nation's supply of food, drugs, medical devices, and other health-related material, such as cosmetics, devices that emit radiation (like TVs and microwaves), and the blood supply. With drugs and devices, the FDA goes one step further and checks to make sure products work for the purpose claimed by the manufacturer. The logic is simple: While protections against egregious fraud are important in any industry, ineffective health-care products pose a particular risk. If a lamp doesn't work, you can take it back to the store and buy another one. But a pacemaker that doesn't work could kill you.

The clear sense of mission—the knowledge that their work can literally be the difference between life and death—infuses the agency with energy. "The FDA has way more than its share of bright, dedicated, competent people," says William Vodra, who worked for the agency's general counsel in the 1970s. "We would have discussions all the time, and ultimately someone would ask: 'Okay, what's in the public interest here?' On Capitol Hill, you never hear issues framed that way." Even critics, like Richard Samp of the Washington Legal Foundation, praise FDA staffers. "I'm generally impressed by their intelligence and public spiritedness," Samp says. "These people don't sit around dawdling in their offices, turning around paperwork all day."

In addition to the widespread acclaim for FDA employees, the agency's basic mission is affirmed by supporters and critics alike. There is widespread agreement that the FDA should remain, in Samp's words, " a centralized government bureaucracy providing an official stamp of approval that a product is certified as safe, based on the best available technology."

The issue with the FDA, then, is not what it should do—the question is how it does what it does. Like all regulatory agencies, the FDA faces the challenge of protecting the public without suffocating commerce. With drugs and medical devices, it faces an additional, more delicate, task: The FDA must protect the public from hazards without holding up useful treatments—keeping a life-saving drug off the market can be as lethal as allowing a flawed drug to go forward.

The famous case of Dr. Frances Kelsey illustrates the tricky business of regulating health products. Between 1959 and 1961, thousands of babies in 20 countries were born with grievous deformities because their mothers had taken a new sedative called thalidomide during pregnancy. In the United States, the drug had never been marketed because Kelsey, the medical officer in charge of the application, had held it up.

Clearly, Kelsey made a huge save. And conscientious work like hers has made FDA approval the worldwide "gold-standard" for medical products. According to a study by Dr. Sidney Wolfe at the Health Research Group of Public Citizen, this country only had to recall 9 drugs between 1970 and 1992. Over that same period in France there were 31 recalls; in Germany, 30; in Britain, 23.

But Kelsey's legacy has another side: According to close watchers of the FDA, she was known for being slow and ponderous—sometimes to excess. We know about the tragedy she stopped. But could she have caused a tragedy by scuttling beneficial new therapies? That question cuts to the heart of the FDA.

Among critics, it is an article of faith that the FDA is slow and getting slower. A commonly-cited Tufts University study shows that the average time required to bring new medicines to market in this country has increased from about eight to 15 years since the early 1960s. It's true that the FDA can be guilty of excessive caution, particularly when keeping a product off the market because they're not 100 percent sure it works. Reviewers have an incentive to err on the side of caution: If they let a bad drug get through, they face a rain of humiliation. If a good drug is stopped or unduly delayed, the only complaints come from industry.

Still, in context, the data cited by critics do not indicate an agency in crisis. Every decade or so, a defective medical product slaps Americans in the face and reminds this country of the necessity of thorough reviews. In 1962, it was thalidomide—which, along with earlier scandals, led Congress to require the FDA to check for the efficacy as well as the safety of drugs. In 1976, it was the Dalkon Shield—an intrauterine device that caused 18 deaths and 66,000 miscarriages and led to FDA regulation of medical devices. In the late eighties came another series of scandals involving heart valves, jaw implants, and breast implants, among others. The resulting clampdown on devices led to a backlog in the early 1990s.

The Tufts study is not inaccurate: it does take longer to develop a drug now than in 1960. But the FDA rightfully is being more cautious than it was in 1960.

It is also crucial when assessing the FDA's speed to distinguish between drugs and devices that truly improve on existing therapies, and those that replicate other products or add the chemical or engineering equivalent of a new bell or whistle. "If you're a drug company," explains Sidney Wolfe, "and you see a lucrative $4 billion market for a drug that treats arthritis and it's nothing really new, but you can repackage it as something radically new, then you're going to go for it." According to the London journal *SCRIP*, of 47 new chemical entities introduced in the world between January 1 and December 8, 1994, only two were breakthroughs. Both were first approved and marketed in the United States. Remember the drugs recalled in Europe but never introduced here? Not one had shown a significant advance over existing therapies. In other words, it's not safe to assume that holding up a drug or medical device means lost lives.

But some FDA-regulated products *are* breakthroughs. The challenge for the agency, then, is to maximize its speed without sacrificing its standards. And according to a recent GAO report, the agency actually has made great strides in its review speed. In 1987, the average review time for a New Drug Application—submitted after a drug has been fully tested in human subjects—took an average of 33 months: in 1992, the average was 19 months. This study also found the FDA to be quicker than the British Medicines Control Agency, to which critics often unfavorably compare the FDA.

When it comes to reviewing products that are, in fact, significant advances, the FDA has a good history: it has even improved in recent years. The agency correctly employs triage—assigning priority to products depending on the seriousness of the illness to be treated and the availability of other therapies. AZT, one of the few drugs available to fight AIDS and HIV was approved in just a few months. Much of the improvement in review times is due to the institution of user fees for drug applications. Just as college applicants pay a fee to have their applications reviewed, drug companies now pay to have their data analyzed and methods reviewed. The FDA uses the funds to augment its staff, which leads to a quicker turnaround time.

Certainly the FDA could improve. It has, for example, a lackluster history with generic drugs, which are radically less expensive than patented drugs and can save consumers thousands of dollars in drug costs. With exploding health-care costs, it makes sense to push generics through as fast as possible. But for years, the pharmaceutical industry pressured the FDA to preserve the industry's competitive edge by holding up generics. The agency obliged, insisting, for example, that a generic undergo the same testing as a new drug, even though it might be identical to a drug already on the market. That practice was changed in 1985, when generics accounted for only 14 percent of prescriptions written. Today, they account for 45 percent, and the FDA now allows generics on the market the day a patent expires. But Congress hasn't granted the agency the authority to charge user fees to test generic drugs, and so it has insufficient resources to review them; that means useful and more affordable generics aren't making it onto the market. Whether through user fees or standard appropriation, the FDA's budget needs to match its responsibilities.

And unlike its steller record on safety, the FDA's record regulating product efficacy—something it has been doing only since 1962—is spotty. Too often the agency takes an all-or-nothing approach. A drug is either fully approved for safety and efficacy, or it is kept out of patients' hands entirely. Once a break-through drug has been proven safe, there's no reason why people shouldn't be able to use it—assuming they're fully informed that the FDA has yet to certify the drug's effectiveness. Along these same lines, compassionate use—exemption from FDA rules due to a clear and pressing need—should also be expanded. Denying dying patients a drug because it might hurt them is clearly a fool's bargain.

On the whole, though, the FDA's record on drug reviews is good. The story with medical devices is somewhat more complicated. Rhetorical fireworks from agency critics have largely centered around devices, in part due to the fact that, unlike drugs, devices tend to be made by small entrepreneurs. A "no" from the FDA—or a delay in approval—can mean the end of a company.

Some of the critics claims have legitimacy, but many do not. The Sensor Pad, intended to help women detect breast cancer, is an example of critics gone awry. FDA "ineptness," the Washington Legal Foundation claimed in ads run in *USA Today* and *Roll Call*, "is *still* killing thousands of women . . . The FDA has obstructed approval—for nine years—of the Sensor Pad. . . . In Canada, the product was approved in less than 60 days."

In fact, the best evidence indicates that the Sensor Pad is no more helpful in detecting lumps in breasts than bare hands and soapy water. The device was once marketed in Canada but ordered withdrawn by officials who echoed the concerns of the FDA: that the product could actually be less effective than traditional methods and might lull women at risk into a sense of complacency. To blame the FDA for thousands of breast cancer deaths, then, is the height of irresponsibility.

But the critics have a point about another device featured in Washington Legal Foundation ads: the CardioPump. An aid for paramedics conducting CPR on victims of cardiac arrest, the pump is sold legally in a dozen countries, including Japan and Germany; in Austria, it is standard equipment on ambulances. Even though many health professionals are convinced that the Cardio-Pump is a valuable, life-saving tool, the FDA has kept the product off-market. The agency defends its decision by pointing to studies showing that, while patients treated with CardioPump do in fact reach the hospital in greater numbers than a control group, they do not *survive* at a higher rate. Unlike the Sensor Pad, however, there is absolutely no evidence that people will suffer from the CardioPump's use. Given that the pump certainly isn't harmful, why not leave the decision to paramedics and hospitals after warning them that the FDA is not convinced of its efficacy?

But if less regulation is required with some devices, other areas show a need for more regulation, specifically the thousands of products that were "grandfathered" into approval. That means they went on the market before the FDA began regulating devices in 1976 and were subsequently granted a reprieve until the agency could get around to checking them. In many cases, they still haven't gotten around to it, and consumer advocates rightly complain about the slow pace. Some types of pacemakers grandfathered into approval, for example, have a 25 percent failure rate. It's a glaring loophole in an otherwise tough regulatory scheme.

THE FOOD WE EAT

Early last February, the makers of Similac infant formula were flooded with calls from frantic parents in Southern California. The formula had produced rashes, stomach aches, and seizures in 54 infants. The FDA staked out warehouses, searched dumpsters, and eventually caught two men selling fake Similac to supermarkets. Within weeks, the fake formula was confiscated.

Such heroic FDA stories are not uncommon, and it's not just consumers who benefit. Just ask Pepsi Co. In 1993, when the FDA exposed as a hoax claims that syringes had been slipped into Pepsi, the company saved the millions it would have cost to recall and dispose of its product.

Yet much of the FDA's work is rarely noticed, let alone shone on by the klieg lights of press conferences. That's partly because their lifesaving work is so prosaic in appearance: At the FDA district office in Baltimore, I watched inspectors matter-of-factly sniff black tiger shrimp from Thailand—that's "organoleptic testing"—and scientists quietly testing baby corn and crab meat for botulism.

But while much of the FDA's work is admirable and underappreciated, the federal regulation of the food supply does need improvement. Spread across three agencies, it is often poorly coordinated. The FDA splits food regulation with the Department of Agriculture, which regulates meat, poultry, and some types of dairy products. The Environmental Protection Agency sets the rules for pesticides, and the FDA enforces them. The Department of Transportation even gets in on the act, setting standards for refrigerated vehicles.

With the resources it has, the FDA does a good job. But the resources are inadequate—and the jury-rigged nature of food regulation is a prime culprit. Take the recently-announced FDA rules on seafood inspection. One hundred and fourteen thousand Americans are poisoned by seafood each year; yet seafood regulations have changed little since the turn of the century. So it is a welcome sign that the FDA has finally overcome pressure from the seafood industry and imposed a new system of lab checks and computer monitoring.

But, believe it or not, the system will actually bring a decrease in inspections. That is because the new system is so complicated that it will double the average inspection time, but the FDA doesn't plan to put any new inspectors on the job.

And the shortage of inspectors isn't confined to seafood. FDA food inspections dropped precipitously from 20,528 in 1981 to 5,741 in 1994. The consequences are alarming: Raw oysters kill at least a dozen people each year, but the FDA has not responded to the problem. [In 1995] in Florida, the Norwalk virus in oysters caused 121 illnesses, but there was no FDA recall. "The reality is," says Caroline Smith DeWaal, director of food safety for the Center for Science in the Public Interest, "they don't have inspectors, and they don't have a program adequate to meet the problem. With the pressure to approve drugs faster, it's only getting worse."

Why would pressure to approve drugs more quickly mean less regulation of food? Because the FDA has to do both jobs with only a limited fund pool. While Congress has piled on mandates for the FDA in monitoring drugs and devices, the blood supply, and medical procedures, lawmakers have made far fewer demands with respect to food safety. And so, with a total budget that is now stagnating in real terms—the agency received no increase for inflation in 1996 appropriations—the FDA has been forced to shift resources away from food. The $220 million the FDA spends on food regulation is only 40 percent of what the Agriculture Department spends on meat and poultry regulation alone.

Even with its comparatively enormous budget, of course, the Agriculture Department does not inspire confidence that it can keep tainted beef out of Americans' mouths. But the FDA shouldn't have to reduce resources on food inspections in order to increase resources on medical products—nor would taxpayers want it to. One sensible solution is to separate the regulation of food and drugs and devices into different agencies. If the FDA does keep all its jobs, Congress needs to make sure the agency is adequately funded for all its responsibilities.

QUESTIONS STILL UNANSWERED

One magazine article can hardly cover all the important ground at the FDA. Consider the early testing of drugs on humans. Before a drug or device is even submitted to the FDA for approval, the "sponsor" has to go through a long series of tests. This is where most of the expense and delay in getting drugs from the laboratory to the pharmacist's shelf happens. How can these tests be done more quickly and at lower cost, and what can the FDA do to streamline the process?

The agency's actions in areas outside its traditional role of regulating food and medical products also need evaluation. Take cigarettes, for example. David Kessler is a hero for facing up to the tobacco companies. But is his agency the most sensible place to conduct such regulation? It seems more appropriate for the agencies responsible for fighting drug abuse—who now deal almost exclusively with illegal drugs—to spend some of their $14 billion annual appropriation curbing the abuse and youth-oriented marketing of cigarettes and alcohol.

Is the FDA hurting job growth in this country?

Drug companies allege that the FDA has gotten slower and more bureaucratic since the thalidomide scandal of the early sixties—hurting their bottom line. So why is the stock of industry giant Merck & Co. 113 times more valuable now than it was in 1962 (in figures not adjusted for inflation)? Investors in drug stocks haven't just done well, they've done *very* well. Consider the story of Anne Scheiber, reported recently in *The Washington Post*. She bought $10,000 worth of shares in Schering-Plough Corp. in 1950. Today, that investment is worth $7.5 million. The industry as a whole has also done quite nicely. In 1980, non-generic drug firms had $12 billion in U.S. sales—a figure that exploded in the next 15 years to $57 billion.

Yes, American pharmaceutical and biotech companies are opening some operations overseas, but it is difficult to tell to what extent, if any, FDA regulations are to blame. Fruit of the Loom is moving overseas, too, but not because of excessive underwear regulation. And it isn't just the drug industry that's booming. A recent report in *The Wall Street Journal* showed that Swiss firms are rushing to invest billions of dollars in American biotechnology. "It is in the U.S.," Ralph King reports, "where the biotechnology industry began and, for the most part, remains."

Some other criticisms are as dubious as the notion that the FDA drives American industry overseas. "The problem with health care in America today is the FDA," the Washington Legal Foundation claims in its ads. If the FDA is *the* problem, one wonders if the tally of 41 million uninsured Americans makes the group's top five? Other critics don't seem to share the basic values that undergird the FDA's existence. Henry Miller, a former FDA official, recently blasted the agency in a *National Review* article as slow and politically motivated. But when I asked him about the study showing France and Britain with triple the number of drug recalls as the U.S., Miller replied that he wouldn't mind more recalls if it meant getting drugs through more quickly. Considering the devastation that a bad drug can cause—Clometacin was withdrawn in France after 130 reports of hepatitis, including nine deaths: Indomethacin-R was withdrawn in Britain after 717 adverse reactions and 36 deaths—this is hardly a trade-off most of us would like to make.

This is not to demonize the agency's critics. The FDA's job is important enough—and the balance between getting good drugs on the market while keeping bad ones off is delicate enough—that vigorous criticism of the agency should be welcomed, not dismissed out of hand. Still, it hardly benefits the public to have the conversation dominated, and too often distorted, by a right-wing fringe. When confusion reigns, groups in the know, such as the regulated industry and big money donors to Congress, benefit. And the public suffers.

Enhancing public understanding of the FDA should be a top priority of government auditors, the press, and the FDA itself. As it is, the only way a major review can get started is for a high official to pressure the GAO or the inspector general at the Department of Health and Human Services. Such reviews are rare. More common is the confusion that characterizes debates over the CardioPump and Sensor Pad. Critics accuse the agency of stonewalling: the FDA responds that its doing a good job. The truth is hard to discern.

What's needed at the FDA is a strong, generously funded inspections office, which at the request of industry or Congress or interested citizens could review the handling of a particular case, produce an explanation in clear language as to what happened, and recommend future action. This would both educate the public and inject a sense of accountability into the FDA's review process. And since government reports can get buried, the press is an even more important engine for honest and constructive evaluations of the agency.

In this heated political climate, tough, fair scrutiny of the FDA is more necessary than ever. Think about it: When you brush your teeth in the morning, you know your gums won't turn black. When you take pain medicine at night, you can be confident that you won't get hurt—and that you haven't been ripped off. You can eat your meals without worrying about salmonella or a surprise serving of rat droppings. We take all these things for granted. We can't afford to do the same with the agency that makes that possible.

PART III

POLITICAL
BEHAVIOR

PUBLIC OPINION AND THE MEDIA

HEAD NOTES/SECTION QUESTIONS

If democracy means rule by the people, then the people's opinion should matter, and by every indication it does. If one uses the number of public opinion polls conducted to measure public opinion as a guide, public opinion is extremely important. In fact, few candidates for public office, and probably none for high public office such as governor, U.S. Senator, or president, go without public opinion polls on a daily or at least weekly basis.

What is public opinion? It is simply the opinions held by people. The way that we know what "the people's" opinion is about any given issue, event, or policy proposal, is to ask them. So, that is exactly what politicians and public opinion polling firms do, all of the time. On any given day, thousands of people are answering questions about everything from whether or not they support the president's foreign policy in the Middle East to whether they can name the Chief Justice of the Supreme Court.

What shapes public opinion? Do people wake up in the morning and find that they have an opinion about the president's Middle East policy, or is there something else that shapes public opinion at a much more general level? Political scientists have conducted many studies to determine what influences public opinion, and they have concluded that the attitudes that people hold about issues are shaped and influenced by their political culture. That is, specific opinions get shaped by the political culture that one has acquired over time. What factors contribute to political culture? One of the most important long-term influences on political culture is family. Another is religion. Others include race, gender, age, major events in life, and the region of the country one is from.

One of the most important influences on public opinion is the mass media, because it is through the mass media that leaders can speak to people and influence their opinion about certain things. Through the mass media, leaders are able to set the public agenda, that is, establish what the important questions are. For example, when leaders talk about the dire situation that the Social Security Trust Fund is in, public opinion pollsters begin to see Social Security emerge as one of the things the public is concerned about. When enough of the public is concerned about Social Security to cause government to take steps to fix it, the public's opinion has had an influence on the course of government. It could be argued that in fact what has happened is that the public's opinion has been manipulated by leaders via the media, and this is what Celinda Lake and Jennifer Sosin examine in their article.

Of course, sometimes the public does not respond to the media. A good example is the Monica Lewinsky scandal, when the media spent an enormous amount of time covering something that many people did not pay much attention to. This is the issue addressed by Michael Gartner. Some think that the media was obsessed with the Lewinsky scandal and went so far as to "pick" on President Clinton. However, Linda Lotridge Levin contends that, when it comes to sex scandals, the press has always been harsh on presidents.

As you read the selections in this section, keep the following questions in mind:

1. Is public opinion really manipulated by the media, or is the media simply an outlet where things the public is concerned about get attention?
2. Is it better for democracy for political leaders to conduct a poll before doing something? Or, would it be better for democracy if political leaders did what they thought was best, and then tried to explain to the public why they did what they did?

LEARN MORE ON THE WEB

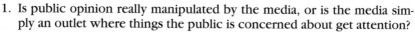

The Polling Report
http://www.pollingreport.com

National Opinion Research Center
http://www.norc.uchicago.edu/

Pew Research Center for the People and the Press
http://www.people-press.org/

The Gallup Organization
http://www.gallup.com/

National Election Studies
http://www.umich.edu/~nes/

CNN
http://www.allpolitics.com

Washington Post
http://www.washingtonpost.com/wp-dyn/politics/

PUBLIC OPINION POLLING
AND THE FUTURE OF DEMOCRACY

CELINDA LAKE AND JENNIFER SOSIN

CONTEXT

Following public opinion can be a dangerous thing for a politician to do, or so we hear. After all, is the public not highly misinformed about things? Consider for example, foreign aid. If you ask people how much foreign aid the United States gives as a percentage of its total annual budget, they respond with numbers much higher than the less than one half of one percent that is reality. So, is it fair to ask the public what they think about foreign aid and to take their concerns seriously when they do not even know the facts?

In addition, is it not true that the public's opinion is easily manipulated? Consider, for example, the numerous television commercials during campaign season in which one candidate is claiming something about another candidate and the truth is not quite what the television commercials claim. If the public knows nothing except what they see on television, does that not make what they know suspect? Ultimately, if this is true, should elected representatives from the president on down pay attention to an ill-informed and easily misled public?

In this selection, Celinda Lake and Jennifer Sosin contend that while there are plenty of people who argue that elected representatives should not pay as much attention to public opinion as they do, polls actually serve two very good purposes. One, polls play a valuable role in setting broad policy and political directions for elected decision makers. Two, since a member of the House of Representatives serves no less than 600,000 people, polls help representatives stay in touch with their constituency. In the end, they admit, the future benefits of public opinion polling for democracy are uncertain.

● *THINK CRITICALLY* ●

1. What do you think: Should representatives pay attention to public opinion polls as much as they do, or should they exercise their own judgment more?
2. Do you agree with the assertion that the public is much more sophisticated and thoughtful than many stereotypes suggest? Why or why not?

During the last thirty years, the use of public opinion polling in American politics has exploded. Practically every day, there is a press briefing in Washington on a new poll. In nearly every contested federal campaign, the candidates spend thousands of valuable campaign dollars on their own polls. Most of the country's biggest newspapers and television stations conduct polls regularly, as do the networks and newsmagazines.

What does all this mean for democracy? For one thing, it starkly reveals two fundamentally differing visions of how representative democracy should work. In one vision, representatives are elected to give direct voice to the people's preferences. In the other, representatives serve more as delegates than representatives; they are invested with the trust to exercise their own judgment.

Some say that, with the proliferation of polling, we are moving more and more toward the first vision of representative democracy. By this analysis, elected officials are functioning increasingly as instruments of a plebiscite, responding directly to what they perceive as public opinion, using the polls to decide what to believe, what to say, and how to say it. At the same time, we know that voters rarely choose their representatives simply on the basis of issue positions. Rather, most voters choose their candidates by combining an inclination toward one political party or the other with an assessment of the individual candidates' character and values. Issues may symbolize values, but few voters arrive at the polls with a checklist of litmus tests.

This raises a question: If voters treat their representatives as delegates, but if polls mean that representatives respond to the public as if they were instruments of a plebiscite, what are the implications for the kinds of decisions that are made? This is the first question we explore in this essay. The second is how this will change as polling and communications change in the twenty-first century.

SHOULD REPRESENTATIVES PAY ATTENTION TO PUBLIC PREFERENCES AS EXPRESSED IN PUBLIC OPINION POLLS?

There are plenty of arguments for a "no" answer to this first question, arguments that good public policy is somehow compromised or undermined when representatives pay slavish attention to polls. Indeed, we frequently hear at least four reasons why public opinion—as measured by public polls—should not guide public policy.

First, it is said that the public is misinformed. A classic example is the American public's belief that foreign aid is a significant drain on the federal budget, even though the true proportion is but a small fraction of federal spending. Moreover, this false impression is not without consequences, since it creates political pressure to reduce international spending.

Second, say others, the public is ill informed. It is not that the public has wrong information, they say; it is that people have too little information. Indeed, there is plenty of evidence that the public pays little attention to the details of public policy issues. For example, the Pew Research Center regularly runs polls on the attention paid to major news stories, and it consistently finds that the public pays far more attention to stories about celebrities than about public policy. In August 1997, for instance, 24 percent said they followed the

Gianni Versace and Andrew Cunanan story very closely, compared to 14 percent who followed the budget debate, and just 6 percent who followed the expansion of NATO.

Third, we hear that public opinion is easily manipulated. This critique emphasizes the popular media's ability to influence public opinion; indeed, the relationship between the news media and public opinion is complicated and circular. Clearly, because television is the dominant source of information in American life, public opinion is influenced by what the news media choose to cover, and how they cover it. For example, many argue that the high level of distrust toward government is fueled in part by the "gotcha" approach of the post-Watergate news media. At the same time, public opinion also influences programming, as television executives seek to maximize viewership.

Fourth, we hear that public opinion polling is easily manipulated. This is true. Sophisticated consumers of public opinion polls are well aware that sampling methodologies, question wording, and timing can have significant impacts on polling results. On top of this, even the same polling results can be interpreted in multiple ways by different observers. This leads some to argue that, whatever the truth of underlying public opinion, survey research is a poor and unreliable instrument for measuring it.

Given these critiques, can one see public opinion polling as anything but a distorting influence on policymaking and democratic decision making? We have two reasons for believing that one can see it otherwise:

1. Public opinion and the polling that captures it play a valuable role in setting direction and in checking political excess.
2. Public opinion polling keeps elected representatives, who are increasingly isolated, more in touch with their constituencies than they would be without it.

First, the public is much more sophisticated and thoughtful than many stereotypes suggest. Although it is true that the American electorate pays little attention to the details of legislative choices, most voters are clear in their minds about their priorities and their values. They then use these priorities and values to make choices about the elected officials they support and the issues they emphasize. Thus, public opinion, as expressed through polling, often provides a valuable check on political excess, and it often sets direction in a way that keeps pressure on elected representatives to accomplish larger goals.

The Republican "revolution" of 1994 provides a striking example of this. The Republican majority in Congress, elected in 1994, took office with an ambitious agenda, and a core of members who sought comparatively dramatic changes in the size and scope of government. Yet in the end, they were not able to implement very much of this agenda—and public opinion was one component of that failure.

As political consultants who work with a large number of Congressional campaigns, we witnessed this dynamic at work in the summer and fall of 1996, particularly on education issues. Public opinion polling consistently revealed that most voters wanted education to be a priority. Even when they disagreed on the specific role the federal government should play, most people opposed cutting spending on things like college loans and were uncomfortable with eliminating the federal Department of Education. How could education be a priority, they asked, if we were abolishing the department charged with responsibility for education?

The clarity of the polling on this issue prompted the Democratic party and most of its candidates to make education issues a centerpiece of their campaigns. The consequence is that the Republican candidates who were challenged on this issue lost ground, an outcome that was visible in our polling across many districts and almost certainly visible in the candidates' own polling. The result of their perceived vulnerability on this issue had a direct consequence for policy: in 1996, the Republican caucus restored every dollar of education funding they had earlier threatened to cut, and their candidates launched an onslaught of political advertisements defending their record on education.

Is this outcome dynamic evidence of a healthy interplay of public opinion and policy making, or is it proof that members of Congress are dangerously vulnerable to the prevailing winds of public opinion? The answer rests in part on how you feel about the funding that was restored. Those who support federal spending on education tend to believe that the pressure of public opinion saved the day; those on the other side decry the education debate as demagoguery.

We have been on both the winning and the losing sides of this kind of dynamic, and we have seen these dynamics at work on many issues, often with vastly differing outcomes. The dynamics of balancing the budget, welfare reform, and health care reform were all similar (although with quite divergent outcomes). In each case, public opinion polling reflected an electorate that was making these issues a priority, and political candidates and elected leaders responded by making these issues legislative priorities as well. Health care is a particularly interesting example. Public opinion pressure played a part in prompting the first Clinton administration to make health care reform a centerpiece, and public opinion also played a role in killing their plan. At the same time, despite this failure, public opinion continues to exert pressure on elected leaders to reform the system, with the consequence that legislative attempts at reform continue, at the federal and state levels. In the end, we believe that—agree or disagree with the specific legislative outcomes—public opinion, and the polling that captures it, plays a healthy role in setting direction and checking excesses.

Our second reason for seeing public opinion polling as making a valuable contribution to democratic decision making is its ability to keep elected officials in touch with the lives of the people they represent, particularly at the federal level. The average congressional district in the 1990s comprises roughly six hundred thousand people—far too many for the average member of Congress to meet individually. (Many new candidates begin campaigns wanting to knock on every door in their district. Assuming the typical district has 250,000 households, then at the rate of ten hours per day, seven days a week, and with no more than five minutes for each door, this would take more than four years.) This means that members often develop their sense of public opinion from the small circles in which they travel, primarily circles of organized interests, donors, and other political elites. These elites are hardly representative of popular opinion. For one thing, they pay much more attention to the details of politics and policy; Gallup polling has suggested that the average American voter spends no more than five minutes a week thinking about politics. No doubt this is considerably less than is spent by people whom members of Congress see often.

In addition, there is plenty of evidence that the opinions of the public at large and political elites differ. Last year, for example, we did a small public opinion poll among donors to federal candidates (an equal number of Democrats and Republicans), using identical questions to national random sample surveys. The opinions of the two populations—donors and voters—were considerably different. For example, although the majority of donors believe that "government regulations go too far now" (58 percent), most of the rest of America believes that "we need to make government regulations tougher" (53 percent). Similarly, by a margin of two to one donors believe that "government spends too much, taxes too much, and interferes in things better left to individuals and businesses" (55 percent to 29 percent). For the public, however, it is more true that "government is too concerned with what big corporations and wealthy special interests want, and does not do enough to help working families" (48 percent to 35 percent).

This divide between what the public thinks and what members hear from the people they come in contact with most often is quite visible to us every time we brief members of Congress on national polling. Invariably, something in the polling surprises them and contradicts their own sense of public opinion. To their credit, however, this is one reason why members of Congress are so eager for polling data. Most work very hard to stay in touch, and they recognize that staying in touch requires effort; their constant quest for new and more thorough public opinion data reflects this.

WHAT DOES THE FUTURE OF POLLING IMPLY FOR THE FUTURE OF DEMOCRATIC PREFERENCES?

Over the past fifty years, most technological changes have improved the accuracy of political polls. Once telephones became nearly universal among voters and computers made possible random-digit-dial sampling methodologies, sampling became more consistent and reliable. Computer assisted telephone interviewing (CATI) technologies have minimized error in questionnaire administration. Faster and more powerful computers allow more sophisticated data manipulation and analysis.

The next fifty years, however, are as likely to bring greater inaccuracy as greater accuracy. First, for example, although nearly universal telephone penetration among voters initially made telephone interviewing the best balance between cost and reliability, changes in telephone use may be introducing new sources of error. Greater use of answering machines to screen calls—as well as telemarketing burnout—may already be reducing incidence rates. Also, the explosion of area codes means there is less and less relationship between telephone exchanges and geography, making it more difficult to control sample distribution.

Addressing these kinds of inaccuracies is possible, but often costly, requiring more aggressive call-back methodologies and greater use of computer assistance in both sample and questionnaire administration. If the cost of accurate polling grows, this in turn suggests that who has access to polling is likely to change, with only wealthier organizations having the ability to commission independent polling.

Campaign finance reform also plays a role. If campaign spending by individual campaigns is capped, while the cost of communicating continues to grow (with the cost of communicating being the largest and most important expense), smaller amounts of money will be available for all the other things that political campaigns must do—which includes research and polling, as well as many other administrative and overhead costs. This means that ever less polling will be done by individual candidates, and that a higher proportion of the polling available to elected officials will be done by advocacy and lobby organizations. It may also mean that more polling is done by political parties, who then share results across multiple candidacies.

This has two potential implications. If candidates must rely more on political parties for information about public opinion, it could enhance the strength of the political parties, giving them stronger tools for developing and enforcing a coordinated party message and platform. At the same time, if elected officials are also relying more on lobby groups for information about public opinion, it increases the influence of the wealthiest groups, while diminishing the voice of constituencies without organized representation to make their case. This is because, the value of polling notwithstanding, any one poll is likely to reflect the biases of its sponsor, while a plethora of polls from a variety of viewpoints paints the most accurate portrait of public opinion.

There is a third change brewing, which has less to do with public opinion polling but a great deal to do with how public opinion is translated into policy choices: the growth—particularly in the west—of both initiative voting and election-day reforms that expand turnout. In many western states, where the idea of direct democracy is most popular, ballots are growing in length each year as more referenda are put to a direct vote. At the same time, these states are among the most aggressive in implementing election-day reforms (including vote-by-mail elections and early voting) that are demonstrably expanding turnout. Thus, in many states, we are often closer to approaching the ultimate in rule by public opinion.

Together, what do these changes—consolidation of polling in the hands of wealthier organizations and political parties, combined with an increase in direct referenda on issues—mean for how public opinion is captured in polls, and how polling influences public policy? In our view, there are both perils and opportunities to these changes. The perils lie in the degree to which public opinion is defined by those who measure it. If fewer can afford independent public opinion research, do we risk muting those voices that are already weakest? On the other hand, an increased emphasis on issues and party positioning offers an exciting opportunity for more often engaging American voters in direct debates on policy priorities and direction. Such debates, we believe, are a sign of a vibrant democracy, and only to be welcomed.

HOW THE MONICA STORY PLAYED IN MID-AMERICA

MICHAEL GARTNER

CONTEXT

Many people, including many in the media, think that the media spent too much time and resources on the Monica Lewinsky scandal than they should have. This criticism comes at a time when some claim the media is partially responsible for Americans' cynicism about government in general. For instance, James Fallows, a former speech writer for President Carter and current editor of the *Atlantic Monthly*, blames the media for mistaking their need to be skeptical with cynicism. The result, he argues, is that the media portrays the political system, and government, in ugly and corrupt terms even when it is not ugly and corrupt, and that portrayal is partly responsible for the public's cynicism toward government.

Others, however, are not as harsh on the media. In this selection, Michael Gartner argues that as far as the coverage of the Monica Lewinsky scandal goes, the media did a fairly good job. He contends that just because the people were not as interested in the scandal and ensuing impeachment story as they were in other stories is not reason to claim the press did a bad job. Part of the media's responsibility to the public is to report on stories of great importance, whether the people want to hear them or not, and the Lewinsky scandal and ensuing impeachment were certainly stories of great importance.

● *THINK CRITICALLY* ●────────────────────────

1. What do you think: Did the press do a good job in covering the Clinton-Lewinsky story?
2. Do you agree with Gartner's assertion that part of the media's responsibility is to report on important stories whether people want to hear about them or not? In your view, is there a point at which the media should not report on important stories if the public is not interested?

The Scandal looked different from Iowa.

The "all-Monica" cable channels aren't even on the systems in Des Moines and Arnes and many other Iowa towns. The talk at dinner parties was about schools and property taxes and city councils. The screaming headlines—on those rare occasions when there were screaming headlines—were about crimes, but not high crimes and misdemeanors.

There was discussion of Bill Clinton and Monica Lewinsky and Kenneth Starr, of course, but it didn't fill up our every inch of newsprint or consume our every second of airtime. We knew the scandal was a grave situation, and we decided for ourselves who were the good guys and who the bad. And we were exceptionally well-informed.

We were well-informed, because in Iowa, like most of the nation outside of Washington and New York, we got most of our news from The Associated Press (which serves 1,550 newspapers in the United States) and The New York Times News Service (which has 350 newspaper clients) and the three traditional broadcast networks (which go into 98 million households).

They did a remarkably good job.

That's the view of this editor, who read the wires day in and day out—and it's the view of Americans answering pollsters' questions.

Sure, the cable channels were often obsessed and dreadful (Chris Matthews is particularly obnoxious, Geraldo Rivera is particularly obsequious, and Larry King is particularly egotistical). But few people watch them. Even the news of Clinton's acquittal was only the twenty-first highest-ranked cable program of that week, and the Senate's voting the articles of impeachment was the fourteenth highest. No other news show in cable was in the top twenty-four. On CNN, the acquittal went into 2,216,000 households, Monday Night Wrestling, on TNT, went into 4,477,000 households. By contrast, around 60 million households buy a newspaper every day, and some 30 million households watch the ABC, CBS, or NBC evening news shows every night.

It is true, as critics note, that the scandal shoved other important news off the front pages and off the evening news. But were those stories more important than the impeachment and the events leading up to it? Probably not. Campaign finance, Social Security, even East Timor and Uganda will still be in the news next month and next year, and you can always get back to them. But impeachment was the story of the year.

The output was prodigious. The Washington bureau of The Associated Press moved 4,109 stories on the scandal in the one year after it broke on January 21, 1998. It had twenty-five reporters working regularly on the story. *The New York Times* had a dozen Washington reporters on it, with another handful working on it in other cities.

Was all of this coverage—as some charge—a "feeding frenzy" by an overeager press pushed by Washington bureau chiefs who delight in seeing big politicians tumble? In my view it's outrageous even to make such a charge. This was the greatest human, moral, political, and constitutional drama in our country since the end of the Civil War. It threatened to bring down a government and, perhaps more significantly, turn the country into a parliamentary democracy. It will reverberate forever. This was not just a lurid story like that of O. J. Simpson or JonBenet Ramsey. This was a drama about democracy.

The impeachment of a president comes along only "once every 130 years," says AP Washington bureau chief Sandy Johnson. "Lord knows that [a big story that comes] once a century is the story of any journalist, the story of his or her career." Who could fault this argument? Well, historian Arthur Schlesinger for one. He likened the press's performance to the yellow journalism of the old Hearst and Pulitzer days. And, he said at a *Columbia Journalism Review* forum on the eve of the impeachment vote: "I've never seen a greater disjunction between the media and the electorate than as we see at this moment."

Schlesinger was only half right. But the mainstream press went out of its way to avoid yellow journalism. Alan Murray, Washington bureau chief of *The Wall Street Journal*, said it was "a race to be last" in printing sex news about the president. Joseph Lelyveld, executive editor of *The New York Times*, told his staff: "This is the only area of news where I can't imagine wanting to be first. I need not just an excuse to do it, I need to be deprived of my last excuse not to do it." Thus the *Times's* news pages barely mentioned the revelations from *Hustler* magazine publisher Larry Flynt of some congressmen's sexual misadventures.

When mainstream newspapers did publish steamy and seamy news, it was usually only after it became general knowledge through the new media—the Internet and the all-news cable networks—and only after it had been verified and deemed relevant.

Still, there was a disjunction. The three traditional networks devoted 1,931 minutes to the Clinton scandal story on their evening news shows in 1998—more than the next seven most-aired subjects combined. Those seven were the year's news from Iraq, Serbia, and the Mideast, the Wall Street gyrations, El Niño, tornadoes, and the embassy bombings in Africa, according to Andrew Tyndall, a New York researcher who meticulously keeps track of such things.

Yet the Pew Research Center for the People and the Press reports the Monica Lewinsky/Bill Clinton investigation barely made the top ten among the stories that Americans said they were "following very closely" in 1998. The top three stories they were interested in, according to a Pew poll of 805 adults interviewed December 19 to 21, were the school shootings in Jonesboro, in Oregon, and at the Capitol. Wars, elections, and the weather also were of more interest than the scandal. The impeachment vote itself "was a non-starter to the American public," the Pew Center reported. More people watched the CBS telecast of the New York Jets-Buffalo Bills football game on the Saturday of the impeachment vote in the House than watched the actual vote on ABC *and* NBC.

That disjunction does not mean the press is neither "accountable" nor "responsible," as Schlesinger charged, but just that the press attached more importance to the story than the public did. That happens all the time. The efforts at campaign-finance changes is just one example.

Good editors and editorial writers and executive producers—unlike many politicians—follow their brains and their instincts, not the polls. And no editor or producer can deny the constitutional, political, and personal importance of this story. Indeed, the responsibility of the press, as Yale law professor Stephen Carter said, "is not to give the American people what they want. It is, instead, to give people what they need."

Today more than ever they need facts and editorial judgment. For increasingly, speculation and rumor are flowing into our homes through the Internet and the all-news cable channels. We do not know whom to believe or what to believe as we dredge up Drudge-like information on the Internet and watch the cable channel chatterboxes.

All of this is made far more complex by the democratization of gossip. In the old days, gossip about the Washington insiders was limited to those insiders. The elite who dined in the salons of Georgetown knew who in Washington was a drunk, an adulterer, an idiot. Today, those salons have moved into our houses.

The shift started in 1982, when Roone Arledge of ABC resuscitated a Sunday morning show called *Issues and Answers* by expanding it to an hour and hiring David Brinkley from NBC. NBC's *Meet the Press* followed, bringing in aggressive reporter Tim Russert and then expanding the show to a full hour. Politicians began clamoring to get on the shows because it increased their visibility, and reporters began competing to be guests because it pleased their publishers and raised their speaking fees. So the politicians and reporters started coming up with tidbits of gossip and inside information that would make them more attractive to the bookers.

This has made Sunday mornings far more fascinating and informative, but it has also put the viewers in the same boat as the Internet surfers: They must become their own editors, establishing their own hierarchy of news, determining their own levels of trust in various sources, and setting up their own methods for separating the wheat of fact from the chaff of rumor. Suddenly, the viewer and the surfer have to be able to recognize and interpret political spin. This is difficult even for an experienced editor. So, thank heavens for the journalists who can do this well.

In my view as an editorial writer, the *New York Times* editorial page did this well, I read every one of the 42 editorials that the *Times* published on the scandal and the impeachment debate in the second half of 1998. Their drumbeat—severe on Clinton, protective of democracy—was as cogent as it was ceaseless and consistent. Remember: *USA Today*, the *Chicago Tribune*, the *Philadelphia Inquirer*, and other major newspapers rushed to judgment and urged that Clinton resign. Meanwhile, the *Times* was merciless in its criticism of his behavior. ("Bill Clinton failed in his duties to the Presidency. He lied under oath. His private character is deeply flawed.") But it was unyielding in its view that that behavior was not a high crime against the nation. It consistently argued against impeachment and in favor of censure. And it was as tough on Kenneth Starr and House Republican bigwig Tom DeLay as it was on Clinton.

Critics fault the press in general with somehow going easy on Starr, not fully reporting his tactics or his politics or his zealotry. The implication is that the press was leaked juicy stuff from the team of the rogue prosecutor and thus gave it a free pass. That, of course, is ridiculous—it's precisely because of the press that we know of Starr's tactics and his politics and his zealotry. Look, for instance, at the piece by Lars-Erik Nelson in *The New York Review of Books* of November 11. He wrote: "If the Starr group's behavior does not rise to Gestapo tactics, it recalls that rascally police detachment on the island of

Grenada that, until it changed its name to Volunteers of the Defense of Fundamental Liberties, was called the Night Ambush Squad." As *The Wall Street Journal's* Murray said, Starr clearly was not handled with kid gloves: "The man's reputation has been damaged a lot by the press."

The press is held "in low repute" these days, said Schlesinger, and perhaps it is. A Pew Research Center poll of 1,203 adults in February [1999] found that 38 percent of them believed that news organizations are generally immoral, nearly triple the percentage who believed that in 1985.

The Freedom Forum's Media Studies Center in January [1999] asked 1,000 people to rate the coverage of five stories: the impeachment of Clinton, the Y2K computer problem, changes in U.S. policy toward Cuba, U.S. military action in Iraq, and the labor dispute in the National Basketball Association.

Of those polled, 57 percent said the press did an excellent or good job on the impeachment story. Here's how the other stories rated: Iraq, 60 percent; the NBA, 48 percent; Y2K, 44 percent; Cuba, 25 percent. Perhaps more telling, 24 percent of those polled rated the press excellent on its impeachment coverage. The others: Iraq, 13 percent; NBA, 9 percent; Y2K, 8 percent; Cuba, 4 percent.

Alas, in another Media Studies Center survey in March [1999], only 40 percent of those polled rated the coverage of the Clinton/Lewinsky story as excellent or good. At the same time, anywhere from 61 percent to 63 percent said that President Clinton, Monica Lewinsky, and Kenneth Starr had been fairly covered by the press. Robert Giles, executive director of the Media Studies Center, said, "As far as the public is concerned, the news media did not play favorites on this story."

Throughout, both the AP and *The New York Times* stuck to their standards. The AP, for instance, adhered to its corporate-wide rule about anonymous material: it must be unobtainable on the record, it must be fact, it cannot be opinion, and it must move the story ahead.

The *Times*, similarly, held to its policy. Washington bureau chief Michael Oreskes described it in a talk to his paper's managers: "Sources had to have direct knowledge of the information they were telling us. We needed at least two clearly separate sources—not, for example, two people in one office. Another news outlet could not count as one of those sources."

And both were quaintly modest. The AP, for instance, didn't write about the infamous incident involving Clinton, Lewinsky, and the cigar when the story was "being pushed by Republican sources," says bureau chief Johnson. "When we had verification from the right sources, we found a way to put a reference into the copy without being too specific about it." When the Starr report came out, the AP flagged for its members every take that had references that might be offensive to readers.

It's odd, in a way, how this yearlong story has brought such wrath upon the press. On inspection, many of the charges seem based on the ideology of the charger. Others were aimed at the new "journalists" of the Internet. Says Oreskes: "Newspapering is a good life . . . but . . . I'd like to be known for my own sins and not for Matt Drudge's." Still other charges came from sweeping conclusions based on occasional sin—particularly the sins of those newspapers that reported an eyewitness to a Clinton-Lewinsky tryst.

In fact, the reporting by the AP and *The New York Times* and, for the most part, by CNN and the over-the-air networks on their nightly news shows was thorough and fair and accurate.

The fact that the public wasn't very interested in the story is immaterial. This was a huge story, swirling in a new atmosphere, but it was the old media using the old rules that carried the day. "It was an unavoidable story, a real story," says Oreskes, "one that tested us and in the end allowed us to show exactly who we really are and why having a news organization worried about what's 'fit to print' matters even more in the age of Matt Drudge than it did in the age of Joseph Pulitzer."

At least, as seen by this editor in the Heartland, the newspeople and the editorial people of the mainstream press performed valiantly and expertly. Their performance should not be diluted by lumping them with the cable babblers whom nobody watches or heeds, or by ascribing to them or their peers furtive motives generated by the seminar and cocktail crowds.

NEWSPAPERS SAVAGED OTHER PRESIDENTS, TOO

LINDA LOTRIDGE LEVIN

CONTEXT

President Clinton has complained about the extent to which the media pried into his private life. He has said that the media treated him far differently than it treated previous presidents. Surely, this is partially true. After all, we know that many reporters saw President Franklin Roosevelt in a wheelchair but never reported it because they did not want to embarrass him. Additionally, we know that many reporters knew of President John F. Kennedy's philandering but did not report it.

Part of the change in coverage of the president dates back to the Watergate scandal, when two reporters for the *Washington Post*, Bob Woodward and Carl Bernstein, were credited with uncovering great abuses of power. Since then, "investigative" journalism, where journalists look for scandal of any kind, has been on the rise.

Some argue, though, that coverage of the president has always been rough and personal. In this article from *Editor & Publisher*, Linda Lotridge

Levin discusses newspaper coverage of the presidents' private life in light of the kind of coverage given to President Clinton's private life. Despite the fact that many Americans, including the president, felt that the media spent too much time covering the Lewinsky sex scandal, the press is no worse today in this regard than in the past. Levin discusses previous presidential sex scandals and media coverage of those scandals. She argues that the press today may in fact be easier on the president than it was in the past. In the end, the press will continue such coverage because right or wrong, people want to know, and the media has the right to report these types of stories.

● *THINK CRITICALLY* ●

1. In your view, should the media pay attention to the private lives of politicians at all? Why or why not?
2. Do you think the media needs to be regulated more than it is? In other words, should the media be required to report on some things and limited on other things?

Did your readers tell you that the media spent too much space and time covering President Clinton's sexual peccadillos and the impeachment proceedings?

Why not tell them you're merely following a long tradition of newspapers beating up on presidents for their alleged sexual sins. If anything, the press of today is far easier on the president than newspapers as far back as the 17th century.

In a letter to the editor of the *New York Evening Post* in 1886, President Grover Cleveland called newspapers purveyors of "silly, mean and cowardly lies" when they attacked his plan to marry a woman more than 30 years his junior.

"They have used the enormous power of the modern newspaper to perpetuate and disseminate a colossal impertinence, and have done it, not as professional gossips and tattlers, but as the guides and instructors of the public in conduct and morals. And they have done it, not to a private citizen, but the President of the United States, thereby lifting their offense into the gaze of the whole world, and doing their utmost to make American journalism contemptible in the estimation of people of good breeding everywhere," Cleveland wrote.

Nor was Cleveland the first president to have his personal life hung out in the nation's media. Truth be told, the media have been in hot pursuit of sex scandals involving heads of state since the American colonies' first newspaper in 1690. A small rag called *Publick Occurrences Both Foreign and Domestick*, it was banned after one issue because Massachusetts Bay Colony authorities found a report of the French king seducing his daughter-in-law to be in bad taste.

George Washington was accused of being a blasphemer—taking the Lord's name in vain—apparently that was all journalists then could dig up on him. His successor, Thomas Jefferson, didn't get off so easily. The press accused him of fathering children by one of his slaves.

Later, newspapers reported that John Quincy Adams had had premarital relations with his wife, and that Andrew Jackson had lived in adultery with his wife before she divorced her first husband.

The *New York World* wrote that Andrew Johnson was totally inebriated at his inauguration and that "in comparison even Caligula's horse would have been respectable." His inauguration address, the *Brooklyn Eagle* reported, was "so indecent that even Republican papers refused to print it." The *Cincinnati Daily Gazette* called it "idiotic babble." But it was Johnson's views on Reconstruction that did him in.

President Rutherford B. Hayes refused to serve alcoholic beverages at White House functions, but that proved minor ammunition for the press, which periodically repeated the story that Hayes had taken several hundred dollars off a deserter later executed, in his Civil War regiment.

Presidents in the 20th century fared little better, especially in the sexual rumor arena. Teddy Roosevelt was spared the press peering into his bedroom, perhaps because he was health conscious, egotistical, emotional, and a bit strait-laced—leaving him little time or inclination for extramarital romps.

But his cousin Franklin did find time for a fling or two, though it wasn't until long after his death that one of his biographers published the details. Gradually, other books reported on Franklin Delano Roosevelt's affairs, or alleged affairs, before and during his White House years. Why was FDR spared media scrutiny during his lifetime? Probably because the women involved were discreet and loyal, or because the media were focused first on the Great Depression, then on a world war. More likely it was because the press, with few exceptions, obeyed a set of strict rules Roosevelt and his press secretary, Stephen T. Early, laid down early on for coverage of the president.

Lyndon B. Johnson also was spared public scrutiny of his sex life—even though Washington journalists were acutely aware of his philandering—because of the turmoil of Vietnam and the protests that marked his presidency. Details were published only after he left the White House.

John F. Kennedy also escaped exposure but for different reasons. Many in the Washington press corps socialized with him and considered him a friend. But when Jimmy Carter told a magazine interviewer that he "lusted in his heart," it was enough to send journalists scurrying, unsuccessfully, in search of scandal.

But the 20th century president whose personal life most closely paralleled Clinton's is Warren G. Harding. Both were married to strong-willed women, but, according to her biographer, Florence Harding "successfully manipulated the press" to win positive coverage of her husband. She remained steadfastly devoted through a succession of his adulterous affairs, some in White House closets and hallways.

Despite the litany of personal excesses, covered or not, of past presidents, why have none led to impeachment until President Clinton? First: Ken Starr, a dogged special prosecutor, and the leaks to the press from his office. Second: a mass media fully transformed from the compliant Washington press corps of Franklin Roosevelt's day, a media far more pervasive with cable TV, the internet and fiercely competitive. And quite simply, the media, including newspapers, have learned anew that sex sells.

Rightly or wrongly, the media will continue to stick their noses into the personal lives of White House residents on the grounds of the public's desire to know and the media's First Amendment rights to report those stories. Conversely, presidents from the birth of this country have suffered the press' "colossal impertinence" before—and the republic has remained intact.

SECTION SIX

POLITICAL PARTIES
AND ELECTIONS

HEAD NOTES/SECTION QUESTIONS

Political parties are nothing more than political factions in society. People, be they elected office holders, community leaders, or laymen, who identify with a common set of principles about government and what government should or should not do, constitute a political faction within society. One does not have to be an activist or involved in politics to identify with or be a part of a political faction.

Political factions become more coherent when represented by a political party. While there are probably hundreds of political factions in America, there are only a few represented by political parties, and only two that are big enough to have any influence on government. Of the two big factions represented by political parties, one believes in limited government and the other believes in a more active government. These two factions are made coherent by the fact that they are represented by the Democratic Party and the Republican Party. Obviously there are also divisions within these factions (and divisions within each of these parties), and Ron Faucheux talks about that and the danger it poses to each party.

The central objective of each faction, or party, is to gain political power and eventually gain control of government, so that it can put into effect its principles about government. The way that political parties achieve, or try to achieve, this central objective is by competing in elections. Elections are at the heart of a democracy because they are the primary way that the people can express their wishes. The United States holds more elections than perhaps any other country in the world. Since we hold so many elections in America, thus putting so many decisions before the people, it is worrisome that voter turnout is low. Martin P. Wattenberg discusses this and suggests some ways that voter turnout might be increased.

Finally, in order for political parties to compete in elections and gain enough power to control government, they have to have resources. The primary resource that the political parties need is money, and the amount of money they need, what they do with it, and where it comes from has become a problem in recent years. Two readings address the issue of money and elections. Magleby and Holt look at how what is called "soft money" (money given to political parties) and issue ads are changing the nature of elections. Joshua Rosenkranz looks at the issue of campaign finance reform and how the Supreme Court is likely to view efforts to reform the current system.

As you read the following selections, think about these questions:

1. In your view, is there a relationship between the low voter turnout and campaign finance issues? If so, what is it?
2. Does America only have two political factions? If not, does it makes sense to you that America only has two major political parties? How many political parties do you think it would take to represent the political factions in America?

LEARN MORE ON THE WEB

The Jefferson Project
  http://www.capweb.net/classic/jefferson/parties/

Political Parties of the Americas
  http://www.georgetown.edu/pdba/Parties/parties.html

Election Calendar
  http://www.ifes.org/eleccal.htm

The U.S. Electoral College Calculator
  http://www.bga.com/~jnhtx/ec/ec.html

Campaign Finance Reform
  http://www.brookings.org/GS/campaign/home.htm

PARTY POLITICS: BOTH ENDS AGAINST THE MIDDLE

RON FAUCHEUX

CONTEXT

Many of the Founders worried about political parties and warned against them. In his farewell address, George Washington warned against the "baneful effects" of political parties. Within a few years, however, political parties had begun to take shape. They did so because of policy disagreements among political leaders and the desire on the part of the political giants of the time, Alexander Hamilton, James Madison, and Thomas Jefferson, to gain as much support as possible in policy debates.

The two parties that emerged, the Federalists led by Alexander Hamilton, and the Democratic-Republicans led by Thomas Jefferson and James Madison, were nothing like the two parties of today. Back then, political parties were really nothing more than groups of like-minded politicians fighting over policy. The parties did not go out and recruit candidates or hold get-out-the-vote (GOTV) drives, as they do today. It took another decade or so, until the presidential election of 1800, before the parties actually began to make appeals to the voters and compete with each other in elections.

Today, political parties spend a great deal of time appealing to voters for support, and each of the two major political parties can count a certain percentage of the population as "strong" supporters. But as Ron Faucheux explains in this article from Campaigns & Elections, the two main parties might see their voters' support decline in years to come if they do not start paying more attention to the voters in the middle who are not extremely partisan either way.

Faucheux says that the Democratic and Republican parties are too busy playing to their narrow bases at the extremes and are ignoring the middle 40 percent of Americans who are not aligned with either extreme. During the Clinton impeachment, Democrats responded to their voter base and Republicans responded to their voter base. However, 40 percent of Americans are in the middle rather than either of the two extremes. Faucheux argues that while the economy remains strong, this 40 percent is not likely to be a problem for either party. When the 40 percent becomes discontented, however, they are likely to look for alternatives to either of the two parties. The result could be a larger independent movement or third party.

● *THINK CRITICALLY* ●───────────────────────

1. Why do you think political parties play to their base rather than the middle?
2. Faucheux says that if the 40 percent of voters in the middle become disenchanted, independents and third-party movements could have a chance to strike. Do you think this is already happening, or are the 40 percent in the middle still content?

The 20th century began with Republicans ascendant. Its middle was marked by a long expanse of Democratic dominance. But as the century comes to a close, no one is in charge: America essentially has two minority parties, with neither commanding the allegiance of a majority of Americans. And that leaves the window of opportunity for third-party candidates open wider than ever.

Beginning with Franklin Roosevelt's election as president in 1932—which itself terminated a long Republican heyday—and ending with the Republican landslide of 1994, the Democrats were the nation's governing party. Even though Republicans often held the White House and, on occasion, a chamber or two of Congress, it was the Democratic Party that steered the course of the nation. Throughout much of this time, Republicans needed to carry a huge share of independent voters just to equal the Democratic base.

Democratic dominance began to crack with Ronald Reagan's election to the presidency in 1980. But it didn't collapse until 1994, when Republicans took control of Congress as well as a slew of state governorships and legislatures. That triumph, however, has not brought on a new Republican era. Instead, it has created a new parity within the electorate, with voters split roughly equally between the two parties. Since 1994, neither party has been able to assemble a governing majority.

For more than a decade, each party has been living off the mistakes of the other party. Victories have been won on the backs of an inept opposition—not on the merits of anyone's leadership agenda or policy vision. The fight for control between these two minority parties has amplified a zero-sum mentality about politics. It has made politics nastier and less fun.

While voters turn off to the importance of politics in general and tune out politicians from both parties, the parties' organizational anti financial muscle has bulked up, nourished by allied interest groups and "soft money." The impeachment fight displayed the double sides of this partisan coin.

Throughout the Clinton-Lewinsky scandal, about 30 percent of the electorate consistently stuck with the president, 30 percent steadfastly opposed him and 40 percent stood in the middle. The 40 percent were astonished by the spectacle and disgusted by both the blind partisanship of the prosecutors and the moral corruption of the prosecuted.

Caught in the middle of an ax fight, cynicism among this 40 percent deepened to the point that they no longer believed or trusted anything that came from anybody in public authority, from Kenneth Starr to the House prosecutors to the White House. This, of course, benefited President Clinton, since the burden of proof rested with a prosecution that seemed to most voters to be acting out of excessive partisan zeal. Despite the strong reaction against partisanship by swing voters—the people who decide most elections—the scandal paradoxically hardened partisan polarities.

Almost all of the Democrats in Congress responded to the voter base they shared with the president, the left-leaning 30 percent, by voting with him all the way. Nearly all Republicans in Congress stood by their base, too, the 30 percent on the right, by voting in favor of impeachment and removal from office despite national polls showing voters breaking 2–1 against their position.

In effect, both sides danced not to the music of the middle, but jumped, instead, to the cracking whips of their own party's organizational and financial base.

The already cynical though somewhat content 40 percent of the electorate in the middle will begin to look for new alternatives.

In recent years, the alternative has been, as many voters view it, the lesser of two evils. But if and when voters begin to shed their contentment with domestic economic conditions, and if the international scene worsens, both major parties need to be careful. Independents and third-party movements will have a chance to strike.

But to flourish, independent movements and third parties will need to recruit capable candidates who can hold their own in the campaign arena. They will also need to surmount an unfriendly campaign finance system and a treacherous terrain of ballot access requirements.

Their task will be exceedingly difficult. But new opportunities may be opening for them.

As partisans wag the dog of electoral power, they need to look out. The 40 percent are coming.

SHOULD ELECTION DAY BE A HOLIDAY?

MARTIN P. WATTENBERG

CONTEXT

Turnout levels, the proportion of the voting age population that votes, have been going down in the United States since the 1950s, when turnout levels were in the high 60 percent range. In recent presidential elections, turnout levels have been around 50 percent. During the 1800s, from the presidential election of 1840 to the presidential election of 1896, turnout hovered between 70 and 80 percent.

What has caused this drop in turnout? Political scientists have advanced a number of explanations, ranging from the difficulty potential voters have in registering to vote, to the high number of elections we have in the United States, to the fact that political parties are weaker today than they have been in the past. In this selection, Martin P. Wattenberg suggests another reason. Wattenberg summarizes turnout levels in the United States and compares current turnout levels with past turnout levels. He notes that younger Americans are much more likely not to vote than older Americans. If all voted who were eligible to vote, the results of recent elections would probably be different than they were. He suggests three ways that voter turnout might be increased, and concludes that the most viable alternative would be to make election day a national holiday.

● *THINK CRITICALLY* ●

1. In your view, does it matter if voter turnout is low? Why or why not?
2. Do you agree with the statement: "If citizens don't vote they must be satisfied with the government"? What are some other possible reasons why citizens do not vote?
3. What do you think about the suggestion that election day be a national holiday? Do you think this would increase voter turnout?

Regardless of who wins in next month's midterm elections, a sure bet is that less than half of the voting-age population will actually participate. The percentage of the electorate casting ballots for the House of Representatives has fluctuated between 33 and 45 percent over the past sixteen midterm elections. Recent turnout rates suggest that the percentage in 1998 will probably be near the bottom of this range, and quite possibly even lower. In 1996 the presidential-election turnout fell below 50 percent for the first time since the early 1920s—when women had just received the franchise and had not yet begun to use it as frequently as men. Last year not a single one of the eleven states that called their citizens to the polls managed to get a majority to vote. The best turnout occurred in Oregon, where a heated campaign debate had taken place on the question of whether to repeal the state's "right to die" law. The worst turnout last year was a shockingly low five percent, for a special election in Texas. This occurred even though Governor George W. Bush stumped the state for a week, urging people to participate and promising that a "yes" vote would result in a major tax cut.

Universal suffrage means that everyone should have an equal opportunity to vote, regardless of social background. But over the past three decades studies have found increasing biases in turnout. In particular, people without college degrees have become less likely to go to the polls. Statistics from the Census Bureau on turnout by educational achievement make the point. Respondents were asked if they had taken part in the most recent election in their area.

	1966	1994
No high school diploma	47%	26%
High school diploma	60%	41%
Some college	65%	50%
College degree	71%	64%

Since 1966 turnout rates have declined most sharply among people at the lower levels of education. In 1994 people with no college education made up 53 percent of the adult population but only 42 percent of the voters.

Turnout is now also greatly related to experience in life. Turnout rates have always been lowest among young people: perhaps this is why there was relatively little opposition in the early 1970s to lowering the voting age to eighteen. But not even the most pessimistic analysts could have foreseen the record-low participation rates of Generation X, as shown in the following census findings on age and turnout:

	1966	1994
18–20	—	17%
21–24	32%	22%
25–44	53%	39%
45–64	65%	57%
over 65	56%	61%

The low turnout among young voters today is paradoxical given that they are one of the best-educated generations in American history. Even those who have made it to college are expressing remarkably little concern for politics. Chelsea Clinton's class of 2001 recently set a new record for political apathy among college freshmen: only 27 percent said that keeping up with politics was an important priority for them, as opposed to 58 percent of the class of 1970, with whom Bill and Hillary Clinton attended college.

Of course, Chelsea's classmates have not seen government encroach on their lives as it did on the lives of their parents—through the Vietnam War and the draft. Nor has any policy affected them as directly as Medicare has affected their grandparents. It is noteworthy that senior citizens are actually voting at higher rates today than when Medicare was first starting up. Political scientists used to write that the frailties of old age led to a decline in turnout after age sixty; now such a decline occurs only after eighty. The greater access of today's seniors to medical care must surely be given some credit for this change. Who says that politics doesn't make a difference?

Yet it is difficult to persuade people who have channel surfed all their lives that politics really does matter. Chelsea's generation is the first in the age of television to grow up with narrowcasting rather than broadcasting. When CBS, NBC, and ABC dominated the airwaves, their blanket coverage of presidential speeches, political conventions, and presidential debates sometimes left little else to watch on TV. But as channels have proliferated, it has become much easier to avoid exposure to politics altogether. Whereas President Richard Nixon got an average rating of 50 for his televised addresses to the nation, President Clinton averaged only about 30 in his first term. Political conventions, which once received more TV coverage than the Summer Olympics, have been relegated to an hour per night and draw abysmal ratings. In sum, young people today have never known a time when most citizens paid attention to major political events. As a result, most of them have yet to get into the habit of voting.

The revolutionary expansion of channels and Web sites anticipated in the near future is likely to worsen this state of affairs, especially for today's youth. Political junkies will certainly find more political information available than ever before, but with so many outlets for so many specific interests, it will also be extraordinarily easy to avoid public-affairs news altogether. The result could well be further inequality of political information, with avid followers of politics becoming ever more knowledgeable while the rest of the public slips deeper into political apathy. This year's expected low turnout may not be the bottom of the barrel.

Some commentators welcome, rather than fear, the decline in turnout rates in America. If people do not vote, they say, citizens must be satisfied with the government. There is a certain logic to this view, because if nonvoters were extremely disgruntled with our leaders, they would undoubtedly take some political action. However, to argue that nonvoters are content with government just because they aren't actively opposing it stretches the logic too far. When the 1996 National Election Study asked people to rate their satisfaction with how democracy works in the United States, nonvoters were *less* positive than voters. Furthermore, young people were more than twice as likely as senior citizens to be dissatisfied with American democracy.

Why should young adults be satisfied with government, given how few benefits they receive from it in comparison with their grandparents? But until they start showing up in greater numbers at the polls, there will be little incentive for politicians to focus on programs that will help the young. Why should politicians worry about nonvoters any more than the makers of denture cream worry about people with healthy teeth? It is probably more than coincidental that Clinton's two most visible policy failures—the 1993 economic-stimulus package and the 1994 effort to establish universal health care—had their strongest backing from people who were not even registered to vote. Congressional Republicans may rationally have anticipated that many of these proposals' supporters were unlikely to be judging them in the 1994 elections.

After the Republican takeover of Congress in 1994, I saw a bumper sticker that read NEWT HAPPENS WHEN ONLY 37 PERCENT OF AMERICANS VOTE. Although I don't usually let bumper stickers determine my research agenda, this one piqued my interest. Would the Republicans have won the majority of House seats if turnout had been greater? A simple way to address this question is to assess how much difference it would have made if voters had mirrored the adult population in terms of education. According to the 1994 National Election Study, 30 percent of voters who lacked a high school diploma and 62 percent of voters with college degrees voted for Republican candidates for the House. Increasing turnout among the least educated citizens would thus have made some difference. If turnout rates had been equal in all education categories, the Republican share of the vote would have fallen from 52.0 to 49.2 percent.

Although it is unlikely that people of differing education levels would ever vote at exactly the same rate, this is only one of many biases in electoral participation. A more comprehensive method of estimating the impact of higher turnout is to gauge the attitudes of nonvoters toward those factors that influenced voters in 1994: party identification, approval of Clinton, stands on issues, and incumbency. Examining only survey respondents who were registered but did not vote. I found that these nonvoters would have favored Democratic candidates by an even greater margin than that by which actual voters supported the Republicans. Had all registered citizens gone to the polls, the Republicans' share of the vote would have been reduced by 2.8 percent—exactly the same estimate as arrived at above. If this loss occurred in all districts, the Republicans would have won only 206 seats—twenty-four fewer than they actually won, and twelve short of a majority.

Such findings, regrettably, suggest that nothing will be done to increase turnout in America. Few Republicans will want to correct a situation that has benefited them in the past. Yet until something is done, the House of Representatives will be representative not of the electorate but only of the minority that actually votes.

What can be done to reverse the decline in turnout? At his first press conference after the 1996 election Bill Clinton was asked about the poor turnout and how to increase participation in the future. The President stumbled over this question—he didn't really have an opinion on what could be done, and he concluded by asking the members of the press corps whether they had any ideas. Clinton's apparent frustration in addressing the question probably stems from his involvement in passing the 1993 Motor Voter Act. He and many others believed that its voter-registration reforms would increase turnout. But although the registration rolls swelled in state after state prior to the 1996 election, the turnout rate fell dramatically on Election Day. (The Census Bureau, paradoxically, found fewer people in 1996 than in 1992 who said they were registered. Apparently, the Motor Voter procedures made registering so easy that many forgot they had placed their names on the voting ledgers.)

Had Clinton been better advised on this subject, he would not have expected turnout to increase simply because registering to vote had become easier. North Dakota has since 1951 not required people to register in order to vote, yet its turnout is not especially high, and it has seen turnout in presidential elections decline by 22 percent since 1960. Minnesota and Wisconsin have allowed citizens to register on Election Day since the mid-1970s, but they have lower turnout rates today than when they had tighter registration laws. In short, not even the most lenient voter-registration procedures are the answer to the problem of low turnout.

Clinton is said occasionally to remark that solutions to most public-policy problems have already been found somewhere—we just have to scan the horizons for them. This certainly applies to increasing turnout. Three possible changes stand out as particularly likely to get Americans to the polls—though, unfortunately, their probable effectiveness is inversely related to the plausibility of their ever being enacted in the United States.

If in an ideal democracy everyone votes, people could simply be required to participate. This is how Australians reasoned when they instituted compulsory voting after their turnout rate fell to 58 percent in 1922. Since then the turnout in Australia has never fallen below 90 percent, even though the maximum fine for not voting is only about $30, and judges readily accept any reasonable excuse. However, American political culture is based on John Locke's views on individual rights, whereas Australian culture was shaped by Jeremy Bentham's concept of the greatest good for the greatest number. Most Americans would probably assert that they have an inviolable right *not* to vote.

Beyond that, it is debatable whether we really want to force turnout rates in America up to 90 percent. People with limited political knowledge might deal with being compelled to vote by making dozens of decisions in the same way they choose lottery numbers. In Australia this is known as the "donkey vote," for people who approach voting as if they were playing the old children's game. Given Australia's relatively simple electoral process, the donkey vote is a small proportion: in America it would probably be greater.

Evidence from around the world indicates that our turnout rates could be increased if we adopted some form of proportional representation. In our winner-take-all system many Americans rightly perceive that their votes are unlikely to affect election outcomes. Proportional representation changes this perception by awarding seats to small voting blocs. The threshold for representation varies by country, but typically any party that receives more than five percent of the national vote earns seats in the legislature. Almost inevitably when proportional representation is instituted, the number of political parties grows. And with a range of viable parties to choose from, people tend to feel that their choice truly embodies their specific interests. Hence they are more likely to vote.

If we were to adopt proportional representation, new parties would be likely to spring up to represent the interests of groups such as African-Americans, Latinos, and the new Christian right. Although this would give members of these groups more incentive to vote, and thus would raise the low turnout rates of minority groups, a price would be paid for this benefit. The current system brings diverse groups together under the umbrellas of two heterogeneous parties: a multi-party system would set America's social groups apart from one another. Proportional representation therefore seems no more practical on the American scene than compulsory voting.

A simple but effective change, however, could be made in election timing. An ordinary act of Congress could move Election Day to a Saturday or make it a holiday, thereby giving more people more time to vote. An 1872 law established the first Tuesday after the first Monday in November as Election Day. At that point in history it made little difference whether elections were on Saturday or Tuesday, because most people worked on Saturday. Only Sunday would have been a day free of work, but with elections in the late nineteenth century being occasions for drinking and gambling, that option was out of the question in such a religious country.

Americans have become quite accustomed to Tuesday elections, just as they have to the nonmetric system for weights and measures and other artifacts of another time. State after state has set primary-election dates on Tuesdays—all twentieth-century decisions, some of them quite recent. It would be difficult to change this custom. Furthermore, there would probably be some resistance from Orthodox Jews and Mormons to putting Election Day on their sabbath.

An alternative would be to declare Election Day a national holiday. This would probably be resisted on the basis of cost. A solution would be to move Election Day to the second Tuesday of November and combine it with Veterans' Day, traditionally celebrated on November 11. This would send a strong signal about the importance our country attaches to voting. And what better way could there be to honor those who fought for democratic rights than for Americans to vote on what could become known as Veteran's Democracy Day?

26

THE LONG SHADOW OF SOFT MONEY AND ISSUE ADVOCACY ADS

DAVID MAGLEBY AND MARIANNE HOLT

CONTEXT

Political campaigns cost money, pure and simple. Without money, candidates could not run for office and political parties could not compete with each other over policy ideas. However, not all money is the same.

Money given to candidates for office is called "hard money." This kind of money is called hard money because it is meant to be spent by the candidate on his or her behalf. "Soft money," on the other hand, is money contributed to political parties, not political candidates. Soft money is supposed to be spent by the political parties not for the benefit of individual candidates but for the benefit of the party as a whole. Soft money is meant to be spent on getting more party loyalists out to the polls on election day and running television commercials advancing the party's issues (called issue advocacy ads).

More money has been contributed to political parties in the soft form in recent elections than to political candidates in the hard form. In this article, Magleby and Holt analyze soft money expenditures and advocacy advertising in selected congressional elections in 1998. They are interested in learning the extent to which soft money and issue advertising are having an influence on elections, especially in competitive districts/states, by causing the elections to move away from being candidate-centered campaigns toward interest group- and party-centered campaigns. The change, they warn, could have a profound impact on the nation's electoral democracy.

● *THINK CRITICALLY* ●

1. What kind of impact could a change from candidate-centered to interest group- and party-centered campaigns have on our electoral democracy?

2. If elections are becoming increasingly party-centered and less candidate-centered, what does this do to the power of political parties? Is
   this a good or bad thing in your view?

The shift from candidate-centered campaigns to interest group- and party-centered campaigns could have profound significance for our electoral democracy.

The most recent national elections marked a watershed in terms of political
parties and interest groups running their own separate campaigns. Their activities changed the strategic environment, influenced the issue agenda and in
some instances spent more money than the candidate campaigns. Because of
narrow party majorities in Congress, especially in the House of Representatives, the campaign dynamics in the most competitive battle-grounds may determine which party controls Congress. This shift from candidate-centered
campaigns to interest group- and party-centered campaigns could have profound significance for our electoral democracy.

With grant support from the Pew Charitable Trusts, we conducted a study of
party soft money and issue advocacy in 16 competitive 1998 congressional
elections (12 House and four Senate races). The sample of contests was drawn
from lists of competitive races published in the *Cook Political Report*, the
Rothenberg Political Report and Congressional Quarterly's *On Politics* weekly
newsletter.

Interviews were also conducted with party committee staff and PAC directors to determine which races were most likely to see issue advocacy or soft
money activity. Respected academics were recruited in each of the
districts/states to monitor the undisclosed campaigns. We also contracted with
Strategic Media Services, a media marketing firm, to utilize its tracking technology of political advertisements to supplement our own media monitoring efforts in the field.

FOUR DEVELOPMENTS

Four important developments emerge from our study of issue ads and soft
money in competitive 1998 congressional elections.

First, soft money has become an essential part of party campaign strategy in
congressional elections. As soft money grows in importance, so do soft money
contributors, especially the large donors, because they give the party the ability to immediately shift millions of dollars into a tight race. The congressional
party committee leaders are therefore more important because of the large
amounts of soft money they spend in competitive races.

Second, there is a fundamental shift under way in competitive congressional
elections from a candidate-centered system of elections to an interest group- and
party-centered system of elections. With the stakes so high and the resources
available, the parties and interest groups now fight for control of Congress in a

relatively few districts or states and these "outside campaigns" can overwhelm the candidate campaigns.

Third, the 1998 elections were decided much more on the "ground" where interest groups and parties mounted a major voter identification and activation effort than in the air through broadcast advertising. Issue ads on television and radio were important in agenda-setting, but in a low turnout midterm election the "ground war," including direct mail and phone banks, was critical. The Democrats and allied interest groups more effectively activated voters in this ground war in 1998.

Finally, the limited disclosure laws and the media's lack of coverage of soft money expenditures and issue advocacy, what we call outside money, makes the reporters' work much more difficult. In most cases the news media entirely missed the story of outside money in the 1998 contest in their state or district.

SOFT MONEY SURGE

Party' committees, building on their record-setting soft money fundraising in 1996, set new fundraising and expenditure records for a midterm election in 1998. Soft money, which had been used primarily by national party committees rather than congressional campaign committees, became a central part of the strategy of both parties' congressional committees, especially the Republicans'. Overall party soft money spending in 1998 was more than double party soft money spent in the 1994 election, while the number of races parties invested in was lower.

The parties raised and transferred record-setting amounts of soft money for a midterm election in 1998—more than double the money that they raised in the 1994 midterm election. The Democrats raised over $89.4 million between January 1, 1997 and November 23, 1998. This represents an 82 percent fundraising increase over the 1993–94 midterm election. The Republicans increased their soft money funds by 112 percent, raising $111.3 million. Most of the increase in soft money fundraising took place in the senatorial and congressional campaign committees.

According to our data set, the Republicans focused their money on television ads and direct mailers while the Democrats had a more diversified approach, including a good deal of radio time and phone banks.

Party committee leaders have always controlled soft money accounts but this control has become more important as soft money contributions have increased over the past 10 years. Essentially, party leaders now control a vast bank of unchecked money; they are personally responsible for deciding which candidates receive these campaign funds or party support.

One of the effects of the soft money boom is to increase the power of party leaders. A good example is Sen. Mitch McConnell of Kentucky, chair of the Senate Republican Campaign Committee, who took a strong personal interest in his home state senatorial race between Jim Bunning (R) and Scotty Baesler (D).

The Republicans spent over $3 million in support of Bunning. McConnell was a key ally and mastermind of the Bunning campaign; he loaned two of his staffers to help design and run Bunning's campaign. He provided strategic campaign advice, consulted on the hiring of campaign advisers, and also helped steer state and national contributors to both the senatorial race of Kentucky and the 6th District race between Fletcher (R) and Scorsone (D).

In some races, soft money actually exceeded hard money spent by the candidates. An example was the central role played by the Democratic Party, also in the Kentucky Senate campaign.

Democratic committees transferred over $1.8 million in soft money contributions to the Kentucky Democratic Party. The state party spent nearly $1.7 million on television ads. The party spent more on television advertisements than Baesler's own campaign.

The Democratic Party's TV ads were attack spots and were an especially important component of the early media campaign. It purchased much statewide radio time—for example, spending more than $90,000 in the Louisville area alone—on behalf of Baesler and its slate of candidates. It also ran a sophisticated, coordinated GOTV campaign that featured targeted phone calls, door-to-door canvassing, and thousands of non-allocable mass mailings using non-profit bulk rates.

Of course, the use of more party money does not mean victory. Republicans waged a vigorous campaign in New Mexico's 3rd District; however, the simple lack of party members in the district doomed these efforts. While the GOP had twice the money to spend, Democrats had deeper roots: nearly three-fifths of all registered voters in the 3rd District are Democrats.

Both the New Mexico Republican Party and the Republican National Committee aired numerous ads; the RNC spent $48,022 on television time discussing incumbent U.S. Rep. Bill Redmond's (R) education and economic development record. The state party spent $296,255. The RNC ran both pro-Redmond and anti-Tom Udall (D) ads. As part of its national endeavor to elect Republicans, dubbed "Operation Breakout," the NRCC ran an ad critical of challenger Udall's support of Goals 2000, a federal program that provides grants for school programs and reforms.

Sometimes, party and candidate efforts collided. An example was what Republican committees did for Larry McKibben (R) in the Iowa 3rd District U.S. House race. Party sources bought numerous television ads and sent a massive amount of direct mail on behalf of McKibben, who was challenging incumbent Leonard Boswell (D). The ads and mail accompanied statewide GOTV efforts.

Ads for the bulk of the campaign consisted of positive spots bolstering McKibben, stressing national issues and advising voters to "call McKibben" to express their support for the Republican agenda in Congress. In addition, the ads mentioned that the GOP sought to save Social Security and has balanced the budget.

These ads, in the main, were not particularly tailored to the needs of the candidate: They did not attack Boswell or run comparisons. The direct mail lambasted Boswell as a criminal-coddling, pro-welfare and pro-quotas, two-faced liberal Democrat. But the softer television ads criticized President Clinton and discussed ethics.

McKibben was not able to run the campaign he wanted because the party campaign was misguided.

McKibben's campaign was whipsawed by outside spending from both sides. The outside money, in the opinion of at least one consultant who has watched the race, constrained loser McKibben's strategic options.

Local party activities that are funded by soft money can make a difference as well. In one Illinois race, the most important non-candidate activity, besides party soft money, was the "17th District Victory Fund." The fund was considered a Democratic Party committee and was designed to help U.S. Rep. Lane Evans (D) and state and local Democrats win re-election.

With a budget of roughly $300,000 and 18 full-time volunteers (with no salaries but expenses paid), this "campaign school" group mattered. The Victory Fund was financed by DNC soft money, labor unions, and other interested groups and individual contributions. Some of these contributors had "maxed out" on direct contributions to the Evans campaign.

The training and setup were provided by Strategic Consulting Group, a Chicago-based consulting firm co-run by Bob Creamer, Citizen Action of Illinois activist and husband of Democratic congressional candidate (now congresswoman) Jan Schakowsky. The group's volunteers focused on phone calling and door-to-door canvassing to reach tens of thousands of voters, culminating in a GOTV effort on election day.

Challenger Mark Baker (R) attacked this group repeatedly, calling it "Lane's imported labor" and "political mercenaries." The group was technically separate from the Evans campaign, but the Democratic incumbent defended it repeatedly by comparing it to the "Freedom Riders" of the 1960s, noting that its goal was to register and get people to vote.

Eric Nelson, Evans' campaign manager, called the Victory Fund "extremely helpful." Nelson noted that the Evans campaign had to spend most of its money on television and his field staff could only do so much mobilization. Having volunteers on the ground identifying and mobilizing supporters and marching in parades greatly benefited the campaign. Proof of that is more elusive, however.

Nelson noted that the Victory Fund had a very good organization in Adams County (Quincy), yet Evans received only 34 percent of its vote. Evans noted, "Perhaps there was nothing more we could have done, or maybe we would have done even worse without them."

Baker cited the Victory Fund as one the reasons for his loss along with eight weeks of negative ads and the national Democratic trends.

U.S. Rep. John Linder, chair of the NRCC, credited labor and the Victory Fund for Evans' win, but Linder also noted that the Democrats caught a "wave" nationwide, leading to their surprise five-seat pickup in the House.

Party campaigning by Democrats through the Kansas Coordinated Campaign in the state's 3rd District House race between incumbent Vince Snowbarger (R) and challenger Dennis Moore (D) demonstrated the benefits of a coordinated campaign strategy, which is allowed under the law.

According to Chris Esposito, Moore's campaign manager, the effort was organized and funded by the state Democratic Party and "allowed the Moore campaign to spend a maximum amount on television." The coordinated campaign's money was spent on phone banks, advance ballots and direct mail. For example, in most Kansas elections there are not party poll watchers present on election day. This year, Democratic poll watchers (not Republicans) could be found in many precincts throughout the district.

In one precinct, the poll watcher left and placed calls to individuals who had not voted by 3 p.m. Some targeted voters said they had been called by the party three or four times during the final two days. In one case, an individual who had yet to vote recalled being contacted at 6:15 p.m., 45 minutes before the polls closed.

"In retrospect," said Moore's campaign manager, "Snowbarger would have beat Moore without paid field organizers to execute the KCC [coordinated campaign] field plan."

A coordinated campaign can save the candidate money. For example, Moore raised and spent $1 million while the coordinated campaign raised and spent an additional $400,000.

INTEREST GROUP SPENDING

Interest group involvement was more than a fundraising foil for the parties. In our sample races, we found 111 active interest organizations. These groups ran 218 different ads on television or radio and mounted 258 phone banks or direct mail efforts. Most records show that groups used direct mail from pre-primary to the day of the election; they used phone banks more in the final month. Television ads aired throughout the election cycle, but most heavily in the final month and a half of campaigning.

Interest group involvement in 1998 was multifaceted, with some of the most important activities aimed at mobilizing voters for election day turnout. In our 16 races, many organizations used their local affiliates for help. For example, six state labor unions actively worked on Labor '98 campaign activities.

The use of outside money illustrates that parties and issue groups have multiple agendas, ranging from helping elect their candidates to pressing legislation. Some groups indicated they would continue to push their agendas through ads, even if tracking polls showed that they were hurting the candidate they presumably were trying to help. Other contests showed that despite a candidate's request that an interest group not join the campaign, the outside campaign went ahead.

A good example of how one group can have a significant presence was in Utah's 2nd District House race. Democrat Lily Eskelsen signed the term limits pledge while GOP incumbent Merrill Cook did not. Cook claimed that Howard Rich, President of U.S. Term Limits, called him and said that if he did not sign the pledge that it would put $100,000 into Eskelsen's campaign. Cook refused and Americans for Limited Terms spent $380,000 in the race: $250,000 on TV ads in the last three weeks, $100,000 on three mailers (sent to registered Republicans and independents), and $30,000 on phone banks.

One ad, tailored to the district, had ordinary citizens asserting that if Cook supported term limits, he should sign the pledge: "What's good for the goose is good for the gander," the spot said. The group's phone banks asked if term limits mattered to the voter called, and then informed the voter of the candidates' stands.

In other races, candidates are quick to take an early pledge so they can keep outside campaigners from showing up in support of their rivals.

U.S. Rep. Jim Maloney signed three pledges in 1998: the Citizens Flag Alliance, which works for a flag protection amendment to the Constitution; Americans for Tax Reform, which opposes increased corporate and individual income taxes; and U.S. Term Limits, which supports term limits.

Because Maloney took the pledges, these groups, and to an extent, their issues, were removed from the campaign.

Environmental groups, such as the Sierra Club and the League of Conservation Voters, were also very active. Each group spent over $5 million on selected races running issue ads on candidates supporting or opposing their environmental agenda.

According to the League of Conservation Voters project director, Gregory Green, the LCV spent the most money in the New Mexico 3rd Congressional District. Its ad was anti-GOP incumbent Bill Redmond, who had been placed on the group's Dirty Dozen list for his votes against approving the San Juan River for consideration as an American Heritage river and for his vote to postpone the Environmental Protection Agency's clean air standards for four more years.

The LCV produced a single 30-second ad that showed 138 times between October 1 and November 2. It spent $129,645 for air time. This ad got quite a bit of press attention, receiving over 18 hits across northern New Mexico newspapers.

The LCV felt the ad was effective; a voter poll indicated that it was well-received by voters and that Redmond's worst issue was the environment. At the same time, the environment was seen as Democrat Tom Udall's second most positive position. This was a marked change in attitudes toward Redmond and Udall from an earlier survey.

The LCV's efforts were not limited to broadcast. It also spent nearly $30,000 on direct mail, phone banking, person-to-person persuasion, and get-out-the-vote efforts. Its main strategy was to reduce Green Party candidate Carol Miller's support which came out of the Democratic base. It sent out letters in Spanish and English appealing for votes against Redmond and for Udall.

GROUND WAR

Issue advocacy in recent election cycles has received attention largely for the television air wars and radio advertisements. But in a low-turnout midterm election, an air war became less efficient, wasting many resources on apathetic voters. The most effective party soft money and issue advocacy efforts were aimed at voter identification and mobilization—the ground war.

Democratic Party committees and their allies in the Labor movement won the organizational battle. Voter turnout for the Democrats surged among African Americans in targeted states. For example, in 1994, blacks were 19 percent of Georgia's voters. In 1998, they made up 29 percent of the votes.

African-American turnout also dramatically increased in North Carolina, South Carolina and Illinois—securing victory in numerous key races. The

DCCC reserved $2 million for minority campaign activities, such as radio ads, direct mail and conference calls.

Republicans also mounted a ground war in competitive races, but it was overshadowed by the attention given to the NRCC's $10 million TV campaign on the Clinton/Lewinsky matter spent in the final days before the election.

Even though the ground war greatly impacted voter turnout, interest groups and parties are likely to continue to use the air war because of its power in agenda setting. Groups like the National Education Association were able to make education a major issue in the Iowa 3rd District race as the League of Conservation Voters used its environmental Dirty Dozen efforts to focus attention on the environment in key races.

Ground efforts by organized labor were particularly notable. The AFL-CIO spent $35 million in 1996 waging war against newly elected freshmen Republicans through broadcast issue advertising. It revised their strategy for 1998 to include fewer targeted races, more grassroots organization, greater voter mobilization and fewer television advertisements.

Labor budgeted $23 million in 1998, $18 million for the ground war and only $5 million for broadcast issue ads. Many of our sample races were among those targeted by labor in which their activities helped set the campaign tone.

The AFL-CIO's televised ads against Republican House member Vince Snowbarger, for example, were centered on Social Security and health care and ran in late September before either of the candidates ran television spots of their own. Of course, these ads set the campaign agenda in a manner compatible with the strategy of Snowbarger's challenger, Moore.

Indeed, the AFL-CIO ads, "officially" not coordinated with the Moore campaign, seemed almost to be lead-ins to Moore's own commercials in early October. For example, one ad invited viewers to call Snowbarger to register their protest. Approximately 15 minutes later, a Moore ad appeared talking about the candidate's support for Social Security and health care choice.

The major union effort, however, was the massive GOTV drive during the final three weeks of the campaign. Particularly impressive were the efforts of the labor-sponsored '98 Project, a coordinated, grassroots effort to mobilize liberal support in the district. The group, keeping a low profile and downplaying its labor connections in a strongly pro-business district, coordinated a number of extensive mass mailings during October, including fliers sent by other groups, such as the National Council of Senior Citizens. The tone was always anti-Snowbarger. Very sophisticated targeting was utilized. For example, a flier dealing with food programs for women and children went only to women in the 25–45 age category.

The state AFL-CIO, based in Topeka, was responsible for a number of mass mailings in the district. In the last weekend of the campaign, labor unions in the Kansas City, Kan., area (Wyandotte County) underwrote a massive GOTV effort, involving direct contact and phone banks.

A variety of outside groups also participated in the Nevada Senate election between incumbent Harry Reid (D) and challenger John Ensign (R).

The coordinated efforts of organized labor appeared decisive to many observers inside and outside of both parties and campaigns. Rather than spending large sums of money under the direction of the national AFL-CIO, local union leaders collaborated with each other, national leaders and the Democratic Party to mount a massive GOTV effort.

The union contribution to the race cannot be accounted for in dollar terms. According to a key union strategist, the effort cost less than $300,000. Aided by experienced national organizers and by hundreds of volunteers, organizers visited more than 30,000 households during the campaign. Each household was contacted at least three times by phone, mail or personal visit. Labor '98 made all the difference in Reid's razor-thin victory.

One of the most strategically important moves the Democratic Party made in its ground war emphasis was to target minority voters. Elections in Kentucky and South Carolina provide interesting snapshots of their tactics.

Jesse Jackson went to Kentucky to lend his support to Democratic candidates and to encourage voter turnout among African Americans. Some national and statewide Democratic leaders also accompanied Senate candidate Baesler on his October Victory '98 Train Trip around the state, tracing the 1948 trip of President Harry Truman. GOTV adds were run by the national party, DCCC, to target African Americans and women.

As part of this GOTV campaign, there were Hillary Clinton phone calls to approximately 30,000 women at a cost of about 45 cents each. Radio ads, phone calls and mailings were paid for by the DNC to the DCCC at a total cost of $25,000. In addition to Tipper Gore, Jackson came to the 6th District as well.

In 1998, South Carolina's voter turnout ranked 29th. In 1994, the state ranked 41st. Approximately 53 percent of the registered voters participated.

The key difference in turnout was among African-American voters. In 1994, African Americans constituted 17 percent of the total turnout; in 1998, they represented 25 percent.

Three of the top five counties in turnout held a majority of African-American voters. For example, Hampton County, which ranked first in turnout, gave Ernest Hollings (D) 79 percent of its vote. Hollings was re-elected by a 52.7 percent to 45.7 percent margin. Instrumental to this re-election, we found, was the GOTV effort of the Democratic Party and the 8 percent increase by African Americans in the voting population.

CONCLUSIONS

The unregulated and undisclosed campaign activities by parties and interest groups in 1998 were not well-covered by the local and state media. More broadly, the Annenberg Center found the media gave less attention to the 1998 elections than past midterm elections.

Voters in competitive contests were inundated with communications by mail, phone, print ads, and radio and television ads about the candidates. Voters find it hard to distinguish candidate ads from those run separately by their parties and also assume many issue advocacy ads are candidate commercials. Getting clear information on who the groups are and how much they are spending is difficult. The consequence for voters is a flood of persuasive ads from unknown sources.

For candidates, the involvement of outside groups is, as one candidate put it, "a double-edged sword." Candidates may benefit from the attack on their opponents, but they may also be harmed if the ads are too negative or if these groups bring baggage with them. The lack of accountability in non-candidate campaigning is a serious problem as is the inability of voters to find out who is attempting to persuade them.

We anticipate additional growth in the use of soft money and advocacy ads in the 2000 presidential elections and the 2002 midterm elections.

Interestingly, this same dynamic may prompt groups to pursue stronger direct campaign involvement in the presidential primaries of 2000. A group willing to spend $3 million to $4 million dollars in New Hampshire or Iowa on its issue could force its viewpoint into the campaign debate and impact candidate campaigns in a number of ways, helpful and harmful. Candidates, fearing this prospect, will not only want to raise money early, but will likely try to ally with friendly groups or PACs that can push issues favorable to them.

Parties will likely spend more of their resources on ground war tactics in the next election, and all party committees will assume they need to have even more soft money in the future than they had in the most recent past.

Candidates of the future will also assume that if they are in a competitive race, they will have a harder time controlling the message of the campaign, and that means they will need more money.

CAMPAIGN FINANCE REFORM AND THE CONSTITUTION: WHAT'S HOT IN THE COURTS

E. JOSHUA ROSENKRANZ

CONTEXT

Before 1971, there were virtually no limitations on campaign contributions and campaign expenditures. However, campaigns, especially presidential campaigns, were becoming increasingly expensive. In fact, after the 1968 presidential elections, the Democratic National Committee found itself nearly $10 million in debt. Increasingly, people started to worry that contributors to political campaigns were getting and would continue to get more attention from elected officials and political parties than regular constituents, who could not or would not contribute large sums of money.

As a result, Congress passed the Federal Election Campaign Act (FECA) in 1971, and amended it in 1974 after the Watergate scandal, in which campaign finance abuses figured prominently. FECA provided for partial funding for presidential campaigns if the candidates agreed to limit spending. It also mandated full reporting and strict limits on contributions and spending in federal elections. In 1976 the Supreme Court, viewing spending on federal elections as a form of speech, ruled that the spending limits part of FECA was unconstitutional because it violated the constitutional guarantee of freedom of speech.

In this selection, Rosenkranz summarizes the Supreme Court's 1976 ruling, *Buckley v. Valeo*, which is the ruling that most campaign finance issues revolve around today. He notes that while the Supreme Court did rule limits on campaign spending to be unconstitutional in that case, it did not rule limits on contributions unconstitutional. The court, he says, made a distinction between free speech based on spending and free speech based on contributing. It is a greater infringement on speech to limit spending than it is to limit contributing. Based on this understanding of *Buckley v. Valeo*, Rosenkranz discusses four hotly contested areas of campaign finance law: contributing limits, issue advocacy, soft money, and public financing, and guesses how the court would decide cases in these areas today.

● *THINK CRITICALLY* ●────────────────────────

1. Which of the four hotly contested areas of campaign finance law discussed by Rosenkranz is most in need of reform in your view?
2. In your view, is there an appearance of corruption in the current campaign finance system? If so, is that not justification enough to reform it? If no, explain why or why not.

Campaign finance reform and the Constitution. When I think of those two forces in the same breath, I cannot help but think of the recently released transcript of a radio communication between a U.S. naval ship and Canadian authorities off the coast of Newfoundland. Each insisted that the other "divert your course 15 degrees . . . to avoid a collision." After several exchanges of escalating hostility, with each authority refusing to budge, the American captain warned: "This is the Captain of . . . the aircraft carrier USS Lincoln, the second-largest ship in the U.S. Atlantic fleet. We are accompanied by three destroyers, three cruisers and numerous support vessels. I demand you change your course 15 degrees north, or counter-measures will be undertaken to ensure the safety of this ship." The Canadians responded, "This is a lighthouse. Your call."

The exchange between campaign finance activists and the courts this decade has often borne an uncanny resemblance to this transcript. Especially early in the decade, reformers forged ahead with damn-the-torpedoes resolve. Armed with the seemingly unstoppable power of public outrage and cynicism, they fashioned reforms that resonated with the average voter, but paid little heed to the First Amendment as interpreted by the Supreme Court. Reformers worked tirelessly to pass their reforms, but no sooner did the victory cry emerge from their lips than they were stopped dead in their tracks with a pronouncement from the proverbial immovable object, "This is a court."

Battle-scarred, reformers in recent years have become increasingly sensitive to First Amendment concerns. Yet the script remains much the same. Offering little guidance and less predictability, the courts are continuing to scuttle even the most sensitively drawn reforms. Opponents of reform have capitalized on the uncertainty. They greet any reform effort by invoking the First Amendment, as if the very invocation of the clause should stop us cold. Often their First Amendment claims are specious, at best, the logical equivalent of warning, "Better not budge. There's a lighthouse out there . . . somewhere."

Obviously, neither approach to constitutional analysis—"damn the torpedoes" nor "better not budge"—is particularly productive. My goal here is to sketch current campaign finance doctrine in order to put some of the current legal controversies in context.

THE *BUCKLEY* FRAMEWORK

The discussion on campaign finance reform and the Constitution begins, and often ends, with *Buckley v. Valeo*, the Supreme Court's 1976 opinion that dominates the field. In *Buckley*, the Supreme Court reviewed the 1974 post-Watergate amendments to the Federal Election Campaign Act. As passed by Congress, FECA was an intricate scheme of four integrated components.

1. Contribution caps—limits on how much a variety of political actors could put directly into each other's pockets.
2. Mandatory spending limits—separate caps: (a) on how much a candidate could spend of his own personal wealth; (b) on the amount a campaign could spend from funds raised in discrete amounts; and (c) on the amount an individual could spend independently advocating for or against a candidate.
3. Public financing (for presidential elections)—conditioned on voluntary spending limits.
4. Stringent disclosure and reporting requirements.

Buckley is most well known for striking mandatory spending limits of all three varieties. But it is just as important to understand that the Court upheld each of the other components of the integrated regulatory scheme. How in the world could the Supreme Court have upheld contribution limits, yet strike spending limits as categorically impermissible? The Court began with the observation that money is the fuel for speech, and, as such, limits on spending or giving money call into play First Amendment concerns.

Next, *Buckley* held that contributions and expenditures are different under the First Amendment. As it does in so many areas of constitutional doctrine, the Court in this context balanced the importance of the speech right against the weightiness of the government's reasons for wanting to infringe on speech.

As to the speech value of these two activities: A contribution, the Court held, has little speech value. It is a mere "signal" of support whose message does not depend very much on the size of the contribution. Spending, the Court believed, has greater speech value. It is much more akin to direct speech, because every dollar spent will actually increase the size of an audience, the number of issues covered, and the depth of their exploration. Or so the Court thought.

As to the reasons for regulating: The Court concluded that contributions are more corrupting than spending. The Court easily saw that a candidate could be corrupted by large contributions. In contrast, the Court could not see how a candidate could be corrupted by unlimited spending. The Court rejected the notion that a candidate might give special consideration to a supporter who independently spends $1 million on television ads supporting his election rather than writing a much smaller check directly to the campaign. Nor did the Court recognize any danger that the endless money chase might corrupt a candidate's agenda or priorities.

Finally, *Buckley* held that preventing corruption (or guarding against the appearance of corruption) is the only rationale that will justify any restrictions on campaign finance. Specifically, the Court rejected any notion that the government might limit the flow of money into elections in the name of equality. The Court famously opined that it is improper to limit the speech of some in order to advance the speech of others.

The upshot of the Court's analysis is that spending limits of any sort are unconstitutional—unless they are imposed as a condition of the receipt of public funds, so that candidates remain free to reject them. But contribution limits are constitutional, so long as they are not set so low as to lose the justification of combating corruption.

I used to say *Buckley* left us with a world where we are basically playing baseball with a huge oak tree in the middle of the field—and whenever you hit the tree, it's an automatic out. But *Buckley* left a lot of questions unanswered, and increasingly the lower courts have turned the case into one of those trees in the *Wizard of Oz* that move freely and snatch balls right out of mid air. To make matters worse, the lower courts are all over the place on many important issues, and the Supreme Court has remained conspicuously silent in the face of the confusion.

This phenomenon makes it hard to predict how the courts will rule, ultimately, with regard to any particular regulatory device. The best I could hope to do is summarize the most hotly contested legal issues right now in campaign finance law and offer some prognostications of how they are likely to play out when they ultimately wind their way up to the Supreme Court.

CONTRIBUTION LIMITS

Perhaps the area that has gotten the most judicial attention of late has been the evaluation of lower contribution limits. Exploiting the latitude to set contribution limits, reformers over the past decade have taken to racheting down contribution limits across the nation. But recall that *Buckley* did not say that *all* contribution limits are constitutional. It held that contribution limits are constitutional as long as they do not go too low. How low is too low? The Court shed no light on this question, except to say that a contribution limit is too low when it becomes "a difference in kind" rather than "a difference in amount"— whatever that means.

Although the Supreme Court declared that courts should defer to legislative judgments on such line-drawing exercises, the courts have been second-guessing the judgments of legislatures and initiatives. Increasingly, the courts have been striking not just the $100 contribution limits that were in vogue for a time, but any limits that depart from the $1,000 limits sustained by *Buckley*.

Even limits fashioned after those approved in *Buckley* are now vulnerable. The case to watch is *Nixon v. Shrink Missouri Government PAC,* which will be argued before the Supreme Court in the fall of 1999. At issue are Missouri's contribution limits, which are currently set at $1,075 for statewide races. Though these contribution limits are higher than the current federal limits, and higher than the very limits the Supreme Court upheld in *Buckley*, a federal appellate court sitting in St. Louis struck the limits as too low. The rationale? A dollar doesn't buy what it used to. What was acceptable to the Supreme Court in 1976, the appellate court concluded, will no longer do. For the first time in history, a court has concluded that constitutional rights must be adjusted for inflation.

I predict the Supreme Court will disagree. I doubt the Supreme Court has the appetite to weaken the hand of legislatures that are grappling with how to guard against corruption or the appearance of corruption, nor the appetite to sit as a super-legislature second-guessing exactly where to draw the line for each race.[1]

My hope is that the Supreme Court will use this case as a vehicle to resolve several baseline analytical questions that are hopelessly splitting the courts. The courts are not speaking with a single voice on questions as fundamental as whether the state must actually prove that large contributions can corrupt, or appear to corrupt, candidates, and, if so, whether the proof must directly support the threshold level the legislature chooses. Nor are the courts in sync on whether a contribution limit, say $500, is valid or invalid in the abstract, or whether its validity depends upon other factors such as the size of the race. The Supreme Court did accept, quite uncritically, the same contribution limits for congressional races as for presidential races. But there is something a bit odd about applying the same analysis both to a $100 contribution limit in Arkansas legislative races that average $22,000 and to a $100 limit in a statewide or a nationwide race than runs in the millions.

These and other questions will continue to bedevil the lower courts unless the Supreme Court seizes this opportunity to clarify them.

ISSUE ADVOCACY

The single thorniest legal issue right now involves so-called "issue advocacy." Is it permissible for government to require disclosure or otherwise regulate electioneering ads—a corporate sponsored ad, for example, that trashes a political candidate by name on the eve of the election—that are thinly disguised as generic political speech?

Buckley and later cases have made this much clear: It is permissible to divide the universe of political speech into two categories—electioneering and everything else. Elections are special. Because of the unique role they play in our democracy, the First Amendment will tolerate regulations in this special context that it would never tolerate in other contexts. When it comes to electioneering, we can limit the source of funds, we can limit fundraising (including an outright prohibition on corporate and union funds), and we can require disclosure of amounts raised and spent.

The question is exactly how we are permitted to define "electioneering" for these purposes. Is it limited to magic words, such as "vote for," "vote against," "elect," or "defeat"? Or may a legislature craft a careful definition that extends beyond those magic words? A lot rides on where exactly the legislature puts the line, and how the courts assess it. If the definition is too narrow, we may as well have no campaign finance laws at all; any sophisticated player could figure out how to craft an electioneering message that would evade election laws. If it is too broad, we risk infringing on speech that should be fully protected—speech for which the special rules governing elections ought not apply.

Put another way, the question comes down to this: May a legislature treat as campaign ads commercials that look, smell, waddle, and quack like campaign ads? Or are we stuck—as a matter of inalterable constitutional command—with a mechanical definition of electioneering that looks only for certain magic words?

Right now, the courts seem to be split, with the weight of authority tilting a bit toward the more restrictive approach. But the lower courts are simply reading tea leaves as to how the Supreme Court will eventually come out. This is a question that only the Supreme Court will be able to answer definitively. My instinct is that when push comes to shove, the Supreme Court will not sanction a rule that says it is permissible to regulate electioneering, but only if we define the concept so narrowly that no regulation could possibly be effective.

SOFT MONEY

A close cousin of the electioneering question is the debate over regulating soft money, the mega-contributions that political parties raise from wealthy interests, corporations, and unions. Lately, these funds have been funneled into ads—again, they tend to be ads aired on the eve of an election attacking particular candidates—that are unmistakably designed to influence elections. Unlike the question of defining electioneering, however, the question whether the government can limit the size and source of contributions to *political parties* is as close to a no-brainer as one finds in First Amendment law.

To see why, let us consider an important case that has, oddly, received little attention. The Republican National Committee (RNC) and the Ohio Democratic Party have challenged the current minimally intrusive restrictions on how soft money is spent, regulations requiring political parties simply to mix a certain amount of hard money into their soft money spending. The attack on these allocation formulas is based on a breathtaking expansive reading of the First Amendment. In essence, the RNC is arguing that they have the right to raise unlimited amounts from any source, corporate, union, or foreign; rely on candidates to raise it; and even spend it in coordination with candidates—so long as the party does not spend the money on ads that use "magic words" such as "vote for" or "vote against." If this theory is vindicated, we can, of course, forget about McCain-Feingold; its soft money ban is far more onerous than the restrictions now under attack.

More importantly, if the RNC prevails, we may as well abolish all campaign finance regulation. Contribution limits will be meaningless if a candidate can just set up a segregated account under the party's auspices and raise money that he can then spend on his own campaign as he wishes. Worse yet, if the RNC is right, then there is nothing to stop a candidate from setting up his own issue campaign, raising enormous sums of completely unrestricted contributions for that campaign, and running his entire election campaign out of that fund. All he would be required to do would be to eschew words like "vote for" or "vote against"—words that are rarely found in modern campaigns anyway.

Seem farfetched? Hardly. At this very moment, presidential aspirants for 2000 are establishing and running issue campaigns. They establish funds in Virginia, which, courtesy of its lax campaign finance rules, has become the Cayman Islands of campaign finance. The candidates are raising money for these issue campaigns in contributions—often in the six figures—that far exceed the contribution limits imposed by FECA. Many of the gifts are from corporate entities and others who are prohibited from contributing to elections. Since these groups are styled as issue groups, they do not disclose the sources of the money or their expenditures. Yet, for each of them, the "issue" seems to be what a good guy the candidate is and how compelling his ideas are. If this is, indeed, legal, candidates need not set up campaign committees. They can simply run their entire election campaigns through their issue funds.

Whether or not the current practice is legal—and I firmly believe it is not— there is no question that Congress may act definitively to end both this practice and the raising of soft money by political parties. For this entire century it has been clear that Congress can preclude corporations (and later, unions) from influencing elections by giving money to candidates or to political parties. And for a generation, it has been clear that Congress can limit the size of contributions by very wealthy players to candidates or to parties. Plus, the Supreme Court has made clear that a legislature can impose restrictions that are designed to ensure that other valid regulations are not evaded. These rules converge to mean that a ban on soft money—which is nothing more than a limit on the amount that any individual could give to a political party and a bar to corporate or labor contributions—would be upheld.

PUBLIC FINANCING

As I noted above, the Supreme Court made it clear in Buckley that a legislature is allowed to entice candidates to cap their own expenditures voluntarily, even though it cannot require them to do it by direct command (or penalize them for not doing it). Because public financing has only recently come into vogue in the states, the courts have yet to resolve numerous constitutional questions that will soon come to the fore. The questions fall into three main categories.

The first set of questions revolves around the voluntariness of the spending limit. Can a deal be too sweet to be considered voluntary? The deal for the presidential general elections has been so attractive that no major party candidate has ever turned it down. Yet, the Supreme Court upheld it as voluntary. That would suggest that whether a spending limit is voluntary or not should be judged on the basis of whether candidates who opt out are in some way punished, not on the basis of some judgment that the rewards of participating are too good to be true. Also subject to challenge have been various techniques—sometimes derisively called "Scarlet Letters"—for identifying those candidates who opt in or opt out of the spending limits. Over the next few years, we can expect cases to address whether those techniques—designations on the ballot or on campaign literature—amount to impermissible penalties for those who opt out.

The second set of questions revolves around so-called "trigger provisions," which increase the public financing available to certain candidates depending upon the conduct of others. Is it permissible, for example, for a state to increase the grant to a candidate who accepts spending limits when his opponent crosses a certain spending threshold? How about increasing the public subsidy to a candidate when an independent speaker spends a considerable sum to attack him? Do those extra grants "punish" the speech of candidates who opt out of public financing, or the speech of independent voices? Traditionally, the grant of subsidies to one group has never been thought of as a punishment of the speech of another, but in this context, the grant depends directly on exactly how much speech that other utters.

The third set of questions concerns the other strings that can be attached to public funding (or other government benefits, such as free television). Can a legislature impose strings that have to do with the content or nature of the political speech rather than with spending? Traditionally, the courts have been hostile to government efforts to influence the content of speech. It seems clear, for example, that a legislature could not condition a grant of funds or resources on a promise to run a positive campaign. But what about a promise to debate? Or format restrictions on length of ads or on the willingness of a candidate to appear in them as a talking head? Such provisions are sure to be tested in the courts.

Scores of other legal issues are wending their way through the courts. Reformers are experimenting with state laws at a fevered pace, unprecedented since the post-Watergate era. All along, though, they are haunted by a vague warning bellowing in the mist from the courts: "This is the Constitution. Your call."

NOTE

1. I hasten to note, in the interest of full disclosure, that my colleagues at the Brennan Center represent a party to the case before the Supreme Court.

SECTION SEVEN

INTEREST GROUPS AND PARTICIPATION

HEAD NOTES/SECTION QUESTIONS

In reading #26, David Magleby and Marianne Holt say that one of the results of soft money and issue advocacy advertising may be a change from candidate-centered campaigns to interest group- and party-centered campaigns. Interestingly enough, campaigns used to be very party-centered and not very candidate-centered. What caused the change was that the size of the federal government got too big for one or two political parties to effectively represent all of the varied interests in society. This happened sometime in the 1960s, and that is when campaigns began to become more candidate-centered than party-centered.

The size of the federal government was relatively small (by today's standards) prior to the Great Depression and World War II. Those two events, however, helped the federal government grow rather large, and after World War II, the size of the federal government (and federal budget) did not shrink, as some thought it should, but rather continued to grow. In the 1960s, the federal government launched a war on poverty that caused the government to grow even larger. In fact, by the mid-1960s, the federal government was so large and doing so many different things, that the two dominant political parties simply could not represent all of the various interests that people had.

Thus, people (and businesses and corporations, etc.) began looking elsewhere for help in dealing with the large (and growing larger and more powerful) federal government. It was only natural for them to turn to, and form, interest groups, groups of people who share a common goal. After all, interest groups were already in existence in Washington anyway, and they were (and still are) an effective way to engage in advocacy at the federal level. In 1960, there were only about 500 representatives of interest groups registered with the government. By the turn of the century, that number had risen to nearly 15,000.

Interest groups have replaced, in some ways, the political parties as ways for groups of people to look out for common goals or protect governmental programs from which they benefit. The selection by Andrew Lawler provides a good example of why interest groups form. If both Democrats and Republicans in Congress are interested in cutting the scientific community's budgets, the scientific community suddenly has a common goal of protecting its budgets from congressional cuts. The scientific community would do a better job of protecting its budgets by forming interest groups to advocate on its behalf than by aligning with either of the two political parties. Why? Neither of the two political parties could effectively represent the goals of the scientific community, because some of the members of each party might be for cutting their budgets. However, as the reading by Lind suggests, people in government have to be careful not to let lobbyists, the agents of interest groups, influence them in ways that are illegal or unethical.

Interestingly enough, just as people have found it more worthwhile to both join and form interest groups to advance their goals, they have also stopped participating in civic life as individuals. The rate of civic activity, everything from voting to attending school board meetings, is down. The reading by Hofferber argues for greater attention to participation in politics, especially local politics.

As you read these selections, keep the following questions in mind:

1. Do you think interest groups do a better or worse job than political parties in representing common goals and pressing government to help fulfill those goals?
2. Why do you think that the rate of individual participation in politics is down at the same time that the number of interest groups is on the rise?

LEARN MORE ON THE WEB

Project Vote Smart
   http://www.vote-smart.org/

League of Women Voters
   http://www.lwv.org/

Center for Responsive Politics
   http://www.crp.org/index.html-ssi

Common Cause
   http://www.commoncause.org/

Government and Politics on the Net Project
   http://www.sscf.ucsb.edu/~survey1/

American Association of Retired People
   http://aarp.org/

SELLING SCIENCE: AT WHAT PRICE?

ANDREW LAWLER

CONTEXT

In Washington, interest groups proliferate. Interest groups are collections of people (retired people, former military officers, members of labor organizations, small business owners, etc.) who share a common goal and organize themselves to press government to help them fulfill that goal. For small businesses, the common goal may be lower taxes and less governmental regulation. For members of labor unions, the common goal may be better wages and safer working conditions.

When interest groups press government for action, they are lobbying. Lobbying is simply the process whereby interest groups attempt to influence legislation and convince political leaders to support their goals. Interest groups hire people to do this for them and those people are called lobbyists. Individual interest groups come and go depending on whether the group's goals are affected by something government does or does not do. For example, the scientific community has not historically had to form interest groups. However, as Andrew Lawler notes in this article from *Science*, that is changing.

Lawler recounts how the scientific community has turned to traditional lobbying and other interest group tactics in an effort to preserve its federal allocation of research money. With Washington interested in reducing the federal budget deficit, the scientific community worries it will suffer major cuts if it does not get more involved in the budget process. Thus, for the first time ever, the scientific community is beginning to do things that other interest groups have done for years. These activities include lobbying members of Congress, providing campaign contributions, holding fundraisers, and rating individual members of Congress on their votes related to the scientific community's concerns. Some in the scientific community worry that these efforts could be counterproductive to science.

● *THINK CRITICALLY* ●

1. Do you think science should have to "make its case" for federal money like everyone else? Why or why not?

> 2. What are some of the potential downsides to what the scientific community is doing? Could you see part of the scientific community aligning with the Republicans and another part with Democrats because of this?

The spacious conference room was filled to capacity with gray-suited university and association lobbyists eager to hear a debate entitled: "Einstein in Gucci Gulch—Can (Should) Science Make Its Case in Washington?" In fact, the size of the crowd disturbed one of the speakers at last month's conference, sponsored by the American Enterprise Institute (AEI). "I worry there is so much interest in this topic," says attorney Ken Kay, noting that the need to lobby the government would be so obvious to most other interest groups that they would see no point in debating the issue.

Not scientists. Until recently, universities and scientific societies assumed that the best way to win their share of federal dollars was to make the low-keyed argument that new knowledge is vital to society and a strong economy. Research would get its fair share of a growing federal pot, so the theory went, and academics could stay above the political fray. But the harsh fiscal environment confronting the 105th Congress that convened this month is forcing many science activists to adopt more aggressive tactics. Among the new approaches are rating lawmakers, setting up networks to alert scientists of pending legislation, and spending enough to make sure the voice of science is heard in the corridors of power. "We've got to do a heck of a lot more lobbying," says Donald Langenberg, chancellor of the University of Maryland. "Our old arguments and our old ways don't work anymore."

However, others say that such efforts could damage the typically bipartisan support science has enjoyed since World War II. "You start with considerable goodwill," Robert Walker, former chair of the House Science Committee, told the AEI group. "I don't think you could find a [congressional] member who is antiscience," says Walker, the Pennsylvania Republican who retired last month after 20 years in office. Playing politics, like other groups do, will only alienate lawmakers, he adds. But even Walker and others who back a more conservative approach to lobbying encourage university administrators and researchers to keep their representatives and senators better informed about progress in science and technology.

The tension within the community stems from the growing belief that lawmakers are finally serious about eliminating the federal deficit—and that they plan to do so largely by cutting domestic discretionary spending. Although that category represents only about one-fifth of the $1.2 trillion federal budget, it includes all of the $35 billion spent on civilian science. In that environment, say lawmakers, academics pleading earnestly for increases that match or exceed inflation are living in the past. "Scientists have not grasped reality: Dollars don't fall out of the sky anymore," says Representative Steven Schiff (R–NM), who chairs the House Science Committee's basic research panel.

COUNTING VOTES

One group that believes it understands the new realities is Science Watch Inc., created last year by a group of senior scientists to analyze the voting records of House members in the last Congress. The result—a report card on 30 science-related votes that found Democrats were solidly pro-science while Republicans were generally unsupportive (*Science*, 27 September 1996, p. 1793)—sparked a controversy that suggests how perilous this kind of approach to lobbying can be for researchers. "It's a case study in good intentions gone awry," says Norm Ornstein, resident scholar at AEI.

Those results, coming just weeks before the congressional elections, were praised by Democrats but denounced by Republicans like Walker, who accused the group of "overt subjectivity." Walker says the report card was really a referendum on Democratic policies rather than on science. Schiff and other Republicans agree that the study was unnecessarily divisive.

Roland Schmitt, a past chair of the National Science Board and chair of Science Watch, says that partisan politics played no role in the report. "The idea that the Democrats put us up to this is 100% totally false," he says. "At no time was there any [analytical] input from any political party or any congressional staff." But Robert Palmer, minority staff director for the panel, says that he advised Science Watch in its search for data because his boss, Representative George Brown (D–CA), has long advocated such a report card. Palmer adds, however, that he did not choose which votes to focus on. Republican staffers say they were not involved at all in the report.

Apart from the controversy over Science Watch's methods and objectivity, some science administrators oppose the very concept of rating lawmakers on their support for science. "I have real doubts about public lists," says Cornelius Pings, president of the Association of American Universities (AAU), which represents 60 research-intensive universities. "They may make enemies where there are no real enemies." Charles Vest, president of the Massachusetts Institute of Technology and a member of the President's Council of Advisers on Science and Technology, told *Science* he worries that the effort was "counterproductive."

But Erich Bloch, former director of the National Science Foundation, defends the idea, if not its implementation. "Science Watch is a wake-up call to the community, although there was much wrong in the first attempt," says Bloch, who is on the organization's board. Kay, a lawyer with Podesta Associates who has worked closely with a number of science and technology groups, says the message should be: "Don't give up the attempt to energize the community—but do it better."

Some research organizations have taken that message to heart over the past few years. The Federation of American Societies for Experimental Biology (FASEB), for example, has emerged in recent years as a lobbying powerhouse on behalf of funding increases for the National Institutes of Health (NIH). "A decision was made several years ago to put a strong emphasis on advocacy of biomedical research," says FASEB executive director Michael Jackson. And the organization is spending money to back up that rhetoric: One year ago, the group set aside $1.5 million for a 3-year series of public affairs projects, including the hiring of a lobbyist.

FASEB has a research and analysis operation to keep track of issues and avoid surprises, and it prods members to make frequent contact with lawmakers. Last fall, it set up a system to reach thousands of university biologists around the country via e-mail to warn them about budget and policy fights. After one notice was sent out about an impending congressional budget decision on NIH, over 1000 letters deluged Capitol Hill urging support for the institutes. And FASEB's activities are bolstered by many other groups. For example, a nonprofit advocacy organization called Research!America has commissioned polls and surveys that record a high level of interest among Americans in greater federal support for biomedical research.

Jackson points to NASA and to defense contractors as models that scientists should consider in toning up their political muscle. NASA has a well-established public relations network and a mission that captured the imagination of a generation of Americans, Jackson notes, while contractors are not shy about touting their role in providing the advanced technology that the nation needs to defend its borders and its interests. In contrast, the science and university community has tended to believe that "its virtues are self-evident," says Langenberg. "There's the feeling that it is demeaning" to worry about politics. He says that while Pings might get a decent response from AAU members if he sends out an urgent notice, "it's hard to generate a flood of 50,000 telegrams."

LEADING FROM STRENGTH

But Western Union and electronic mail aren't the only ways to be effective in politics. Two of the greatest assets that the scientific community holds, say Kay, Bloch, Pings, and others, are its high credibility with the public and lawmakers, and the large, almost ubiquitous presence of its major employer—the university. Some, like Vest, sense an increased willingness over the past few years to marshal such clout. His university, for example, has begun to convene meetings with congressional staffers to discuss a particular topic. But others like Langenberg are skeptical that the implications of the federal budget squeeze have sunk in.

Schiff believes that scientists cannot wait to overhaul their message and their tactics. "People have to pull together a more detailed case about what direction research is taking and why it is important," he says. "And the case has to be more than clichés." Arguing that more funding for science today will provide bigger paybacks in the future, he says, is trite and, even if true, doesn't set science apart from the rest of those seeking federal funds.

Whether researchers cope successfully with the changing fiscal environment in Washington will depend not just on what they say, but also their willingness to sell it. "There is a reluctance to do the hard, slogging work to win the hearts and minds of elected officials," Langenberg says. Kay thinks that the community can learn a lesson from the Science Watch imbroglio. "The bottom line," he says, "is that if you are going to be political, you'd better be good."

WASHINGTON MEAL TICKET

MICHAEL LIND

CONTEXT

There are thousands of interest groups in Washington that employ thousands of lobbyists and support staff to look out for their goals and influence the course of public policy. One of the chief ways that interest groups and lobbyists attempt to influence the course of public policy is through campaign contributions. Another way that lobbyists attempt to influence the course of public policy is by cultivating personal relationships with policy makers. In a world where thousands of lobbyists are attempting to influence policy, it helps to have personal connections.

However, policy makers (elected officials and their staff, high government official, etc.) have to be careful about the kinds of relations they have with lobbyists. One reason they have to be careful is the appearance of an improper relationship. The public often believes that votes are available to the highest bidder, and if an elected official is thought to being too close to a lobbyist, that might reinforce the public's perception. In order to quell public perception, Congress passed the Lobbying Disclosure Act of 1995. This law required lobbyists to register with Congress, report who they worked for, the issues they were interested in lobbying government about, and estimate their pay for lobbying, among other things. In addition, the House and the Senate both strengthened their rules related to members and staffers accepting gifts from lobbyists.

In this selection, Michael Lind looks at the Senate Ethics Manual, a 562-page rule book governing relations between lobbyists and Senators or their staffers. He points out several areas where Senate rules on accepting gifts are easily circumvented by crafty lobbyists. He concludes that the ethics manual has both clarified what lobbyists, Senators, and Senate staffers can and cannot do and also how to break the rules.

┌───┐
● *THINK CRITICALLY* ●───

1. If you could add one rule to the Senate Ethics Manual, what would it be? How do you think your rule would play out in reality?
2. Interest groups play an important role in Washington. Can you think of a way that interest groups can do what they do without spending money on elected officials as they do?
└───┘

Far beneath the Dirksen Senate Office Building, just a few paces from the subway that transports senators and their staffers through the tunnels beneath Capitol Hill, the dining room available to the Senate staff doesn't present, at least not at first glance, the appearance of a public trough. The doors open through an entrance beneath raised letters that spell, with an economy that belies the government's reputation for waste, CAFETERIA, into what might be mistaken for an upscale Luby's in one of those states with square corners, or the restaurant of a two-star hotel in New Zealand.

Having come to talk to a Senate legislative assistant, an acquaintance of long standing, about what changes the 1996 Senate gift ban had effected in the buying of meals and other favors for senators dear to one's heart or self-interest, I remarked on the unimpressiveness of the restaurant: not at all the sort of place in which I could imagine tax exemptions being bought or sold.

"The rules have cut out a lot of the more blatant abuses," the aide told me. A soberly dressed, trim man in early middle age, he had the quiet, measured voice of someone who deals frequently with toddlers, or senators. "Back before the gift ban passed, there was a senator from a certain western state who spent an entire evening dining and drinking with a bunch of his cronies at one of the better Washington restaurants. When the check came, the senator phoned a lobbyist at home, woke him up, and ordered him to get his butt down to the restaurant and take care of the bill. You don't see that sort of thing anymore."

Certainly not in the Senate cafeteria. The fare—rice, potatoes, spinach, macaroni and cheese, mummified fried chicken, and lettuce that appeared to have been shaved from scuba-diving flippers—was as modest as the surroundings. Each meal was priced below ten dollars, and here, I thought, was proof that populist rage at the corrupt political class was overblown. If only those mad-as-hell retirees in Florida who speed-dial C-Span to denounce their elected representatives could see the Blue Plate Special in the basement of Dirksen, their suspicions about Beltway insiders would vanish.

Or so, for a fleeting moment, I believed.

"Here's the scam," the legislative assistant explained, after we had ordered drinks from a waitress and were standing in line at the trough, rather like the hogs wearing vests and watch chains in those old Thomas Nast cartoons. "The meals here are priced below ten dollars apiece, so they don't count for purposes of the gift ban. If you're a Senate staffer and a lobbyist takes you out to eat at a fancy restaurant, that counts toward the total you're permitted to receive from one source during the year. But if you eat here it's all off the books."

"So in theory a lobbyist could buy you a meal here in the Senate cafeteria every day, and it would be perfectly legal?"

The legislative assistant nodded. "There's a popular saying around here: We respect the rules, *as written*."

I. IS THE TROUGH HALF EMPTY OR HALF FULL?

Curious about what other gift-giving measures might still be available to today's working lobbyist, I secured for myself a copy of the 562-page *Senate Ethics Manual* and undertook an earnest examination of the rules.

> (1) No Member, officer, or employee of the Senate shall knowingly accept a gift except as provided in this rule.
> (2) A Member, officer, or employee may accept a gift (other than cash or cash equivalent) which the Member, officer, or employee reasonably and in good faith believes to have a value of less than $50, and a cumulative value from one source during a calendar year of less than $100. No gift with a value below $10 shall count toward the $100 annual limit. No formal recordkeeping is required by this paragraph, but a Member, officer, or employee shall make a good faith effort to comply with this paragraph.
>
> SENATE RULE 35.1 (A)

> [T]he term "gift" means any gratuity, favor, discount, entertainment, hospitality, loan, forbearance, or other item having monetary value. The term includes gifts of services, training, transportation, lodging, and meals, whether provided in kind, by purchase of a ticket, payment in advance, or reimbursement after the expense has been incurred.
>
> SENATE RULE 35.2 (B)(1)

Like all rules or laws, even the simplest, these have required a certain degree of interpretation, and to that end the Senate Select Committee on Ethics has provided some minor masterpieces of the hermeneutical art. To wit:

> EXAMPLE 1. Over the course of one year, company Z offers Senator B the following gifts: in January, theater tickets worth $45, in April, a paper-weight worth $8.50; in September, a bottle of wine worth $40; and in December, a crystal vase worth $35. The paperweight does not count towards the $100 aggregate because it is worth less than $10. All the other gifts count. If the Senator accepts the theater tickets and the wine, he must return the crystal vase to avoid exceeding the gift limit.

Such examples are of immense value to the lobbyist, not so much for the information they convey but because of what they imply: that despite demands from right, left, and center that our dirty political system be cleaned up, despite cries from Ralph Nader, Jerry Brown, Common Cause, the Perotistas, and the Buchanan brigades alike, the result has been the reinvention not of government but of the seventh-grade word problem. Which is not to say that the rules are entirely free of real snares for the gift taker. Consider the "hors d'oeuvres" rule:

> Section 1(c)(22) allows a Member, officer, or employee to accept food or other refreshments of a nominal value that are offered not as part of a meal. The Committee

has adopted a reasonable, common sense interpretation of this exception, to include a reception where the attendees consume food (typically, hors d'oeuvres) or drink while standing up, as opposed to a sit-down meal; and a "continental" style breakfast, where coffee and donuts, bagels, etc., are served, as opposed to service of a hot meal.

This raises all sorts of troubling questions. What if a senator took one of those little hot-dog thingies on a toothpick from the caterer—but *sat down* while consuming it? And what about this curious opposition between "a hot meal" and a "'continental' style breakfast, where coffee and donuts, bagels, etc. are served"? Is one to assume that continental-style coffee is served cold? Would the tender of a bagel still warm from the toaster confront the Senate member or staffer with a politico-ethical dilemma? Could a career in public service be derailed by a doughnut?

But just as I began to think that it was no longer possible to feed a senator or Senate staffer in anything approaching pre-gift-ban style, I came upon the following:

(1) A Member, officer, or employee may accept an offer of free attendance at a widely attended convention, conference, symposium, forum, panel discussion, dinner, viewing, reception, or similar event, provided by the sponsor of the event, if—

(A) the Member, officer, or employee participates in the event as a speaker or a panel participant, by presenting information related to Congress or matters before Congress, or by performing a ceremonial function appropriate to the Member's, officer's, or employee's official position; or

(B) attendance at the event is appropriate to the performance of the official duties or representative function of the Member, officer, or employee.

SENATE RULE 35.1 (D)

Under the "widely attended event" exemption, a lobbyist can pay for an expensive meal at The Monocle or The Capital Grille, and as long as there are enough people in attendance and the subject of the discussion has even the remotest connection to the work the Senate staffer is doing, the gift ban does not apply. A lobbyist can buy a Senate aide lunch in the Senate cafeteria, then later that evening he can pay for the staffer's dinner. And we're not just talking about a warmed-over buffet of the sort one finds in the basement of Dirksen. We're talking a three-course dinner at a big table in a private dining room with waiters who hold the platter on your left side and say absolutely nothing while you accidentally scoop out so much of the foie gras that there isn't enough left to go around. The only catch seems to be that witnesses are required.

II. COFFEE, TEA, OR PORK?

Foreign lobbyists should keep in mind that although campaign contributions and similar cash exchanges are now frowned upon, gifts of free travel are still encouraged.

The Foreign Gifts and Decorations Act (5 U.S.C. section 7342) permits the acceptance from foreign governments of gifts of travel or expenses for travel taking place entirely outside the United States if such acceptance is appropriate, consistent with the interests of the United States and is permitted by the Senate Select

Committee on Ethics (as the employing agency for Members, officers, and employees of the Senate) . . .

The only tangible barriers to this sort of gift are that papers need to be filed: the gift taker must inform the Senate Select Committee within thirty days of accepting a junket, and the gift giver must seek approval from the United States Information Agency. Fortunately, such requests are seldom denied, and, at least on the staffer's part, the hassle of paperwork is a small price to pay for a jaunt across the sea.

Asian countries have a reputation for bankrolling the best junkets, and on some of these a lowly Senate staffer can get first-class passage, a suite in a luxury hotel with a pool on the roof, even a butler. All the staffer has to do is attend a few meetings, and then he or she can spend the rest of the trip sightseeing and shopping.

In truth, a lot of these staffers have no business going on trips abroad, and the rules suggest that Senate travelers be "experts in fields of specialized knowledge or skill, and other influential or distinguished persons . . ." But the real experts on international issues often don't have time to go, and if they do, they don't have time to shop and lie around by the pool. Hence, in the spirit of eliminating waste, it makes more sense to send an unimportant staffer.

III. HAVE SOME LUMBER, SIR

Food and travel are the most obvious gift-giving opportunities, but the rules provide a variety of others. For instance, the lobbyist will find it remarkably easy to get around the restrictions on giving staffers tickets to special events.

EXAMPLE 22. The Washington Press Club invites Members to attend its annual Press Awards dinner, which will be attended by representatives of numerous press organizations, and their spouses. The Press Club will provide two tickets to each Member interested in attending, one for the Member, and one for the spouse. The Members may accept the tickets, and may bring their spouses.

Say you're a major corporation, and you want to invite a staffer to a gala dinner put on by a nonprofit organization or foundation. You can't buy tickets to the event and give them to the staffer, but you can give a list of names to the foundation and have the foundation invite the staffer. The big night arrives, and the staffer is sitting right there at the table with you!

This can be done with tickets to sporting events as well. Let's say a major tennis tournament will be played in the Washington area. A lobbyist can't invite the Senate staffer directly, so he gets the tournament's sponsor to invite the staffer to watch the match from the skybox. For a typical Senate staffer of modest means, this might be the closest he's ever going to get to luxury. All the proles are out there sweating in the stands, trying to get the popcorn vendor's eye, and here he is in the air-conditioned suite with caterers offering exquisite finger food on toothpicks. There may even be celebrities on hand, though the Senate Select Committee on Ethics seemingly has taken steps to lessen this incentive by assuring Senate staffers that the very people they work for are, in fact, celebrities. As a result, senators may be the only class of individuals in our society who have been certified "celebrities" by the federal government:

EXAMPLE 30. The sponsor of a charitable golf tournament invites several Senators, along with numerous other celebrities, to participate in the tournament. The sponsor offers to pay the Senators' entrance fee of $150 in order to induce other people to contribute to the charity in return for the opportunity to play with the celebrities. The Senators may accept because the invitation comes from the sponsor of the charity event.

As if being certified celebrities were not enough, senators are also granted the same shot at sudden wealth as the rest of the citizenry:

Rule 35, section 1(c)(10) allows a Member, officer, or employee to accept an award or prize won in a contest or event that is open to the public. Thus, the staffer who appears on *Jeopardy* and becomes a grand champion may keep her prize money and other winnings, as may the Senator who purchases the winning Powerball ticket.

Although this regulation potentially grants Alex Trebek an extraordinary amount of power over the Senate, it is unfortunately of little use to the working lobbyist. But I would like to think that the creative influence peddler could do wonders with the following:

Similarly, under the new Rule . . . home state products (e.g., apples, peanuts, popcorn, coffee, candy, orange juice) are not regarded as gifts to the Senator or staff. These products must be from the Senator's home state, must be from home state producers or distributors, and must be available to office visitors.

Senator Kay Bailey Hutchison of Texas, I suppose, is permitted to accept the gift from a Midland/Odessa wildcatter of a barrel of West Texas crude so long as Styrofoam cups and a ladle are provided for guests. I imagine walking into Washington Senator Slade Gorton's office and admiring the tasteful display of logs. "Yes, Mr. Lind, the timber industry is one of the major employers in our state. Please, help yourself to some lumber on the way out."

The lobbyist's art is not a matter of simple brute bribery, as in, "I buy you lunch; you get the senator to co-sponsor my legislation." Rather, it is a somewhat more delicate, less short-sighted form of quid pro quo. No one in Washington actually believes that a senator must receive advice on how to vote over a three-course meal at The Monocle, or that a skybox is a better site for legislative research than, say, the Library of Congress. It is simply understood that long-term relationships between lobbyists and staffers determine who gets what in Washington, and that gifts are a means of establishing those relationships.

Nor has there ever been much confusion about whose friendship to cultivate. For reasons both moral and practical, some senators refuse to see lobbyists. But a lot of Senate offices are staff-driven, and Senate-staff hierarchy is relatively straightforward. At the top is the chief of staff (busy, and possibly as moral or practical as the senator); just below him is the legislative director (a good target, but difficult to reach). On the next rung are perhaps five to seven legislative assistants, or senior policy advisers, and a few legislative aides, who are glorified legislative assistants (all very good bets; especially big on junkets).

Below these are four or five legislative correspondents (invite these to "widely attended events"). At the very bottom are the senator's scheduling assistant, a clerk, and one or two receptionists (send flowers).

But until two years ago, the lobbyist's task was at least theoretically complicated by the fact that the Senate ethics rules existed only in the form of 443 separate "Interpretative Rulings" and thousands of private letters to Senate staffers from the Ethics Committee. The introduction to the *Ethics Manual* promises

> for the first time, to consolidate all forms of the Committee's previously issued advice and rulings, and to present it in an easy to use and understandable format.

That promise has been kept, and in keeping it the Ethics Committee has ensured not only that senators and their staffers will run less risk of getting into trouble but, perhaps unwittingly, that the lobbyist will have an easier time of it as well. After all, he now has what he always wanted: a how-to manual, courtesy of the United States Senate.

THE PRACTICE OF COUNTRY POLITICS

MICHAEL HOFFERBER

CONTEXT

At times it might seem that our political system is so dominated by institutional players (interest groups, lobbyists, etc.), that there is no room left for individual citizens. This is far from the truth, however. In fact, even though Washington is a considerable distance from where most people live, there are still numerous ways to become involved in civic life in your own hometown, and this local involvement may be as vital to American democracy as anything you could do in Washington, DC.

In this selection, Michael Hofferber talks about the many opportunities to participate in local politics and how important that participation can be. Smaller town and county governments often make many important decisions related to growth, taxation, and education that can have lasting influence. Yet, civic participation among citizens in small-town politics is low. Hofferber argues that citizen participation in small-town politics can be very rewarding. It is also very important for the kind of democracy that we have in America because our democracy cannot survive without citizen involvement.

● *THINK CRITICALLY* ●————————————————————

1. When you hear the term "public life" what does it mean to you?
2. In your view, is civic participation more important locally or nationally? Why?
3. Hofferber says that for democracy to function properly, average citizens must be active in public affairs. Do you agree with this? Why or why not?

The drive through Shoshone, Idaho (pop, 1,250), on a midwinter weeknight is uneventful. The shops along highway 26 have all closed their doors and only a couple of taverns on the north side of the railroad tracks are still illuminated. The town's main thoroughfare is deserted, save for a handful of vehicles crowded around city hall, where the lights inside are glowing.

Five male townsfolk, a mayor and four city councilmen, sit on one side of a long table in the one-room city hall. They face the city clerk, a quiet woman taking notes at a desk before them. The town's police chief and its city attorney are seated to one side.

"Is there any public comment on Ordinance 425?" asks the town's mayor.

A row of metal folding chairs aligned opposite the city council are mostly empty. Only the city's maintenance supervisor and a reporter for the town's weekly newspaper have turned out for the public hearing on an ordinance regulating the size of new homes. Without comment, the city council unanimously approves an ordinance that will shape the future of the town for decades.

Something similar is happening in small towns and rural counties all across America. Local councils, school boards, and commissions are deciding where roads will be built, how school will be taught, and what water will cost. Such decisions affect the day-to-day lives of their communities far more than the machinations of Congress or the changing tide of stock-market trading.

As a small-town newspaper reporter, I have watched rural governments match wits with deep-pocketed developers, debate the merits of public access, and negotiate contracts for sewer line improvements. These issues occupy urban and suburban governments, too, of course, but their councils are often composed of professional politicians, strangers to most of the people who elected them. And they remain strangers.

In small-town America the people who elect mayors and commissioners often know the candidates by their first names and work beside them on their jobs. Many went to school with the people they chose to run their government.

I have reported on small-town elections where the outcome was decided by one vote and have often seen city council decisions swayed by the words of a single citizen. I've followed the successful grassroots campaign of a small group of country people thwarting the condemnation of public land for an Air

Force bombing range, and I've seen rural assemblies rally to save trees, protest corporate crop monopolies, and raise awareness about the plight of family farms, among other concerns.

There are campaigns and elections and protests before city governments as well, but there it is much harder for one voice to be heard above the din of the crowd. Elections are decided by margins of hundreds and thousands rather than by the handful. Results are less immediate and personal.

It is in the rural courthouse or city hall that the democratic principles of self-determination and representative government are more visible. Here a determined individual can affect his government. Here the citizen can elect a trusted friend or family member as his representative.

A good friend once advised me of the three elements that constitute a full life; raising a family, operating a small business, and running for public office. Most folks complete the first two steps in that prescription with nary a thought of the third. "Politics? That's for lawyers and celebrities. I haven't the time."

The concept of public life as a central element in a healthy lifestyle has been greatly ignored for decades. Most Americans today are focused on their private lives and abhor public life. They do so at great cost to their communities and their own sense of meaning and belonging.

The goal of the republic, according to Thomas Jefferson, is "to make each person feel that he is a participator in the government of affairs, not merely at an election one day in the year, but every day." In that sense our national government is sadly lacking. There are few opportunities for one person to feel like a participator amid a crowd of millions. But in our small towns and rural countries the chance for involvement is much greater.

The government leaders I have known have mostly been small-town merchants, tradespeople, real estate agents, retirees, housewives, farmers, and ranchers. Many were driven into politics by some local issue like land use planning, street improvements or school issues.

One town councilman told me he started following local government when he and his neighbors were campaigning against plans for a subdivision development. To keep on top of the issue, he ran for a council seat and was elected, then reelected seven times. He became instrumental in writing the town's planning and zoning ordinances.

Others became involved in government by invitation. A manager of an eyewear shop with no prior political experience was asked to serve on a committee studying her town's parking problems. Her work on the committee led to an appointment to the planning and zoning commission. The more she learned, the more she wanted to have a voice in its policies, she told me. After four years on the planning commission, she was running for a council seat.

My own political career began with a call one evening from the chairman of the library board asking if he could nominate me for town alderman. The library board was seeking more support from the town council, and local libraries are a resource I cherish. I agreed, never suspecting I would win.

For those who are new to a town, or who have just recently taken an interest in its politics, it is important to familiarize yourself with the local government entities and how they operate. If your town is incorporated, it will have a city hall and perhaps a city clerk. In most towns a mayor and city council set policies and draft ordinances that are then enforced by police, firefighters, and other city-paid professionals.

Ask at city hall for an agenda to the next city council meeting and inquire as to where legal notices are published. Usually the local newspaper will carry the notices in or near its classified ads section and include coverage of public meetings in its news pages. A good newspaper can keep you up to date on public meetings, provide background on issues being discussed, and familiarize you with local politicians.

Counties or townships are being governed from a central courthouse that may or may not be located near by. Elected commissioners govern the unincorporated rural properties and preside over county-wide services like landfills, ambulances, and weed control.

Check at your town library for information on local governments, including the names and addresses of elected officials. You may want to write to them about issues that affect you.

In addition to the city and county governments, there may be special taxing districts for school, water and sewer systems, recreational facilities, hospitals, airports, fire protection, and even historic preservation. Each of these will have its own board or commission and will hold regular meetings that are open to the public.

The best way to find out what's going on with any of these government entities is to attend their public meetings, which are usually held at least once a month. You may be asked what business you have at the meeting, to which you should respond, "I'm just observing."

Attend several meetings or follow local government for just a few weeks and you'll undoubtedly begin to form strong opinions on particular issues. If you want to have a voice in how they are resolved you'll have to speak out. Write a letter to the local newspaper editor as a start. Send copies of it to the boards of elected officials who will be making the key decisions.

Don't hesitate to call your mayor or city council member if you have an opinion to express. Or, if you feel up to speaking in public, prepare a statement to make during the next open meeting. Most government entities will make time for you at their meeting if you contact them in advance to be included on their agenda.

If you want to have a full public life and make progress on issues dear to your heart, be prepared to join groups. Like-minded people will come forward or become apparent once you begin to speak your mind. You may be asked to join a special interest group, or you may want to start one yourself.

The group you join could be a political party. You might be asked to help with a campaign by distributing literature or making phone calls. Or you may be asked to run for public office.

Getting elected to a small-town public office that offers little or no monetary compensation is a pretty simple matter. All you need is about a dozen signatures of registered voters on a nominating petition and a few dozen more citizens willing to vote for you on Election Day. Many offices go unopposed at the ballot box, in which case the nomination virtually ensures election and the start of your political involvement.

Unlike big-city elections, small-town campaigns are usually inexpensive and personal. When I ran for city alderman I gave no speeches and bought no advertising. The local newspaper interviewed me and so did the radio station, but otherwise I just answered questions like, "What do you want to do that for?" from local townsfolk.

My response was something like: "I believe in small-town government. I think it's as close to true democracy as we get. After being an observer for a long time, I figure it's time to be an actor."

The responsibilities of public office vary tremendously. Some boards and councils meet for an hour or so once each month while others require attendance at lengthy meeting two or three times a month. When a developer proposed a massive new subdivision at the edge of our town and sought annexation, there was considerable discussion at the council table and even more on the streets. Everywhere I went, it seemed, folks wanted to talk about the subdivision and what it would mean to the future of the town and its real estate.

Research and preparation for meetings may take several hours, especially when there are complex legal issues involved or when there is a lot of public comment. Some people take this preparation time seriously, while others always vote whichever way their conscience carries them at the moment. I served on a six-member council in which I was outnumbered 5 to 1 on many issues. To advance my own causes, I'd take time before a vote to enlist the support of at least three other council members (or two and the mayor).

When I learned I had won election in my town's governing council I was stunned. It was like opening a door on a surprise party. Folks I respected and trusted—and many I barely knew—had chosen me for a role in their government. There are few moments in life when you get such a public affirmation from your neighbors.

Later that night I walked down to city hall and sat for a while on its darkened front steps. And that's when I remembered my friend's recipe for a full life.

Isn't it enough to make a living and raise a family? No, not in a democracy. Our form of government depends on average citizens leading active public lives. It requires a community of individuals willing to serve on school boards, county commissions, and local committees. It will not survive in the hands of celebrities and professionals, no matter how well-meaning.

Without a public life we endanger the well-being of those we care most about in our private lives. Without a public life we give away powers of decision-making and, ultimately, the freedoms we enjoy.

PART IV

PUBLIC POLICY

POLICY DEBATES

HEAD NOTES/SECTION QUESTIONS

Government exists for a reason. The English political philosopher John Locke argued that people choose to live with other people and by doing so enter into a social contract in order to gain the security that is not available alone in a state of nature. In other words, we choose to live in a community rather than as individuals on our own. By doing so, we agree to live by the will of the majority, and thus government exists as an expression of the will of the people.

As an expression of the will of the people, government produces things. We can call the products of government by many names: laws, rules, statutes, regulations, orders, or public policies. Public policy is the preferred term for describing the products of government because it is an all-encompassing description for what government does and what it produces. Public policy is what government does and how government goes about doing it.

In a democracy, it only stands to reason that what government does and how government goes about doing what it does will be open to debate. After all, it is a rare day that everyone agrees on something from the start. Debate is a vital part of democracy, which is why Americans have debated public policies from the very first days of the republic. Over the years, Americans have had literally thousands of public policy debates. Most of the time these debates have been resolved peacefully. For example, in the early 20th century, Americans debated the changing nature of child labor as it related to new factories that sprang up all over the country during the Industrial Revolution. Prior to the Industrial Revolution, the need to debate child labor had not existed because the only kind of work children did was on the family farm. The result of this debate was public policy regulating child labor.

At times, however, public policy debates have not been resolved peacefully. For instance, at root, the Civil War was the result of an unresolved policy debate about whether the federal government had the power to take away states' rights to regulate slavery. After years of debate, people could still not agree on the issue of slavery, and war resulted. In the end, the debate over slavery was resolved, but not in the ideal way that debates are resolved in a democracy.

Debates over public policy evoke strong feelings on all sides of issues. In a democracy, it is expected that as a result of the public debate, a consensus will emerge. In this section we read about five current public policy debates revolving around welfare reform, health care, immigration, the environment and business, and the United States' role in the world. Each article presents a side of the debate, or an overview, and from it you can develop alternative arguments. As you read these selections, consider the following questions:

1. Earlier you read about divided party control of the Congress and the White House. How do you think divided power affects policy debates? Does divided power make public policy debates easier or more difficult, and do you think it matters?

2. Other than the policy debates you read about in this part, name one other public policy issue that you are concerned about. What are the issues being debated? Can you see where a compromise might develop?

LEARN MORE ON THE WEB

Policy.Com
   http://www.policy.com

Electronic Policy Network
   http://epn.org/

HAS WELFARE REFORM HELPED THE POOR?

CECILIO MORALES

CONTEXT

One of President Clinton's campaign promises in 1992 was that he would "reform welfare as we know it." This was a rather dramatic departure for a Democrat, but Clinton promised that he was a different kind of Democrat. In keeping with this campaign promise, the Clinton administration proposed a new welfare plan in 1994 that had as its key component the requirement that

400,000 welfare recipients find jobs by the year 2000. Welfare recipients who refused to work or participate in work training programs would have their benefits cut off after two years.

Clinton's welfare reform proposals were not satisfactory to Republicans in Congress, however, and after the 1994 midterm elections, when Republicans captured a majority in both the House and the Senate, additional reforms were added. Republicans increased the number of welfare recipients who would have to find work by the year 2000 from 400,000 to 1.5 million, denied public aid to legal immigrants who were not citizens, and gave states much more control over welfare programs than they previously had had.

President Clinton was not happy with the Republican plan, but feared a public backlash if he did not do something to reform welfare. In August 1996, he signed the Personal Responsibility and Work Opportunity Act (PRA) into law, thus transforming sixty-one years of federal welfare policy. He promised to make any necessary changes to the program after the 1996 elections, but little change has been made, partially because of a lack of information about what changes need to be made.

In this selection, Cecilio Morales discusses the lack of information about welfare reform. Morales says that too little is known about whether welfare reform has been successful or not. Some in conservative circles argue that welfare reform has been successful because the number of people receiving welfare assistance has declined. Others argue that what really is important in determining the success of welfare reform is whether those formerly on welfare have seen an increase in income since going off welfare. Morales says that welfare reform happened too recently to determine yet whether it has been successful or not.

● *THINK CRITICALLY* ●

1. Which is more critical in determining the success of welfare reform, the number of people on/off welfare, or the income of people recently removed from the welfare rolls?
2. Does America have an obligation to help the poor? Why or why not?

Proving that welfare reform has either decisively helped or hindered the poor, or even society at large, has become one of the rhetorical hinges of congressional debate concerning plans to cut Federal social spending by at least $11 billion, starting with fiscal year 2000, while increasing military spending by multiples of that figure. When experts are asked their opinion, however, the answers are conflicting. The star-crossed alignment of politics and contradictory policy assessments that has become emblematic of the Federal dialogue on welfare reform was demonstrated in Washington on May 27, when four leading House Republicans claimed victory over poverty—only to be followed in day-long testimony by specialists who, relying on the same relatively narrow base of available data, drew widely differing, often directly opposed conclusions.

The current program of welfare reform goes back to August 1996, in the middle of a Presidential campaign, when Republicans in Congress forced onto President Clinton's desk a hardened version of his proposal to "end welfare as we know it," known as *ewawki* among White House staffers. The Personal Responsibility and Work Opportunity Reconciliation Act ended the decades-old legal entitlement to Federal aid, required work search and preparation, set a maximum lifetime limit on assistance and allowed a variety of more stringent state rules, including a controversial cap on aid to children born to recipient mothers.

By December 1998 the welfare caseload dropped nationally from its 1994 peak of 5 million families to under 3 million, a decline of 45 percent. What brought about the decline in the rolls—the abundance of jobs or welfare policies? Where did these people go? What are they doing now? Will they be back for more help? Have caps on aid regardless of the number of children turned out to be the abortion incentive some expected? What happens when someone loses a job after exhausting the allowable lifetime supply of assistance?

These are among the questions to which Cynthia Fagnoni, the General Accounting Office's director of education, workforce and income security issues, would like answers before her agency can return a full appraisal to Congress. In response to such questions, lawmakers' aides joke that if one were to ask a G.A.O. analyst what color Elsie the cow was, the report would come back "spotted, on the side we saw." But Ms. Fagnoni's queries cannot be so neatly dismissed.

After decades of functioning essentially as a machinery to process benefit checks—the words "income maintenance" were until recently part of welfare agencies' official name in many states—the new law began to demand work activities and enforce time-limits, yet without significantly altering the way clients are tracked. To complicate matters, because each state has been free to experiment, the meager and outdated information the U.S. Department of Health and Human Services has been able to collect is increasingly more difficult to use for nationwide comparisons. Corrective regulations have just begun to be issued. When the G.A.O. set out to answer questions for the House Ways and Means Subcommittee on Human Resources in May, the agency found only seven states whose data is complete enough to begin assembling a tentative picture.

Based on Census Bureau and H.H.S. data, a jointly authored report by Republican Representatives Nancy Johnson of Connecticut, Bill Archer of Texas, E. Clay Shaw of Florida and House Speaker Dennis Hastert of Illinois claimed on May 27 that low-income families have increased their consumption and that child poverty has declined, thereby "refuting the claim that low-income female-headed families are worse off now than they were before welfare reform, even though they receive less income from welfare and more from earnings."

The argument echoes a report issued two weeks earlier by the Heritage Foundation, *The Determinants of Welfare Caseload Decline*, by Robert Rector and Sarah E. Youssef. This report offered Republicans a complex, scientific-appearing mathematical model with which to deny President Clinton's claim that prosperity under his Administration's policies is leading to a drop in the welfare rolls. The Republican lawmakers stopped short of adopting in their own report, though, the following major conclusion offered by Rector and Youssef concerning poverty: "In reality, decreases in dependence have beneficial effects on children's long-term development, even if they are accompanied by decreasing family income." Put more simply, these two authors believe poverty builds character.

A very different picture was provided by Wendell Primus, director of income security at the Center on Budget and Policy Priorities, in testimony before the Ways and Means panel, Primus, who resigned from H.H.S. in 1996 in protest against the welfare reform law, stated that caseload reduction is an inadequate measure of welfare reform's success. "The ultimate criteria should include whether the economic well-being of children and families has been enhanced," he said. According to Primus, the disposable income of the poorest fifth of single-mother families rose "substantially and across the board" from 1993 to 1995; but once the rules under the new welfare law began to have their effects on welfare population, that income fell despite the fact that national economic growth and expansion continued.

Primus's views, like those of the lawmakers, are supported by parallel findings. The Children's Defense Fund stated in a 1998 report, *Welfare to What: Early Findings on Family Hardship and Well-Being*, that welfare reform has not made a noticeable dent in poverty. The C.D.F. concluded that among those who recently received welfare, employment rose from 20 percent to almost a third of this population group, but 92 percent still had earnings below the poverty level. "Some treat the news of the dramatic reduction in welfare caseloads as proof that the new welfare policies are a success," said Deborah Weinstein, C.D.F. family income division director. "We ask 'welfare to what?' because we believe that success cannot be judged until we know what is happening to children and families."

Despite the dearth of solid information, the tenor of the discussion has changed considerably since the mid-1980's when I found myself, as a reporter covering then-experimental reform programs in Massachusetts and California, penning the phrase "welfare-to-work program" to avoid the politically loaded term *workfare*; to the caseworkers with whom I spoke, the latter term evoked images of Dickensian workhouses. Today, scarcely an eyebrow rises in Washington when personages like Rector suggest that welfare reform should not be focused on reducing poverty at all, but on public assistance "dependency." Part of the reason that such a startling view is difficult to counter lies in Fagnoni's factual questions about what has happened to all those who left welfare. Even anecdotally, there simply is no credible answer.

Right after reform was passed, food banks stocked up for the catastrophe predicted by advocates for the poor. Continued reporting over the past two years, though, has failed to find on the food lines a substantial trace of the millions who left welfare. Shelters for the homeless have not reported a massive influx that could be expected if two million families were on the streets.

Welfare time limits have not been reached yet by most recipients, but food stamp cutoffs took place with nary a blip on the social services screen. Without benefits, without training, where did former recipients go? No one really knows for sure. Even more controversial issues, such as the possibility of abortions induced by reductions in child benefits, yield no decisive conclusion. Studies concerning developments in New Jersey, an early experimenter in this area, are inconclusive.

A groundswell is growing in policy circles to reduce the expense of welfare still further. Although nationally the average caseload drop is 45 percent, some states have lost as much as 70 percent of their welfare clientele. In Michigan, Republican Governor John Engler has been propelling his "Project Zero," and just about each month a county or two has been reporting that it has no welfare recipients at all. Funds distributed to states on the basis of projected needs are consequently accumulating in state coffers. A number of governors, including Engler, have expressed the desire to keep them for a "rainy day." Indeed, one of the great unknowns is what would happen to state welfare reform programs during an economic downturn. By the time one occurs, Fagnoni suggested, many welfare recipients may have exhausted their legal lifetime limit and be ineligible for aid, regardless of need.

Congress has begun to make noises suggesting that it may consider recalling public assistance surpluses or at least cutting off the bonanza for the foreseeable future. For now, the public issue involves surpluses, dependency, ratios, regression analyses—anything but poverty. About that, very little can be said for certain.

CODE BLUE: HOW MANAGED CARE IS PUTTING EMERGENCY CARE IN SHOCK

HOWARD ISENSTEIN

CONTEXT

Responding to the skyrocketing costs of health care, presidential candidate Bill Clinton promised in 1992 to overhaul the nation's health care system, making it more affordable and more accessible to the millions of Americans who did not have health care. By the end of 1994, President Clinton's health care reform proposal had died in Congress. However, the problem that candidate Clinton had identified, high costs and difficult accessibility, still existed.

The health care industry began to reform itself in order to deal at least with the high cost problem. One result of the reforms enacted by the health care industry was the explosion of managed care plans, or health maintenance organizations (HMOs). HMOs are prepaid health care plans that deliver comprehensive health care to members through designated providers. One of the benefits of HMOs to members is that a fixed periodic payment (usually monthly) is required so that a major sickness does not threaten financial ruin. The benefit to HMOs is that they pay a fixed fee to a physician for services.

Because HMOs are receiving fixed payments from subscribers, they have an incentive to hold costs down. The difference between what subscribers pay in fixed monthly fees and what the HMO pays out in services (to doctors, hospitals, labs, etc.) is profit. Thus, HMOs have an incentive to hold costs down to increase profits. In this selection, Howard Isenstein looks at the effects of managed care plans on emergency services. In order to control costs, managed care programs discourage hospital stays and have begun refusing to cover fully the costs of some emergency room care. The result has been a serious financial burden on many hospitals, which have responded by closing down their emergency services.

● *THINK CRITICALLY* ●

1. Should access to health care be contingent on one's ability to pay, or should health care be available to all without regard to cost?
2. If you could make one reform to the health care system in the United States, what would it be?

Most Americans take it for granted that if they have a heart attack or get in an accident, highly qualified help in an emergency room is but a short drive away. Don't believe it. Growing numbers of hospitals around the country—and their emergency departments—are shutting their doors due to financial pressures. Those that remain are reducing emergency services by pooling their resources with other hospitals or simply by cutting quality.

Emergency departments are the bulwark of the country's health care system. Not only are they the first line of defense when there are actual emergencies, such as plant explosions, airline disasters, and the like, but they are also critical in saving more routine heart attack and auto accident victims. Emergency physicians say that patients such as these need to be seen in the so-called "golden hour" immediately after the onset of their problem or risk irreparable harm. Emergency departments also serve as the primary health care provider to tens of millions of poor and uninsured Americans who lack the means to access more conventional settings like doctors' offices.

But such a safety net doesn't come without a price. Emergency departments must maintain high levels of readiness 24 hours a day, seven days a week, by employing skilled teams of physicians, nurses, administrators and other highly trained staff, and by keeping up with the latest life-saving technology. While surgical and other hospital departments are equally or more expensive to maintain, they enjoy well-insured patients who can pay their bills. Emergency departments, by contrast, are perennial money losers because their patients often cannot.

Until the 1990s, insurance companies and their employer clients were willing to shell out to support emergency departments and pricey health care in general. But that changed with the rise of managed care, a euphemism for rationing. Employers, stunned by double-digit premium increases, answered the siren call of managed care organizations, including HMOs and preferred provider organizations, which promised negligible rate increases. Today, about 85 percent of all employees with health insurance are in some sort of managed care plan.

For much of the mid-to-late 1990s, HMOs delivered on their claims by negotiating steep discounts with hospitals, doctors, and other health care providers. HMOs also delivered by limiting—sometimes harshly—access to and time spent in hospitals. In May, for example, the New York state attorney general's office said it was investigating some managed care plans for allegedly telling patients and doctors that patients must first get approval from their primary care doctor to be covered for an emergency room visit. New York, like many other states, passed legislation that requires health plans to provide coverage of emergency room visits for people who have symptoms that a prudent layperson would consider an emergency. This investigation jibes with a study that surveyed academic departments of emergency medicine across the country. Thirty-seven percent of the respondents reported that HMOs routinely discouraged their enrollees from using 911 services, and 16 percent reported that HMOs provided 911 services to take patients only to participating hospital emergency departments.

Hospitals that couldn't or wouldn't find ways to make up for the shortfall in revenue caused by managed care's hardball tactics closed their doors. Between 1995 and 1996, 180 medical-surgical hospitals with licensed emergency services disappeared, according to the American Hospital Association (significantly more than the 141 closings in 1994-1995).

Those that remained open scrutinized expenses and focused on the biggest ways to get rid of money-losing services. Not surprisingly, emergency services were at the top of the list. Hospitals merged emergency services with those of affiliated or nearby hospitals, reduced staffing levels, substituted less qualified employees for those more qualified, and took other measures. The result is that getting emergency services is harder than ever.

"One of the big concerns of these consolidations of hospital systems and closure of beds is that those that remain may not be able to provide the [emergency] care needed," said Dr. Francis L. Counselman, chairman of the department of emergency medicine at Eastern Virginia Medical School in Norfolk, Va. "People just go to another [emergency] department, which puts . . . incredible strain on the remaining hospitals."

Patients pay the price of that strain most visibly, Counselman said, through increased wait times and possibly through tardy intervention. "Instead of an hour and a half wait, it's going to be a two and a half hour wait or a three hour wait. Then the concern is that there's somebody out there [in the waiting room] who can't wait that length of time, like someone with abdominal pain that ends up being an ectopic pregnancy," a dangerous condition.

The situation is most acute in areas where managed care has made the greatest inroads. Take the Bay Area around San Francisco. In early 1997, a series of patient deaths in emergency rooms was attributed to inadequate nurse staffing, inexplicable delays in transport, lack of doctors on call, and nonexistent quality assurance, as reported in *Modern Healthcare*. For example, on Feb. 12, 1997, Willa Hives, a resident of Vallejo, Calif., drove to Kaiser Permanente's hospital in Richmond, Calif. only to learn that its emergency room wasn't staffed to treat her condition—chest pain—because it was a "standby" emergency room and not a full-scale emergency room. Kaiser's larger Oakland hospital had no beds available, so Hives was taken to Summit Medical Center in Oakland. She was dead on arrival.

And in affluent Marin County in September 1997, an auto accident victim had to be taken to three hospitals to find an ER properly staffed to care for her. She died after surgery at the third.

These and other incidents prompted the state's Emergency Medical Services Authority to conclude in a draft report that California's emergency systems and hospitals don't have enough capacity to handle catastrophes—no slight possibility in an area prone to earthquakes, forest fires, and freeway accidents.

Such problems are directly attributable to falling emergency capacity in the state. Between 1995 and 1996 coverage in terms of emergency department hours dropped 10.4 percent, and 12 emergency departments closed (2.8 percent of the state total), according to a study headed by Dr. A. Antoine Kazzi, an associate professor of medicine in the division of emergency medicine at the University of California at Irvine.

While coverage is down, doctors are being forced to do more at the same time, including filling out reams of paperwork to satisfy managed care companies and seeing about 5 percent more patients per hour than a few years ago, which could hurt their ability to spot problems, Kazzi said.

Not surprisingly, some legislators in California are incensed. A bill that would have given county governments the right to restrict the closure or reduction of emergency care services failed to pass the California Assembly by one vote on June 3, after intense lobbying against the measure by California hospitals.

But it's not clear that this kind of regulation will work even if the bill is brought up again and passed. The real issue is funding. Managed care won't put up with subsidizing money-losing emergency rooms and Medicare, the other major hospital payer, has stated loudly and clearly that the days of hefty reimbursement rate increases are over. So hospitals, even if regulated, will have no other choice but to cut corners if they want to remain viable. More than likely, legislators at the state and national level will ignore the issue until a full scale emergency wreaks havoc, exposing the lack of emergency capacity. Only then will they have the gumption to consider funding an essential service.

STOPPING THE FLOOD
YEH LING-LING

CONTEXT

Immigration has been a public policy issue in the United States almost from the founding of the republic. George Washington and Thomas Jefferson, while both sympathetic to immigrants, worried that too many would threaten America's democracy and expose the new country to corrupting influences from Europe.

Over the years, immigration policy has become very restrictive while at the same time less biased against immigrants of certain racial and ethnic groups. The first restrictive immigration policy was the Chinese Exclusion Act of 1882, which limited the number of Chinese who could migrate to America. The policy was based on racial stereotypes of Chinese people. From 1882 through 1965, immigration policy was based on national origin preferences, whereby immigrants from European countries were favored over immigrants from non-European countries.

In 1965, Congress passed the Immigration and Nationality Act, which eliminated national origin preferences and replaced them with per country limits. The result was an increase in the number of immigrants from non-European countries. The 1965 law still governs immigration policy today, and some argue that it is bad for the United States.

In this article from *A. Magazine: Inside Asian America*, Yeh Ling-Ling argues that current U.S. immigration policy is damaging America economically and is bad for all Americans. A much larger percentage of new arrivals are dependent on welfare, and abuse of the welfare system is rampant. In addition, immigrants strain the public school systems in many parts of the country. Ling-Ling argues that despite the calls for more liberal immigration from the high-tech portions of the economy, in reality there is little need for more high-tech workers. In the end, Ling-Ling contends, immigration reform is needed for the long-term benefit of all Americans.

● *THINK CRITICALLY* ●

1. Do you agree with Yeh Ling-Ling's arguments? Why or why not?
2. Do immigrants provide benefits to the United States? What are some of the benefits they provide?

American society can be enriched by many Asian virtues. However, by promoting welfare and mass immigration, Asian American activists are unintentionally hurting the Asian American community as well as America at large.

Some of our community's most respected scholars have reported that Asian Americans are among the hardest hit by mass immigration. Sociologists Hsiang-Shui Chen, Min Zhou, and Peter Kwong have all written books acknowledging the adverse economic impact of large-scale immigration on Chinese Americans and Chinese immigrants. Even UCLA's Professor Paul Ong, a strong advocate of liberal immigration policy, admitted at a forum in 1991 that minorities and established immigrants suffer the most impact from immigration's adverse effects on wages and employment. So why, I ask, do so many oppose a most sensible alternative—namely, immigration reform?

Every year, the human race is burdening Mother Earth with an additional 95 million people in need of food, housing, jobs, education and many other services. China and India alone are homes to one-third of the world's population. Asian American activists who are truly concerned about the well-being of all Asians on a global scale should work on curbing population growth in the U.S. and abroad through family planning and immigration reduction. Leaders in developing nations should also be pressured into improving life for their own citizens to stop the impetus for their exodus.

According to the U.S. Census Bureau, if the U.S. continues to grow at its current rate, this country's population can exceed 519 million people by 2050—some 25 million more people than India had in 1966. In fact, two-thirds of this nation's future population growth will result from immigration since 1994. Even if all immigrants are arguably assets, do we really want immigration to turn the U.S. into an overpopulated, overburdened nation like China, India, or the Philippines? They are, remember, all countries with consistently high rates of flight—often, not surprisingly, to the U.S.

In California, the largest populations of elderly, non-refugee legal immigrants receiving SSI benefits are Chinese, Korean, and Filipino—at 55 percent, 50 percent, and 39 percent, respectively. Among refugee groups, seniors from Vietnam topped the list of welfare users, at 74 percent. And despite the pledge from all non-refugee legal immigrants (including myself) of economic self-sufficiency as a condition for immigrating to the U.S., immigration advocates have continuously (and successfully) pressured Washington into reinstating welfare benefits for a skyrocketing number of immigrants. This despite census data clearly demonstrating extensive welfare abuses among elderly legal immigrants. Is this compatible with our image of Asians as a "model minority"?

The effects of over-immigration touch lives at every level. Just as legal immigrants and U.S.-born citizens on welfare are receiving smaller checks from their government, those currently in the workforce face increasing competition from the influx of recent immigrants. Case in point: The Information Technology Association of America, a powerful immigration lobby, claims that the U.S. has a shortage of programmers. This claim has fueled their call for the admission of unlimited numbers of programmers. However, UC Davis Computer Science Professor Norman Matloff has demonstrated that many mid-career programmers, including Asian Americans, are being displaced by new graduates and foreign-born workers who accept lower wages. Moreover,

Sun Microsystems, a prominent Silicon Valley company which lobbies vigorously for large-scale immigration, has boasted publicly that it has hired 50 Russian programmers at "bargain prices." Can there be a real shortage of programmers if Microsoft only hires two percent of applicants for its software openings?

But small businesses also experience the economic dilemma between hiring from the American labor pool and from among less expensive, recent immigrant labor. Immigrant advocacy groups often speak of the "revitalizing" of neighborhoods by immigrant entrepreneurs. But what they don't mention is that many immigrants subsidize their businesses with illegally obtained welfare dollars and hire only their own family members. Those business owners pay little payroll and income taxes, and benefit from the depositing of welfare checks received by elderly family members into their own company coffers. Meanwhile, they and their employees send their children to public schools, which cost U.S. taxpayers approximately $5,000 per child per year. Even if all low-skilled immigrants pay taxes, the cost of various public services they use generally far exceeds the tax dollars they generate.

With the arrival of immigrant workers, of course, comes the burden of their children. Largely due to immigration-derived growth, many public schools (K–12) in states with large numbers of immigrants are overwhelmed by children coming from all over the world speaking over 80 languages but little English. In fact, there are districts in California that hire ethnic teachers without the necessary credentials to cope with limited-English students. Mass immigration has undoubtedly contributed to the rapid decline of academic performance in California's public schools. Once ranking at the top among states on standardized test scores, California public schools now hover near the bottom.

But rather than recognizing the wisdom of reducing immigration, many ethnic activists are pointing fingers at the 1978 passing of California's Proposition 13, the referendum setting a limit on the amount of taxes government entities can collect. The National Research Council recently estimated that an average household in California pays over $1,000 a year for services rendered to immigrants. Yet, many ethnic activists still pressure our governments to allot additional billions of tax dollars to fund overcrowded schools. Where are the Asian ideals of parsimony and fiscal responsibility in that?

Immigration advocates must be reminded that their children will bear the direct consequences of their actions. According to the Census Bureau's 1994 Population Survey, the poverty rate among the foreign-born arriving since 1989 was at 37.5 percent, a number more than double that of American natives. The liberal press have also begun to recognize the culturally balkanizing effects caused by mass migration from over 100 countries. The United States now is the greatest debtor nation on Earth. Do we wish to leave our children a heavily indebted and culturally splintered America?

Immigration has long been the backbone of the Americas' success. And immigration can still be beneficial—if the level is socially and economically sustainable. Advocates can continue resorting to name-calling and allow historically high levels of immigration to sink us all. Or for the sake of Asian Americans and other Americans, we should set aside ethnic and political differences to support an immigration policy that reflects the interests of the majority. Ultimately, no law on Earth can please all the governed.

(34)

PANNING YELLOWSTONE'S POOLS FOR SCIENCE AND PROFIT

TODD WILKINSON

CONTEXT

Americans strongly support public policy designed to improve the quality of the environment. In recent surveys, as many as 80 percent of Americans have labeled themselves as environmentalists. Part of the reason for such strong support among Americans for the environment is that many are able to see the direct relationship between their own quality of living and the quality of the environment around them. Thus, Americans are also generally in favor of environmental policies designed to ensure clean air, clean water, and the proper removal and storage of hazardous and solid waste.

Many economists and members of the business community see the relationship between economic growth and environmental protection as a zero-sum game. Increased environmental protection necessarily means less economic growth, and greater economic growth is dependent upon less restrictive environmental protection laws. Many in the business community think that economic growth is more important than environmental protection, especially if the amount of environmental protection is very small and the level of restriction on economic growth is great. Many environmentalists, on the other hand, oppose economic growth if it comes at the expense of environmental quality.

Some policymakers believe that economic growth and environmental protection can work in tandem rather than in opposition to one another. In this selection from *National Parks*, Todd Wilkinson discusses a new agreement between the National Park Service and a bioengineering company called a Cooperative Research and Development Agreement (CRADA). CRADA will allow the bioengineering firm to conduct research on Yellowstone National Park microbes for possible commercial applications. The National Park Service contends that this agreement will allow it to learn more about the endemic organisms in the national parks and potentially earn millions of dollars in royalties if products are developed as a result of the research. Critics worry about the long-term consequences of such research and wonder whether the national parks should be used this way at all.

● *THINK CRITICALLY* ●

1. Do you see this as an acceptable compromise between environmental protection and economic growth? Why or why not?
2. Would it not be better to protect national parks like Yellowstone from everything to guard against any potential harms? Why or why not?

Cures for Cancer.

Cosmic parallels with the planet Mars.
Even microscopic clues for how to brew a better beer.

As John Varley, the chief scientist of Yellowstone National Park, watches researchers fill test tubes from a steamy emerald pool in the park interior, he isn't thinking about those important discoveries hovering on the horizon.

Gripping his attention is a paradox—the "happy accident," as he calls it—that has enabled this realm of America's first national park once thought barren to be recognized as one of the richest vaults of biological diversity on earth. "What we have here," Varley says, "is a panoply of organic life that exists on an order of magnitude greater than anyone could have imagined in the 1870s," when the park was first explored.

In a teaspoon of mud or water drawn from a single hot spring, recent analysis has shown thousands of different microbial species. Extrapolating that across Yellowstone's array of 10,000 geysers, hot springs, and fumeroles, Varley estimates conservatively that far less than 1 percent of the microbes surviving in park waters have been cataloged.

In the summer of 1997, Varley, Vice President Al Gore, Secretary of the Interior Bruce Babbitt, National Park Service (NPS) Director Robert Stanton, and Yellowstone Superintendent Mike Finley marked the occasion of Yellowstone's 125th birthday with a monumental announcement aimed at narrowing that microbe information gap. Under the terms of a novel scientific contract—officially known as a Cooperative Research and Development Agreement (CRADA)—the federal government plans to license "bioprospecting" rights to private companies seeking to conduct research on Yellowstone microbes for commercial applications.

Never before used in a national park, the first CRADA was reached with San Diego-based Diversa Corporation. In exchange, Yellowstone will receive information about endemic organisms it could not afford to inventory, collect about $20,000 annually over the next five years from Diversa to support research activities, and earn potentially millions of dollars in product royalties in the future.

Consider that just one park microorganism, *Thermus aquaticus*, was used in the development of DNA fingerprinting that has revolutionized genetic research and produced billions of dollars for the biotech industry. With Yellowstone's innumerable microbes, the potential windfall for the park is tremendous.

Although last summer's agreement has landed the Park Service in hot water with some environmentalists and groups philosophically opposed to bioengineering, Varley hopes that those agreements will enable the private sector to become a lucrative partner in making limited public research dollars go farther. Other parks that are rich in genetic resources valuable to science could benefit as well.

In fact, although the Yellowstone pact alone holds far-reaching implications, it is actually part of a much larger federal strategy to inventory and preserve the full range of biological diversity in national parks that has, until recently, been largely ignored.

"In 1872, Congress had the foresight to protect Yellowstone based on the aesthetic wonders of its thermal basins," Varley notes. "Today, we value geysers and hot springs in more profound ways because of the things inside of them that we cannot see with the naked eye. We've also learned that you cannot protect something effectively unless you know it exists."

Park Service Director Stanton has taken those words to heart, unveiling an ambitious, multimillion-dollar initiative titled, "Revitalizing Natural Resource Stewardship in the National Park Service." The centerpiece of Stanton's proposal is an unprecedented survey called the All-Taxa Biodiversity Inventory already under way in Great Smoky Mountains National Park—soon to be applied to other national parks.

The idea is to compile a "living encyclopedia" of organisms in Great Smoky's 500,000 acres to better understand how the ecosystem functions on a macrocosmic and microcosmic scale. Park spokesman Bob Miller says the all-taxa inventory represents a significant shift away from focusing scarce public research dollars solely on large, popular animals.

"Great Smokies has one of the most comprehensive black bear research programs in the world," Miller says. "We've also contributed significantly to the understanding of deer, but beyond those two species, we don't know much about the rest of our flora and fauna." Conservationists consequently say the need is urgent because Great Smokies is among the most imperiled wildland preserves in the United States—and also among the most biologically diverse— where species are being lost before they can be cataloged.

Another impetus for more scientific research is the 1997 publication of Park Service historian Richard West Sellars's book, *Preserving Nature in the National Parks: A History* (Yale University Press), which highlighted serious shortcomings in the NPS research agenda.

"The central dilemma of national park management has long been the question of exactly what in a park should be preserved," Sellars writes. "Is it the scenery—the resplendent landscapes of forests, streams, wildflowers, and majestic mammals? Or is it the integrity of each park's entire natural system, including not just the biological and scenic superstars, but also the vast array of less compelling species, such as grasses, lichens, and mice?"

During high-level meetings between members of the Park Service's National Leadership Council and Interior Secretary Bruce Babbitt, Alaska Regional Director Bob Barbee (formerly the superintendent of Yellowstone) has said the foremost threat to park protection is the agency's own ignorance.

Unless resource managers can provide a more compelling picture of what is at stake, how systems are threatened by development pressures, and what holds them together, decision makers who support resource protection are destined to lose political battles. If the superintendent of Great Smoky Mountains, for instance, can show that air pollution is causing species to disappear, he or she can make a more compelling argument for looking at smokestacks upwind.

Ironically, this effort comes at a time when parks are under greater threats than ever before, and Congress continues to trim back public land research budgets. This spring, NPCA called on Congress to authorize $150 million annually for efforts to promote science-based decision making in the National Park Service.

In related testimony before the Senate Subcommittee on National Parks, Historic Preservation, and Recreation, NPCA praised efforts to bolster research in national parks but said current legislation does not authorize nearly enough to meet its natural resources protection mandate. The subcommittee was debating provisions of the National Parks Restoration Act that would set aside just $15 million annually for agency research. This is an amount that "does not come close to approximating what the Park Service needs to become a science-driven and resources stewardship-focused agency," according to William J. Chandler, NPCA vice president for conservation policy.

In the absence of increased congressional funding, supporters of bioprospecting say the CRADA helps ensure that valuable research will not come to a halt.

But in spite of these potential benefits of commercial contracts, what might be the costs? Specifically, what impact might bioprospecting have on Yellowstone's surreal thermal landscape?

"Hikers crossing a thermal basin will have more liquid evaporate off their boots than Diversa, or any other company, will sample," Yellowstone's Varley says emphatically. "For our critics to imply that we are inviting consumptive resource extraction to occur is just plain false. The best way to ensure long-term protection is to know what we have, and the best, most cost-effective way to get that done is by letting private enterprise bear the bulk of the expense. This agreement sets a new standard for how limited use of park resources is compatible with the goals of preservation."

During a typical research expedition, scientists collect a couple of teaspoons of liquid material from a hot spring and take it back to their lab. There, they try to identify the unique features of a given organism. Debate over intellectual property centers not on the question of whether private companies will "own" a microbe (they cannot) but how the information and genetic material gleaned from park specimens are used commercially.

In some ways, searching for a commercially promising microbe is like panning for microscopic flakes of gold in a mighty stream. Thousands of different

Yellowstone microbes, known as "thermophiles," may inhabit a tiny amount of water. Some might have special enzymes that enable them to persist at especially hot or cold temperatures; others might have preservative properties or the ability to strip other materials away, as in detergents or paint thinners.

Dozens of products have already been developed from park microbes. At Lechuguilla Cave in Carlsbad Caverns, microbial research has shown promise in fighting cancer. Even NASA is examining these primitive organisms on the theory that they could be related to life forms able to live in extreme conditions on Mars.

Although the CRADA has been hailed by many as a catalyst to a more enlightened age, critics say it has ushered American parks into a brave but perilous new world of scientific exploration. Two lawsuits have been filed against the U.S. Department of the Interior to nullify the agreement, and watchdogs like Edward Hammond of the Rural Advancement Foundation International say researchers shouldn't be experimenting with the genetic makeup of any species, no matter its size.

Hammond and others such as Mike Bader of the Alliance for the Wild Rockies argue that the CRADA opens the door to the mining of park resources. And they claim that officials at Yellowstone entered into a secret deal with Diversa when it failed to solicit public comment or release the full details of the royalty provisions.

"It's not just a matter of adversarie and who has a right to what intellectual property," wrote Beth Burrows of the Institute for Agriculture and Trade Policy in the journal *The Boycott Quarterly*. "It's a question of whether intellectual property is an appropriate way to think about life and life forms of any kind. It's a matter of environmental justice at the very deepest level."

However, Preston Scott of the World Foundation for Environmental and Development, which brokered the landmark agreement based on similar contracts forged in the tropics and at the National Institutes of Health, says that opposition is based more on emotion than substance. He argues that the CRADA actually affords greater resource protection for Yellowstone, not less.

Before 1997, any company could withdraw microbes from the park free of charge, isolate them in a lab, develop them for their commercial potential, and turn a tidy profit without sharing any proceeds with the public. The best example is the patent for *Thermus aquaticus* owned by the pharmaceutical giant Hoffman-La Roche. The company now takes in more than $100 million annually from the patent for DNA fingerprinting, but Yellowstone receives nothing.

According to the terms of the CRADA, Diversa and other companies that enter into similar pacts are limited in what they can remove, are obligated to turn over any scientific knowledge they gather to the Park Service, must pay a substantial annual fee, and will return as much as a 10 percent royalty on commercial profits. Diversa's rate, for example, is set on a sliding scale based on the extent of its profits.

Furthermore, Scott asserts that every aspect of the contract has been made public, except for the precise amount of royalties yet to be paid on a given product. Although an advocate of full disclosure, he says that publicly revealing the exact percentage of royalties tips off Diversa's competition on what products it intends to develop. He also argues that it takes away leverage from the government's ability in the future to negotiate better, more generous deals with larger biotech companies that can afford to pay more. If negotiators of those firms know precisely how much Diversa paid, they could demand to pay less.

Elizabeth Fayad, counsel for NPCA, has scrutinized the CRADA issue. "Our position is that generally speaking, the CRADA seems to be a good agreement," Fayad says, noting that NPCA has chosen not to be a part of lawsuits to stop the CRADA from being implemented. "But we also believe, strongly, that all details of the agreement need to be made public. These are publicly owned resources, and the public has a right to know what the government has agreed to."

Mark Peterson, NPCA's Rocky Mountain regional director, sees another advantage to the agreement. He says that expanding knowledge about Yellowstone's thermophiles provides a greater impetus for prohibiting geothermal energy development on the perimeter of the park that could affect nearby geysers and hot springs.

Five years ago, a bill in Congress called the Old Faithful Geothermal Protection Act, drafted to protect Yellowstone's geysers and hot springs, went down in defeat because lawmakers recognized neither a scientific nor economic imperative. Peterson notes that the dividends of bioprospecting add another element to the debate. In the coming months, NPCA plans to rally support among conservation groups to resurrect the geothermal protection legislation. This time around, he believes legislation will have strong bipartisan support.

Environmentalist Dennis Glick of the Greater Yellowstone Coalition agrees, but based on his work with the World Wildlife Fund in Costa Rica, he says the American public still has not fully recognized the potential of bioprospecting in advancing the value of national parks beyond aesthetics.

Glick says not only are fears that bioprospecting will lead to resource degradation misguided but that the biotech industry provides a strong argument against traditional resource exploitation. He also suggests it is naive for critics to assert that bioprospecting will go away if they succeed in nullifying the CRADA. Bioengineering, from his perspective, is part of the modern world, whether society likes it or not, and now hallowed preserves like Yellowstone have an important role to play in the ongoing philosophical debate.

"There is much we can learn from the lessons of the tropics," he notes. "In Costa Rica, which modeled its parks after Yellowstone, the government and the people realize that they can derive just as many economic benefits by leaving the landscape alone as by developing it in a heavy-handed manner. The average citizen in Costa Rica understands this and appreciates the concept of biodiversity in a way most Americans presently do not. They have taken the idea of Yellowstone and made it better."

In 1870, when members of the famed Hayden Expedition trekked across the same geyser basins to survey park wonders for a special report to Congress, they were oblivious to the "invisible" treasure trove of organic richness. Little did they know that their footsteps on the path to preserving the planet's mother park were leading ultimately into a brave new world.

35

THE TIME OF THE PRIMITIVES

JAMES CHACE

CONTEXT

Since the end of the Cold War, America has been engaged in a public policy debate about its role in world affairs. For much of its early history, America's foreign policy was not to have one at all. America simply did not get involved in the affairs of other nations and expected other nations to leave it alone as well. Of course, World War I, World War II, and the Cold War changed all of that. By the end of the Cold War in 1989, America was by far the most powerful country in the world and actively involved with countries around the globe.

Despite the half-century of active involvement in world affairs from which America has just emerged, elements of the old isolationist value persist. Some would like to see the United States go back to the days when it left other countries alone and expected them to leave it alone. Others argue that because of the way the international economy has integrated all countries, America simply cannot go back to an isolationist position. America's vision of its place in the world is not clear.

In this article from *World Policy Journal*, James Chace argues that at a time when the United States is as powerful as it has ever been, it is faltering in the exercise of that power. Much of the blame for this faltering lies with the Congress, which does things like attach anti-abortion measures to foreign-policy bills knowing that they will cause the bills to be vetoed by the president. Chace argues that the Republican-controlled Congress of today resembles in many ways the Republican-controlled Congress of the 1950s, with a mission of opposing any foreign-policy measure the president proposes. Chace says that America must decide what its vision of the world is and how it will work toward that vision. Such a decision is dependent upon America's sense of power and purpose.

● *THINK CRITICALLY* ●───────────────────────────

1. Chace argues that the root cause of the United States acting like a crippled giant lies within Congress. What does he mean by this? Do you agree with him or disagree?
2. Regardless of whether America has a clear sense of power and purpose or not, should the United States pay its United Nations' dues? Why or why not?

It is an irony of history that at a time when the United States possesses an over-whelming preponderance of power, it so often acts like a crippled giant. The root cause of this behavior lies with Congress. At this writing in early May 1998, Congress has been reluctant to approve legislation to pay the $819 mil-lion in back dues that Washington owes the United Nations. By attaching an anti-abortion amendment to this legislation, the Republican Congress will surely force the White House to veto it.

The Republicans are also opposed to granting the administration's request to add $18 billion to the coffers of the International Monetary Fund, which have been depleted by more than $100 billion in loans to East Asia, unless President Clinton cooperates with a House inquiry into Democratic fundraising for the 1996 presidential campaign.

Even when Congress has given the administration what it wants in order to pursue its post–Cold War foreign policy, the attention paid to the issues have been inadequate or wrongheaded. Although the Senate approved by a wide margin the enlargement of NATO to include the three Central European coun-tries of Poland, Hungary, and the Czech Republic, the debate was, according to George Kennan, the dean of America's Russian experts, "superficial and ill informed." Aside from the central question of whether or not NATO enlarge-ment is desirable—many believe it was unwarranted because it has the poten-tial of causing new problems where none existed—the NATO debate was char-acterized by provocative references to Russia as a country dying to attack Western Europe. Such statements were wholly at variance with the truth of the matter: that Russia is hoping desperately to get into Europe peacefully, not to threaten it with another Cold War.

What we are seeing at the dawn of the millennium is a general refusal by Congress—and especially by Republicans, many of whom were elected in 1994 with little knowledge of or interest in the outside world—to accept the international role of the American leviathan.

Increasingly, the policy of the Republican leadership in the House and Sen-ate resembles that of another era—that of Senator Robert Taft in the wake of the 1948 presidential election. The heyday of bipartisanship was actually be-tween 1946 and 1948, when the Republicans, emboldened by their winning of a majority in Congress for the first time in 18 years, prepared for another elec-toral triumph in the presidential campaign of 1948. When Harry Truman upset all predictions and defeated the internationalist former governor of New York, Thomas Dewey, the bitterness of the Republicans showed itself not only in the ad hominem attacks by Senator Joseph McCarthy in his hysterical anticommu-nist crusade, but also in Senator Taft, who hoped to gain the Republican presi-dential nomination in 1952, a prize he had vainly sought since 1940.

Taft was not an easy man. He was humorless in debate and determined to curb America's involvement in the outside world. He believed it was the duty of the opposition to oppose—and to do little else. He voted against the Mar-shall Plan and the North Atlantic Treaty Organization, and he was adamant in opposing the Bretton Woods agreements that set up the World Bank and the International Monetary Fund. Taft's main quarrel with the Fund was that it would not and could not stabilize shaky currencies. "If we try to stabilize conditions with this fund it will be only pouring money down a rathole," he said. He did not think the United States should play "Santa Claus."

Like so many senators today, Taft did not seem to comprehend that foreign financial turmoil, if it occurs on a sufficiently large scale, could adversely affect the domestic economy of the United States. Stable monetary values promote a vibrant trading system, which might well allow America to export its goods in order to provide jobs at home, as well to reduce its ballooning trade deficit.

Among the know-nothings of today, there is a paradoxical view that the United States is so involved in the global economy that its government's foreign policy is all but irrelevant. But, as Thomas Friedman has pointed out in the *New York Times* (April 18, 1998), the new world order has not yet rendered the nation-state superfluous. The trade and financial integration that American workers and "techies" see as the engine generating enormous wealth in the country today is running, as Friedman described it, "in a world stabilized by a benign superpower called the United States of America, with its capital in Washington, D.C."

An American company like IBM, no matter how many subsidiaries it has from Canada to Australia, is still an American company, dependent on American power and purpose. If IBM gets in trouble, who does it call? Not America Online, as Friedman put it. It would most likely call Washington to put pressure on international institutions in which the United States holds the decisive weight of voting power, or, in the worst case, on the U.S. Marines.

The question before us—and before much of the world—is whether American hegemony is indeed "benign." The answer to that question rests squarely on how the United States supports, sustains, and reforms international institutions. And that, in turn, depends on America's sense of its power and purpose.

THE CONSTITUTION OF THE UNITED STATES

We the People of the United States, in Order to form a more perfect Union, establish Justice, insure domestic Tranquility, provide for the common defence, promote the general Welfare, and secure the Blessings of Liberty to ourselves and our Posterity, do ordain and establish this CONSTITUTION for the United States of America.

ARTICLE I

Section 1. All legislative Powers herein granted shall be vested in a Congress of the United States, which shall consist of a Senate and House of Representatives.

Section 2. (1) The House of Representatives shall be composed of Members chosen every second Year by the People of the several States, and the Electors in each State shall have the Qualifications requisite for Electors of the most numerous Branch of the State Legislature.

(2) No Person shall be a Representative who shall not have attained to the Age of twenty-five Years, and been seven Years a Citizen of the United States, and who shall not, when elected, be an Inhabitant of that State in which he shall be chosen.

(3) [Representatives and direct Taxes[1] shall be apportioned among the several States which may be included within this Union, according to their respective Numbers, which shall be determined by adding to the whole Number of free Persons, including those bound to Service for a Term of Years, and excluding Indians not taxed, three fifths of all other Persons.][2] The actual Enumeration shall be made within three Years after the first Meeting of the Congress of the United States, and within every subsequent Term of ten Years, in such

---

[1]The Sixteenth Amendment replaced this with respect to income taxes.
[2]Repealed by the Fourteenth Amendment.

Manner as they shall by Law direct. The Number of Representatives shall not exceed one for every thirty Thousand, but each State shall have at Least one Representative; and until such enumeration shall be made, the State of New Hampshire shall be entitled to choose three, Massachusetts eight, Rhode-Island and Providence Plantations one, Connecticut five, New York six, New Jersey four, Pennsylvania eight, Delaware one, Maryland six, Virginia ten, North Carolina five, South Carolina five, and Georgia three.

(4) When vacancies happen in the Representation from any State, the Executive Authority thereof shall issue Writs of Election to fill such Vacancies.

(5) The House of Representatives shall choose their Speaker and other Officers; and shall have the sole Power of Impeachment.

Section 3. (1) The Senate of the United States shall be composed of two Senators from each State, [chosen by the Legislature]³ thereof, for six Years; and each Senator shall have one Vote.

(2) Immediately after they shall be assembled in Consequence of the first Election, they shall be divided as equally as may be into three Classes. The Seats of the Senators of the first Class shall be vacated at the Expiration of the second Year, of the second Class at the Expiration of the fourth Year, and of the third Class at the Expiration of the sixth Year, so that one-third may be chosen every second year; [and if Vacancies happen by Resignation, or otherwise, during the Recess of the Legislature of any State, the Executive thereof may make temporary Appointments until the next Meeting of the Legislature, which shall then fill such Vacancies].⁴

(3) No person shall be a Senator who shall not have attained to the Age of thirty Years, and been nine Years a Citizen of the United States, and who shall not, when elected, be an Inhabitant of that State for which he shall be chosen.

(4) The Vice President of the United States shall be President of the Senate, but shall have no Vote, unless they be equally divided.

(5) The Senate shall choose their other Officers, and also a President pro tempore, in the Absence of the Vice President, or when he shall exercise the Office of President of the United States.

(6) The Senate shall have the sole Power to try all Impeachments. When sitting for that Purpose, they shall be on Oath or Affirmation. When the President of the United States is tried, the Chief Justice shall preside: And no Person shall be convicted without the Concurrence of two thirds of the Members present.

(7) Judgment in Cases of Impeachment shall not extend further than to removal from Office, and disqualification to hold and enjoy any Office of honor, Trust or Profit under the United States: but the Party convicted shall nevertheless be liable and subject to Indictment, Trial, Judgment and Punishment according to Law.

Section 4. (1) The Times, Places and Manner of holding Elections for Senators and Representatives, shall be prescribed in each State by the Legislature

---

³Repealed by the Seventeenth Amendment.
⁴Changed by the Seventeenth Amendment.

thereof; but the Congress may at any time by Law make or alter such Regulations, except as to the Places of choosing Senators.

(2) The Congress shall assemble at least once in every Year, and such Meeting shall [be on the first Monday in December,][5] unless they shall by Law appoint a different Day.

Section 5. (1) Each House shall be the Judge of the Elections, Returns and Qualifications of its own Members, and a Majority of each shall constitute a Quorum to do Business; but a smaller Number may adjourn from day to day, and may be authorized to compel the Attendance of absent Members, in such Manner, and under such Penalties as each House may provide.

(2) Each House may determine the Rules of its Proceedings, punish its Members for disorderly Behavior, and, with the Concurrence of two thirds, expel a Member.

(3) Each House shall keep a Journal of its Proceedings, and from time to time publish the same, excepting such Parts as may in their Judgment require Secrecy; and the Yeas and Nays of the Members of either House on any question shall, at the Desire of one fifth of those Present, be entered on the Journal.

(4) Neither House, during the Session of Congress, shall, without the Consent of the other, adjourn for more than three days, nor to any other Place than that in which the two Houses shall be sitting.

Section 6. (1) The Senators and Representatives shall receive a Compensation for their Services, to be ascertained by Law, and paid out of the Treasury of the United States. They shall in all Cases, except Treason, Felony and Breach of the Peace, be privileged from Arrest during their Attendance at the Session of their respective Houses, and in going to and returning from the same; and for any Speech or Debate in either House, they shall not be questioned in any other Place.

(2) No Senator or Representative shall, during the Time for which he was elected, be appointed to any civil Office under the Authority of the United States, which shall have been created, or the Emoluments whereof have been increased during such time; and no Person holding any Office under the United States, shall be a Member of either House during his Continuance in Office.

Section 7. (1) All Bills for raising Revenue shall originate in the House of Representatives; but the Senate may propose or concur with Amendments as on other Bills.

(2) Every Bill which shall have passed the House of Representatives and the Senate, shall, before it becomes a Law, be presented to the President of the United States; If he approve he shall sign it, but if not he shall return it, with his Objections to that House in which it shall have originated, who shall enter the Objections at large on their Journal, and proceed to reconsider it. If after such Reconsideration two thirds of that House shall agree to pass the Bill, it

---

[5]Changed by the Twentieth Amendment, Section 2.

shall be sent, together with the Objections, to the other House, by which it shall likewise be reconsidered, and if approved by two thirds of that House, it shall become a Law. But in all such Cases the Votes of both Houses shall be determined by Yeas and Nays, and the Names of the Persons voting for and against the Bill shall be entered on the Journal of each House respectively. If any Bill shall not be returned by the President within ten Days (Sundays excepted) after it shall have been presented to him, the Same shall be a Law, in like Manner as if he had signed it, unless the Congress by their Adjournment prevent its Return, in which Case it shall not be a Law.

(3) Every Order, Resolution, or Vote to which the Concurrence of the Senate and House of Representatives may be necessary (except on a question of Adjournment) shall be presented to the President of the United States; and before the Same shall take Effect, shall be approved by him, or being disapproved by him, shall be repassed by two thirds of the Senate and House of Representatives, according to the Rules and Limitations prescribed in the Case of a Bill.

Section 8. (1) The Congress shall have Power To lay and collect Taxes, Duties, Imposts and Excises, to pay the Debts and provide for the common Defense and general Welfare of the United States; but all Duties, Imposts and Excises shall be uniform throughout the United States;

(2) To borrow money on the credit of the United States;

(3) To regulate Commerce with foreign Nations, and among the several States, and with the Indian Tribes;

(4) To establish an uniform Rule of Naturalization, and uniform Laws on the subject of Bankruptcies throughout the United States;

(5) To coin Money, regulate the Value thereof, and of foreign Coin, and fix the Standard of Weights and Measures;

(6) To provide for the Punishment of counterfeiting the Securities and current Coin of the United States;

(7) To establish Post Offices and post Roads;

(8) To promote the Progress of Science and useful Arts, by securing for limited Times to Authors and Inventors the exclusive Right to their respective Writings and Discoveries;

(9) To constitute Tribunals inferior to the supreme Court;

(10) To define and punish Piracies and Felonies committed on the high Seas, and Offenses against the Law of Nations;

(11) To declare War, grant Letters of Marque and Reprisal, and make Rules concerning Captures on Land and Water;

(12) To raise and support Armies, but no Appropriation of Money to that Use shall be for a longer Term than two Years;

(13) To provide and maintain a Navy;

(14) To make Rules for the Government and Regulation of the land and naval Forces;

(15) To provide for calling forth the Militia to execute the Laws of the Union, suppress Insurrections and repel Invasions;

(16) To provide for organizing, arming, and disciplining the Militia, and for governing such Part of them as may be employed in the Service of the United States, reserving to the States respectively, the Appointment of the Officers,

and the Authority of training the Militia according to the discipline prescribed by Congress;

(17) To exercise exclusive Legislation in all Cases whatsoever, over such District (not exceeding ten Miles square) as may, by Cession of particular States, and the Acceptance of Congress, become the Seat of the Government of the United States, and to exercise like Authority over all Places purchased by the Consent of the Legislature of the State in which the Same shall be, for the Erection of Forts, Magazines, Arsenals, dock-Yards, and other needful Buildings;—And

(18) To make all Laws which shall be necessary and proper for carrying into Execution the foregoing Powers, and all other Powers vested by this Constitution in the Government of the United States, or in any Department or Officer thereof.

Section 9. (1) The Migration or Importation of such Persons as any of the States now existing shall think proper to admit, shall not be prohibited by the Congress prior to the Year one thousand eight hundred and eight, but a tax or duty may be imposed on such Importation, not exceeding ten dollars for each Person.

(2) The Privilege of the Writ of Habeas Corpus shall not be suspended, unless when in Cases of Rebellion or Invasion the public Safety may require it.

(3) No Bill of Attainder or ex post facto Law shall be passed.

(4) No Capitation, or other direct, Tax shall be laid, unless in Proportion to the Census or Enumeration herein before directed to be taken.[6]

(5) No Tax or Duty shall be laid on Articles exported from any State.

(6) No Preference shall be given by any Regulation of Commerce or Revenue to the Ports of one State over those of another; nor shall Vessels bound to, or from, one State, be obliged to enter, clear, or pay Duties in another.

(7) No Money shall be drawn from the Treasury, but in Consequence of Appropriations made by Law; and a regular Statement and Account of the Receipts and Expenditures of all public Money shall be published from time to time.

(8) No Title of Nobility shall be granted by the United States: And no Person holding any Office of Profit or Trust under them, shall, without the Consent of the Congress, accept of any present, Emolument, Office, or Title, of any kind whatever, from any King, Prince, or foreign State.

Section 10. (1) No State shall enter into any Treaty, Alliance, or Confederation; grant Letters of Marque and Reprisal; coin Money; emit Bills of Credit; make any Thing but gold and silver Coin a Tender in Payment of Debts; pass any Bill of Attainder, ex post facto Law, or Law impairing the Obligation of Contracts, or grant any Title of Nobility.

(2) No State shall, without the Consent of the Congress, lay any Imposts or Duties on Imports or Exports, except what may be absolutely necessary for executing its inspection Laws: and the net Produce of all Duties and Imposts, laid

---

[6]Changed by the Sixteenth Amendment.

by any State on Imports or Exports, shall be for the Use of the Treasury of the United States; and all such laws shall be subject to the Revision and Control of the Congress.

(3) No State shall, without the Consent of Congress, lay any duty of Tonnage, keep Troops, or Ships of War in time of Peace, enter into any Agreement or Compact with another State, or with a foreign Power, or engage in War, unless actually invaded, or in such imminent Danger as will not admit of delay.

ARTICLE II

Section 1. (1) The executive Power shall be vested in a President of the United States of America. He shall hold his Office during the Term of four Years, and, together with the Vice-President, chosen for the same Term, be elected, as follows:

(2) Each State shall appoint, in such Manner as the Legislature thereof may direct, a Number of Electors, equal to the whole Number of Senators and Representatives to which the State may be entitled in the Congress; but no Senator or Representative, or Person holding an Office of Trust or Profit under the United States, shall be appointed an Elector.

[The Electors shall meet in their respective States, and vote by Ballot for two persons, of whom one at least shall not be an Inhabitant of the same State with themselves. And they shall make a List of all the Persons voted for, and of the Number of Votes for each; which List they shall sign and certify, and transmit sealed to the Seat of the Government of the United States, directed to the President of the Senate. The President of the Senate shall, in the Presence of the Senate and House of Representatives, open all the Certificates, and the Votes shall then be counted. The Person having the greatest Number of Votes shall be the President, if such Number be a Majority of the whole Number of Electors appointed; and if there be more than one who have such Majority, and have an equal Number of Votes, then the House of Representatives shall immediately choose by Ballot one of them for President; and if no Person have a Majority, then from the five highest on the List the said House shall in like Manner choose the President. But in choosing the President, the Votes shall be taken by States, the Representation from each State having one Vote; A quorum for this purpose shall consist of a Member or Members from two-thirds of the States, and a Majority of all the States shall be necessary to a Choice. In every Case, after the Choice of the President, the Person having the greatest Number of Votes of the Electors shall be the Vice-President. But if there should remain two or more who have equal Votes, the Senate shall choose from them by Ballot the Vice-President.][7]

(3) The Congress may determine the Time of choosing the Electors, and the Day on which they shall give their Votes; which Day shall be the same throughout the United States.

---

[7]This paragraph was superseded in 1804 by the Twelfth Amendment.

(4) No person except a natural born Citizen, or a Citizen of the United States, at the time of the Adoption of this Constitution, shall be eligible to the Office of President; neither shall any Person be eligible to that Office who shall not have attained to the Age of thirty-five Years, and been fourteen Years a Resident within the United States.

(5) In case of the Removal of the President from Office, or of his Death, Resignation, or Inability to discharge the Powers and Duties of the said Office, the same shall devolve on the Vice-President, and the Congress may by Law provide for the Case of Removal, Death, Resignation or Inability, both of the President and Vice-President, declaring what Officer shall then act as President, and such Officer shall act accordingly, until the Disability be removed, or a President shall be elected.[8]

(6) The President shall, at stated Times, receive for his Services, a Compensation, which shall neither be increased nor diminished during the Period for which he shall have been elected, and he shall not receive within that Period any other Emolument from the United States, or any of them.

(7) Before he enter on the Execution of his Office, he shall take the following Oath or Affirmation:—"I do solemnly swear (or affirm) that I will faithfully execute the Office of President of the United States, and will to the best of my Ability, preserve, protect and defend the Constitution of the United States."

Section 2. (1) The President shall be Commander in Chief of the Army and Navy of the United States, and of the Militia of the several States, when called into the actual Service of the United States; he may require the Opinion in writing, of the principal Officer in each of the executive Departments, upon any subject relating to the Duties of their respective Offices, and he shall have Power to Grant Reprieves and Pardons for Offenses against the United States, except in Cases of Impeachment.

(2) He shall have Power, by and with the Advice and Consent of the Senate, to make Treaties, provided two-thirds of the Senators present concur; and he shall nominate, and by and with the Advice and Consent of the Senate, shall appoint Ambassadors, other public Ministers and Consuls, Judges of the supreme Court, and all other Officers of the United States, whose Appointments are not herein otherwise provided for, and which shall be established by Law: but the Congress may by Law vest the Appointment of such inferior Officers, as they think proper, in the President alone, in the Court of Law, or in the Heads of Departments.

(3) The President shall have Power to fill up all Vacancies that may happen during the Recess of the Senate, by granting Commissions which shall expire at the End of their next Session.

Section 3. He shall from time to time give to the Congress Information of the State of the Union, and recommend to their Consideration such Measures as he shall judge necessary and expedient; he may, on extraordinary Occasions, convene both Houses, or either of them, and in Case of Disagreement between them, with Respect to the Time of Adjournment, he may adjourn

---

[8]Changed by the Twenty-fifth Amendment.

them to such Time as he shall think proper; he shall receive Ambassadors and other public Ministers; he shall take Care that the Laws be faithfully executed, and shall Commission all the Officers of the United States.

Section 4. The President, Vice President and all civil Officers of the United States, shall be removed from Office on Impeachment for, and Conviction of, Treason, Bribery, or other high Crimes and Misdemeanors.

ARTICLE III

Section 1. The judicial Power of the United States, shall be vested in one supreme Court, and in such inferior Courts as the Congress may from time to time ordain and establish. The judges, both of the supreme and inferior Courts, shall hold their Offices during good Behavior, and shall, at stated Times, receive for their Services a Compensation which shall not be diminished during their Continuance in Office.

Section 2. (1) The judicial Power shall extend to all Cases, in Law and Equity, arising under this Constitution, the Laws of the United States, and Treaties made, or which shall be made, under their Authority;—to all Cases affecting Ambassadors, other public Ministers and Consuls;—to all Cases of admiralty and maritime Jurisdiction;—to Controversies to which the United States shall be a Party;—to Controversies between two or more states;—[between a State and Citizens of another State];[9]—between Citizens of different States;—between Citizens of the same State claiming Lands under Grants of different States, and [between a State, or the Citizens thereof, and foreign States, Citizens or Subjects].[10]

(2) In all Cases affecting Ambassadors, other public Ministers and Consuls, and those in which a State shall be Party, the supreme Court shall have original Jurisdiction. In all the other Cases before mentioned, the supreme Court shall have appellate Jurisdiction, both as to Law and Fact, with such Exceptions, and under such Regulations as the Congress shall make.

(3) The trial of all Crimes, except in Cases of Impeachment, shall be by Jury; and such Trial shall be held in the State where the said Crimes shall have been committed: but when not committed within any State, the Trial shall be at such Place or Places as the Congress may by Law have directed.

Section 3. (1) Treason against the United States, shall consist only in levying War against them, or in adhering to their Enemies, giving them Aid and Comfort. No Person shall be convicted of Treason unless on the Testimony of two Witnesses to the same overt Act, or on Confession in open Court.

(2) The Congress shall have Power to declare the Punishment of Treason, but no Attainder of Treason shall work Corruption of Blood, or Forfeiture except during the Life of the Person attained.

---

[9]Restricted by the Eleventh Amendment.
[10]Restricted by the Eleventh Amendment.

ARTICLE IV

Section 1. Full Faith and Credit shall be given in each State to the public Acts, Records, and judicial Proceedings of every other State. And the Congress may by general Laws prescribe the Manner in which such Acts, Records and Proceedings shall be proved, and the Effect thereof.

Section 2. (1) The Citizens of each State shall be entitled to all Privileges and Immunities of Citizens in the several States.

(2) A Person charged in any State with Treason, Felony, or other Crime, who shall flee from Justice, and be found in another State, shall on demand of the executive Authority of the State from which he fled, be delivered up, to be removed to the State having Jurisdiction of the Crime.

(3) [No Person held to Service or Labor in one State, under the Laws thereof, escaping into another, shall, in Consequence of any Law or Regulation therein, be discharged from such Service or Labor, but shall be delivered up on Claim of the Party to whom such Service or Labor may be due.][11]

Section 3. (1) New States may be admitted by the Congress into this Union; but no new State shall be formed or erected within the Jurisdiction of any other State; nor any State be formed by the Junction of two or more States, or Parts of States, without the Consent of the Legislatures of the States concerned as well as of the Congress.

(2) The Congress shall have Power to dispose of and make all needful Rules and Regulations respecting the Territory or other Property belonging to the United States; and nothing in this Constitution shall be so construed as to Prejudice any Claims of the United States, or of any particular State.

Section 4. The United States shall guarantee to every State in this Union a Republican Form of Government, and shall protect each of them against Invasion; and on Application of the Legislature, or of the Executive (when the Legislature cannot be convened) against domestic Violence.

ARTICLE V

The Congress, whenever two-thirds of both Houses shall deem it necessary, shall propose Amendments to this Constitution, or, on the Application of the Legislatures of two-thirds of the several States, shall call a Convention for proposing Amendments, which, in either Case, shall be valid to all Intents and Purposes, as part of this Constitution, when ratified by the Legislature of three-fourths of the several States, or by Conventions in three-fourths thereof, as the one or the other Mode of Ratification may be proposed by the Congress; Provided that no Amendment which may be made prior to the Year One thousand eight hundred and eight shall in any Manner affect the first and fourth Clauses

---

[11]This paragraph was superseded by the Thirteenth Amendment.

in the Ninth Section of the first Article; and that no State, without its Consent, shall be deprived of its equal Suffrage in the Senate.

ARTICLE VI

(1) All Debts contracted and Engagements entered into, before the Adoption of this Constitution, shall be as valid against the United States under this Constitution, as under the Confederation.

(2) This Constitution, and the Laws of the United States which shall be made in Pursuance thereof; and all Treaties made, or which shall be made, under the Authority of the United States, shall be the supreme Law of the Land; and the Judges in every State shall be bound thereby, any Thing in the Constitution or Laws of any State to the Contrary notwithstanding.

(3) The Senators and Representatives before mentioned, and the Members of the several State Legislatures, and all executive and judicial Officers, both of the United States and of the several States, shall be bound by Oath or Affirmation, to support this Constitution; but no religious Test shall ever be required as a Qualification to any Office or public Trust under the United States.

ARTICLE VII

The Ratification of the Conventions of nine States, shall be sufficient for the Establishment of this Constitution between the States so ratifying the Same.

DONE in Convention by the Unanimous Consent of the States present the Seventeenth Day of September in the Year of our Lord one thousand seven hundred and Eighty seven and the Independence of the United States of America the Twelfth. In Witness whereof We have hereunto subscribed our Names.

Go. WASHINGTON
President and deputy from Virginia

ARTICLES IN ADDITION TO, AND AMENDMENT OF, THE CONSTITUTION OF THE UNITED STATES OF AMERICA, PROPOSED BY CONGRESS, AND RATIFIED BY THE LEGISLATURES OF THE SEVERAL STATES, PURSUANT TO THE FIFTH ARTICLE OF THE ORIGINAL CONSTITUTION.

AMENDMENT I[12]

Congress shall make no law respecting an establishment of religion, or prohibiting the free exercise thereof; or abridging the freedom of speech, or of the press; or the right of the people peaceably to assemble, and to petition the Government for a redress of grievances.

---

[12]The first ten amendments were adopted in 1791.

AMENDMENT II

A well regulated Militia, being necessary to the security of a free State, the right of the people to keep and bear Arms, shall not be infringed.

AMENDMENT III

No Soldier shall, in time of peace be quartered in any house, without the consent of the Owner, nor in time of war, but in a manner to be prescribed by law.

AMENDMENT IV

The right of the people to be secure in their persons, houses, papers, and effects, against unreasonable searches and seizures, shall not be violated, and no Warrants shall issue, but upon probable cause, supported by Oath or affirmation, and particularly describing the place to be searched, and the persons or things to be seized.

AMENDMENT V

No person shall be held to answer for a capital, or otherwise infamous crime, unless on a presentment or indictment of a Grand Jury, except in cases arising in the land or naval forces, or in the Militia, when in actual service in time of War or public danger; nor shall any person be subject for the same offense to be twice put in jeopardy of life or limb; nor shall be compelled in any criminal case to be witness against himself, nor be deprived of life, liberty, or property, without due process of law; nor shall private property be taken for public use without just compensation.

AMENDMENT VI

In all criminal prosecutions, the accused shall enjoy the right to a speedy and public trial, by an impartial jury of the State and district wherein the crime shall have been committed, which district shall have been previously ascertained by law, and to be informed of the nature and cause of the accusation, to be confronted with the witnesses against him; to have compulsory process for obtaining witnesses in his favor, and to have the Assistance of Counsel for his defense.

AMENDMENT VII

In Suits at common law, where the value in controversy shall exceed twenty dollars, the right of trial by jury shall be preserved, and no fact tried by a jury, shall be otherwise reexamined in any Court of the United States, than according to the rules of the common law.

AMENDMENT VIII

Excessive bail shall not be required, nor excessive fines imposed, nor cruel and unusual punishments inflicted.

AMENDMENT IX

The enumeration in the Constitution, of certain rights, shall not be construed to deny or disparage others retained by the people.

AMENDMENT X

The powers not delegated to the United States by the Constitution, nor prohibited by it to the States, are reserved to the States respectively, or to the people.

AMENDMENT XI[13]

The Judicial power of the United States shall not be construed to extend to any suit in law or equity, commenced or prosecuted against one of the United States by Citizens of another State, or by Citizens or Subjects of any Foreign State.

AMENDMENT XII[14]

The Electors shall meet in their respective states and vote by ballot for President and Vice-President, one of whom, at least, shall not be an inhabitant of the same state with themselves; they shall name in their ballots the person voted for as President, and in distinct ballots the person voted for as Vice-President, and they shall make distinct lists of all persons voted for as President, and of all persons voted for as Vice-President, and of the number of votes for each, which lists they shall sign and certify, and transmit sealed to the seat of the government of the United States, directed to the President of the Senate;—The President of the Senate shall, in presence of the Senate and House of Representatives, open all the certificates and the votes shall then be counted;—The person having the greatest number of votes for President, shall be the President, if

---

[13]Adopted in 1798.
[14]Adopted in 1804.

such number be a majority of the whole number of Electors appointed; and if no person have such majority, then from the persons having the highest numbers not exceeding three on the list of those voted for as President, the House of Representatives shall choose immediately, by ballot, the President. But in choosing the President, the votes shall be taken by states, the representation from each state having one vote; a quorum for this purpose shall consist of a member or members from two-thirds of the states, and a majority of all the states shall be necessary to a choice. [And if the House of Representatives shall not choose a President whenever the right of choice shall devolve upon them, before the fourth day of March next following, then the Vice-President shall act as President, as in the case of the death or other constitutional disability of the President.][15]—The person having the greatest number of votes as Vice-President, shall be the Vice-President, if such number be a majority of the whole number of Electors appointed, and if no person have a majority, then from the two highest numbers on the list, the Senate shall choose the Vice-President; a quorum for the purpose shall consist of two-thirds of the whole number of Senators, and a majority of the whole number shall be necessary to a choice. But no person constitutionally ineligible to the office of President shall be eligible to that of Vice-President of the United States.

AMENDMENT XIII[16]

Section 1. Neither slavery nor involuntary servitude, except as a punishment for crime whereof the party shall have been duly convicted, shall exist within the United States, or any place subject to their jurisdiction.

Section 2. Congress shall have power to enforce this article by appropriate legislation.

AMENDMENT XIV[17]

Section 1. All persons born or naturalized in the United States, and subject to the jurisdiction thereof, are citizens of the United States and of the State wherein they reside. No state shall make or enforce any law which shall abridge the privileges or immunities of citizens of the United States; nor shall any State deprive any person of life, liberty, or property, without due process of law; nor deny to any person within its jurisdiction the equal protection of the laws.

Section 2. Representatives shall be apportioned among the several States according to their respective numbers, counting the whole number of persons in each State, excluding Indians not taxed. But when the right to vote at any

---

[15]Superseded by the Twentieth Amendment, Section 3.
[16]Adopted in 1865.
[17]Adopted in 1868.

election for the choice of electors for President and Vice-President of the United States, Representatives in Congress, the Executive and Judicial officers of a State, or the members of the Legislature thereof, is denied to any of the male inhabitants of such State, being twenty-one years of age, and citizens of the United States, or in any way abridged, except for participation in rebellion, or other crime, the basis of representation therein shall be reduced in the proportion which the number of such male citizens shall bear to the whole number of male citizens twenty-one years of age in such State.

Section 3. No person shall be a Senator or Representative in Congress, or elector of President and Vice-President, or hold any office, civil or military, under the United States, or under any State, who, having previously taken an oath, as a member of Congress, or as an officer of the United States, or as a member of any State legislature, or as an executive or judicial officer of any State, to support the Constitution of the United States, shall have engaged in insurrection or rebellion against the same, or given aid or comfort to the enemies thereof. But Congress may by a vote of two-thirds of each House, remove such disability.

Section 4. The validity of the public debt of the United States, authorized by law, including debts incurred for payment of pensions and bounties for services in suppressing insurrection or rebellion, shall not be questioned. But neither the United States nor any State shall assume or pay any debt or obligation incurred in aid of insurrection or rebellion against the United States, or any claim for the loss or emancipation of any slave; but all such debts, obligations and claims shall be held illegal and void.

Section 5. The Congress shall have power to enforce, by appropriate legislation, the provisions of this article.

AMENDMENT XV[18]

Section 1. The right of citizens of the United States to vote shall not be denied or abridged by the United States or by any State on account of race, color, or previous condition of servitude.

Section 2. The Congress shall have power to enforce this article by appropriate legislation.

AMENDMENT XVI[19]

The Congress shall have power to lay and collect taxes on incomes, from whatever source derived, without apportionment among the several States, and without regard to any census or enumeration.

---

[18]Adopted in 1870.
[19]Adopted in 1913.

AMENDMENT XVII[20]

The Senate of the United States shall be composed of two Senators from each State, elected by the people thereof, for six years; and each Senator shall have one vote. The electors in each State shall have the qualifications requisite for electors of the most numerous branch of the State legislatures.

When vacancies happen in the representation of any State in the Senate, the executive authority of such State shall issue writs of election to fill such vacancies: *Provided*, That the legislature of any State may empower the executive thereof to make temporary appointments until the people fill the vacancies by election as the legislature may direct.

This amendment shall not be so construed as to affect the election or term of any Senator chosen before it becomes valid as part of the Constitution.

AMENDMENT XVIII[21]

Section 1. After one year from the ratification of this article the manufacture, sale, or transportation of intoxicating liquors within, the importation thereof into, or the exportation thereof from the United States and all territory subject to the jurisdiction thereof for beverage purposes is hereby prohibited.

Section 2. The Congress and the several States shall have concurrent power to enforce this article by appropriate legislation.

Section 3. This article shall be inoperative unless it shall have been ratified as an amendment to the Constitution by the legislatures of the several States, as provided in the Constitution, within seven years from the date of the submission hereof to the States by the Congress.

AMENDMENT XIX[22]

The right of the citizens of the United States to vote shall not be denied or abridged by the United States or by any State on account of sex.

Congress shall have power to enforce this article by appropriate legislation.

AMENDMENT XX[23]

Section 1. The terms of the President and Vice-President shall end at noon on the 20th day of January, and the terms of Senators and Representatives at

---

[20]Adopted in 1913.
[21]Adopted in 1919. Repealed by Section 1 of the Twenty-first Amendment.
[22]Adopted in 1920.
[23]Adopted in 1933.

noon on the 3rd day of January, of the years in which such terms would have ended if this article had not been ratified; and the terms of their successors shall then begin.

Section 2. The Congress shall assemble at least once in every year, and such meeting shall begin at noon on the 3rd day of January, unless they shall by law appoint a different day.

Section 3. If, at the time fixed for the beginning of the term of the President, the President elect shall have died, the Vice-President elect shall become President. If a President shall not have been chosen before the time fixed for the beginning of his term, or if the President elect shall have failed to qualify, then the Vice-President elect shall act as President until a President shall have qualified; and the Congress may by law provide for the case wherein neither a President elect nor a Vice-President elect shall have qualified, declaring who shall then act as President, or the manner in which one who is to act shall be selected, and such person shall act accordingly until a President or Vice-President shall have qualified.

Section 4. The Congress may by law provide for the case of the death of any of the persons from whom the House of Representatives may choose a President whenever the right of choice shall have devolved upon them, and for the case of the death of any of the persons from whom the Senate may choose a Vice-President whenever the right of choice shall have devolved upon them.

Section 5. Sections 1 and 2 shall take effect on the 15th day of October following the ratification of this article.

Section 6. This article shall be inoperative unless it shall have been ratified as an amendment to the Constitution by the legislatures of three-fourths of the several States within seven years from the date of its submission.

AMENDMENT XXI[24]

Section 1. The eighteenth article of amendment to the Constitution of the United States is hereby repealed.

Section 2. The transportation or importation into any State, Territory, or possession of the United States for delivery or use therein of intoxicating liquors, in violation of the laws thereof, is hereby prohibited.

Section 3. This article shall be inoperative unless it shall have been ratified as an amendment to the Constitution by conventions in the several States, as provided in the Constitution, within seven years from the date of the submission hereof to the States by the Congress.

---

[24]Adopted in 1933.

AMENDMENT XXII[25]

Section 1. No person shall be elected to the office of the President more than twice, and no person who has held the office of President, or acted as President, for more than two years of a term to which some other person was elected President shall be elected to the office of the President more than once. But this Article shall not apply to any person holding the office of President when this Article was proposed by the Congress, and shall not prevent any person who may be holding the office of President, or acting as President, during the term within which this Article becomes operative from holding the office of President or acting as President during the remainder of such term.

Section 2. This article shall be inoperative unless it shall have been ratified as an amendment to the Constitution by the legislatures of three-fourths of the several States within seven years from the date of its submission to the States by the Congress.

AMENDMENT XXIII[26]

Section 1. The District constituting the seat of Government of the United States shall appoint in such manner as the Congress may direct:
A number of electors of President and Vice-President equal to the whole number of Senators and Representatives in Congress to which the District would be entitled if it were a State, but in no event more than the least populous State; they shall be in addition to those appointed by the States, but they shall be considered, for the purposes of the election of President and Vice-President, to be electors appointed by a State, and they shall meet in the District and perform such duties as provided by the twelfth article of amendment.

Section 2. The Congress shall have power to enforce this article by appropriate legislation.

AMENDMENT XXIV[27]

Section 1. The right of citizens of the United States to vote in any primary or other election for President or Vice-President, for electors for President of Vice-President, or for Senator or Representative in Congress, shall not be denied or abridged by the United States or any state by reasons of failure to pay any poll tax or other tax.

Section 2. The Congress shall have power to enforce this article by appropriate legislation.

---

[25]Adopted in 1951.
[26]Adopted in 1961.
[27]Adopted in 1964.

AMENDMENT XXV[28]

Section 1. In case of the removal of the President from office or of his death or resignation, the Vice-President shall become President.

Section 2. Whenever there is a vacancy in the office of the Vice-President, the President shall nominate a Vice-President who shall take office upon confirmation by a majority vote of both Houses of Congress.

Section 3. Whenever the President transmits to the President pro tempore of the Senate and the Speaker of the House of Representatives his written declaration that he is unable to discharge the powers and duties of his office, and until he transmits to them a written declaration to the contrary, such powers and duties shall be discharged by the Vice-President as Acting President.

Section 4. Whenever the Vice-President and a majority of either the principal officers of the Executive departments or of such other body as Congress may by law provide, transmit to the President pro tempore of the Senate and the Speaker of the House of Representatives their written declaration that the President is unable to discharge the powers and duties of his office, The Vice-President shall immediately assume the powers and duties of the office as Acting President.

Thereafter, when the President transmits to the President pro tempore of the Senate and the Speaker of the House of Representatives his written declaration that no inability exists, he shall resume the powers and duties of his office unless the Vice-President and a majority of either the principal officers of the executive departments or of such other body as Congress may by law provide, transmit within four days to the President pro tempore of the Senate and the Speaker of the House of Representatives their written declaration that the President is unable to discharge the powers and duties of his office. Thereupon Congress shall decide the issue, assembling within forty-eight hours for that purpose if not in session. If the Congress, within twenty-one days after receipt of the latter written declaration, or, if Congress is not in session, within twenty-one days after Congress is required to assemble, determines by two-thirds vote of both houses that the President is unable to discharge the powers and duties of his office, the Vice-President shall continue to discharge the same as Acting President; otherwise, the President shall resume the powers and duties of his office.

AMENDMENT XXVI[29]

Section 1. The right of citizens of the United States, who are 18 years of age or older, to vote shall not be denied or abridged by the United States or any state on account of age.

---

[28]Adopted in 1967.
[29]Adopted in 1971.

Section 2. The Congress shall have power to enforce this article by appropriate legislation.

AMENDMENT XXVII

No law, varying the compensation for the services of the Senators and Representatives, shall take effect, until an election of Representatives shall have intervened.

CREDITS

Benjamin R. Barber, "More Democracy! More Revolution!," *The Nation* (October 26, 1998), pp. 12-15. Reprinted with permission. All rights reserved.

Michael Lind, "75 Stars: How to Restore Democracy in the U.S. Senate," *Mother Jones Magazine* (Jan-Feb 1998), pp. 42-47. Reprinted by permission of Foundation for National Progress. All rights reserved.

Martha Derthick, "American Federalism, Half-Full or Half-Empty?," *Brookings Review* (Winter 2000), pp. 24-27. Reprinted with permission of the Brookings Institution. All rights reserved.

Carl Tubbesing, "The Dual Personality of Federalism," *State Legislatures* (April 1998), pp. 22-27. Reprinted with permission of the National Conference of State Legislatures. All rights reserved.

Noam Chomsky, "You Say You Want a Devolution," *The Progressive* (March 1996), pp. 18-19. Reprinted with permission of The Progressive, 409 E. Main St., Madison, WI 53703. All rights reserved.

Anne Martinez, "Putting the Innocent Behind Bars," *USA Today* (May 1995), pp. 43-44. Reprinted from USA Today magazine by the Society for the Advancement of Education Inc. Copyright © 1995.

Wilfred M. McClay, "The Worst Decision Since 'Dred Scot'?" *Commentary* (October 1997), pp. 52-54. Reprinted with permission of Commentary. All rights reserved.

Karen Goldberg Goff, "Does Athletic Equity Give Men a Sporting Chance?" *Insight on the News* (January 1999), p. 38. Reprinted with permission from Insight. Copyright © 1999 News World Communications, Inc. All rights reserved.

Hamil R. Harris, "Voter Lockdown," *Black Enterprise* (August 1999), p. 20. Reprinted with permission of Black Enterprise Magazine, New York, NY. All rights reserved.

Gabriel Rotello, "Gay and Lesbian Rights," *Social Policy* (Spring 1998), pp. 56-59. Reprinted with permission. All rights reserved.

John Diconsiglio, "The World's Hardest Job," *Scholastic Upfront* (September 1996), pp. 2-5. Copyright © 1996 by Scholastic Inc. Reprinted with permission.

Charles O. Jones, "The Separated System," *Society* (Sept/Oct 1996), pp. 18-23. Copyright © 1996 by Transaction Publishers. Reprinted with permission.

Stephen M. Leahy, "The Historical Battle Over Dispatching American Troops," *USA Today* (July 1999), pp. 10-12. Reprinted with Permission of the Society for the Advancement of Education.

Gordon S. Jones, "The Changing Role of the Committee," *World and I* (September 1998), pp. 52-57. Reprinted with permission from World and I. Copyright © News World Communications, Inc. All Rights Reserved.

Claiborne Pell, "Civil Discourse Is Crucial for Democracy to Work," *Insight* (September 25-October 2, 1995), p. 13. Reprinted with permission from Insight. Copyright © 1995 News World Communications, Inc. All Rights Reserved.